READERS' GUIDES TO ESSENTIAL CRITICISM

CONSULTANT EDITOR: NICOLAS TREDELL

Published

Thomas P. Adler	Tennessee Wi on a Hot Tir
Pascale Aebischer	Jacobean Dra...
Lucie Armitt	George Eliot: Adam Bede/The Mill on the Floss/ Middlemarch
Simon Avery	Thomas Hardy: The Mayor of Casterbridge/Jude the Obscure
Paul Baines	Daniel Defoe: Robinson Crusoe/Moll Flanders
Brian Baker	Science Fiction
Annika Bautz	Jane Austen: Sense and Sensibility/Pride and Prejudice/Emma
Matthew Beedham	The Novels of Kazuo Ishiguro
Richard Beynon	D. H. Lawrence: The Rainbow/Women in Love
Peter Boxall	Samuel Beckett: Waiting for Godot/Endgame
Claire Brennan	The Poetry of Sylvia Plath
Susan Bruce	Shakespeare: King Lear
Sandie Byrne	Jane Austen: Mansfield Park
Sandie Byrne	The Poetry of Ted Hughes
Alison Chapman	Elizabeth Gaskell: Mary Barton/North and South
Peter Childs	The Fiction of Ian McEwan
Christine Clegg	Vladimir Nabokov: Lolita
John Coyle	James Joyce: Ulysses/A Portrait of the Artist as a Young Man
Martin Coyle	Shakespeare: Richard II
Sarah Davison	Modernist Literatures
Sarah Dewar-Watson	Tragedy
Justin D. Edwards	Postcolonial Literature
Michael Faherty	The Poetry of W. B. Yeats
Sarah Gamble	The Fiction of Angela Carter
Jodi-Anne George	Beowulf
Jodi-Anne George	Chaucer: The General Prologue to The Canterbury Tales
Jane Goldman	Virginia Woolf: To the Lighthouse/The Waves
Huw Griffiths	Shakespeare: Hamlet
Vanessa Guignery	The Fiction of Julian Barnes
Louisa Hadley	The Fiction of A. S. Byatt
Sarah Haggarty and Jon Mee	William Blake: Songs of Innocence and Experience
Geoffrey Harvey	Thomas Hardy: Tess of the d'Urbervilles
Paul Hendon	The Poetry of W. H. Auden
Terry Hodgson	The Plays of Tom Stoppard for Stage, Radio, TV and Film
William Hughes	Bram Stoker: Dracula
Stuart Hutchinson	Mark Twain: Tom Sawyer/Huckleberry Finn
Stuart Hutchinson	Edith Wharton: The House of Mirth/The Custom of the Country/Age of Innocence
Betty Jay	E. M. Forster: A Passage to India
Aaron Kelly	Twentieth-Century Irish Literature
Elmer Kennedy-Andrews	Nathaniel Hawthorne: The Scarlet Letter
Elmer Kennedy-Andrews	The Poetry of Seamus Heaney
Daniel Lea	George Orwell: Animal Farm/Nineteen Eighty-Four
Rachel Lister	Alice Walker: The Color Purple
Sara Lodge	Charlotte Brontë: Jane Eyre
Philippa Lyon	Twentieth-Century War Poetry
Merja Makinen	The Novels of Jeanette Winterson

Matt McGuire	Contemporary Scottish Literature
Timothy Milnes	Wordsworth: *The Prelude*
Jago Morrison	The Fiction of Chinua Achebe
Merritt Moseley	The Fiction of Pat Barker
Carl Plasa	Toni Morrison: *Beloved*
Carl Plasa	Jean Rhys: *Wide Sargasso Sea*
Nicholas Potter	Shakespeare: *Antony and Cleopatra*
Nicholas Potter	Shakespeare: *Othello*
Nicholas Potter	Shakespeare's Late Plays: *Pericles/Cymbeline/The Winter's Tale/ The Tempest*
Steven Price	The Plays, Screenplays and Films of David Mamet
Berthold Schoene-Harwood	Mary Shelley: *Frankenstein*
Nicholas Seager	The Rise of the Novel
Nick Selby	T. S. Eliot: *The Waste Land*
Nick Selby	Herman Melville: *Moby Dick*
Nick Selby	The Poetry of Walt Whitman
David Smale	Salman Rushdie: *Midnight's Children/The Satanic Verses*
Patsy Stoneman	Emily Brontë: *Wuthering Heights*
Susie Thomas	Hanif Kureishi
Nicolas Tredell	Joseph Conrad: *Heart of Darkness*
Nicolas Tredell	Charles Dickens: *Great Expectations*
Nicolas Tredell	William Faulkner: *The Sound and the Fury/As I Lay Dying*
Nicolas Tredell	F. Scott Fitzgerald: *The Great Gatsby*
Nicolas Tredell	Shakespeare: *A Midsummer Night's Dream*
Nicolas Tredell	Shakespeare: *Macbeth*
Nicolas Tredell	The Fiction of Martin Amis
David Wheatley	Contemporary British Poetry
Martin Willis	Literature and Science
Matthew Woodcock	Shakespeare: *Henry V*
Gillian Woods	Shakespeare: *Romeo and Juliet*
Angela Wright	Gothic Fiction

Forthcoming

Nick Bentley	Contemporary British Fiction
Alan Gibbs	Jewish-American Literature since 1945
Keith Hughes	African-American Literature
Wendy Knepper	Caribbean Literature
Britta Martens	The Poetry of Robert Browning
Pat Pinsent and Clare Walsh	Children's Literature
Jane Poyner	The Fiction of J. M. Coetzee
Nicolas Tredell	Shakespeare: The Tragedies
Kate Watson	Crime and Detective Fiction
Andrew Wylie	The Plays of Harold Pinter

Readers' Guides to Essential Criticism
Series Standing Order ISBN 978–1–4039–0108–8
(*outside North America only*)

You can receive future titles in this series as they are published by placing a standing order. Please contact your bookseller or, in the case of difficulty, write to us at the address below with your name and address, the title of the series and the ISBN quoted above.

Customer Services Department, Macmillan Distribution Ltd, Houndmills, Basingstoke, Hampshire, RG21 6XS, UK

Modernist Literatures

A Reader's Guide to Essential Criticism

SARAH DAVISON

Consultant Editor: NICOLAS TREDELL

First published 2015 by
PALGRAVE

Palgrave in the UK is an imprint of Macmillan Publishers Limited, registered in England, company number 785998, of 4 Crinan Street, London, N1 9XW.

Palgrave Macmillan in the US is a division of St Martin's Press LLC, 175 Fifth Avenue, New York, NY 10010.

Palgrave is a global imprint of the above companies and is represented throughout the world.

Palgrave® and Macmillan® are registered trademarks in the United States, the United Kingdom, Europe and other countries.

ISBN 978–0–230–28400–5   hardback
ISBN 978–0–230–28401–2   paperback

This book is printed on paper suitable for recycling and made from fully managed and sustained forest sources. Logging, pulping and manufacturing processes are expected to conform to the environmental regulations of the country of origin.

A catalogue record for this book is available from the British Library.

A catalog record for this book is available from the Library of Congress.

Typeset by MPS Limited, Chennai, India.

Printed in China

For Bram

CONTENTS

Outlines the structure and approach of the Guide, glosses key terms and introduces debates about the nature of modernism.

PART I

Critical Declarations and Contemporary Responses

Modernist Beginnings

Introduces foundational statements of early modernism and examines the critical reception of the literary and dramatic works and movements they engendered, from Charles Baudelaire to Walt Whitman, Decadence, Naturalism, Aesthetic Criticism, Henry James, Joseph Conrad, Oscar Wilde, Symbolism, Edward Gordon Craig and the Abbey Theatre.

High Modernism

Examines the critical pronouncements of the writers who brought modernism to an aesthetic peak and reactions to their work, including key statements on: 1910, Literary Impressionism (Ford Madox Ford and Virginia Woolf), short fiction and the epiphany (Virginia Woolf, Katherine Mansfield, James Joyce and Sherwood Anderson), consciousness in fiction (Dorothy Richardson and James Joyce), psychoanalysis and sex (Sigmund Freud and D.H. Lawrence), Futurism, modernist classicism (T.E. Hulme, Ezra Pound and T.S. Eliot), Imagism, Vorticism, Noh theatre, Gertrude Stein, Dada, *Ulysses*, the New York avant-garde (the Provincetown Players and New York Dada), American modernism (Mina Loy, Marianne Moore and Wallace Stevens), 'Tradition and the Individual Talent' and *The Waste Land*.

Explores the more explicitly political and socially conscious literatures produced in the 1920s and 1930s. Considers key critical statements on: localism and American modernism (William Carlos Williams and William Faulkner), Surrealism, the fates of 'the men of 1914', the Jazz Age and the lost generation (F. Scott Fitzgerald and Ernest Hemingway), the Harlem Renaissance (including W.E.B. Du Bois, Jean Toomer, *The New Negro*, Carl Van Vechten and Zora Neale Hurston), sexual politics (Radclyffe Hall and Virginia Woolf) and the 'Revolution of the Word' (Eugène Jolas and James Joyce).

PART II

Literary Criticism from 1930–Present

Investigates the institutionalisation of modernism as an academic discipline, exploring the impact of New Criticism, poststructuralism, deconstruction and feminism on the formation of the canon.

Considers how critics have responded to modernist constructions/explorations of gender and sexuality, examining the politics of modernist form, New Woman fiction, the impact of the First World War on femininity and masculinity, and modernist sexualities.

Contemplates the geographical range of modernism, its relationship with colonial occupation and its multiple timeframes, investigating themes of space, place and race.

CHAPTER SEVEN 166

Modernist Literatures and Mass Culture

Overturns notions of modernism as an elite art at a remove from mass culture by exploring its interactions with popular media, such as jazz, music hall and cinema, and its relations to the market economy (including conditions of publication and circulation).

CONCLUSION 190

Summarises the Guide and indicates the likely direction of future developments in the field.

Introduction

If there is one essential critical insight that comprehends the diverse literatures we consider to be modernist it is Ezra Pound's exhortation 'Make It New'.[1] Simple and memorable, Pound's maxim is the clearest, most widely applicable and readily quotable formulation of modernist aesthetics. 'Make It New' is a call to modernise, to remake or break with the past, in order to respond to, and indeed sculpt, the experience of living in a palpably modern world. And it is telling, therefore, that the slogan was not Pound's own invention: he translated it from the inscription on an ancient Chinese emperor's bathtub.

Many ages have been conscious of their modernity. 'Modern' is, after all, a term that is constantly updated, and so 'modernity' makes itself felt when the turnover is rapid and the displacement is violent. Ezra Pound (1885–1972) was writing in a time of pervasive cultural and scientific upheaval and 'Make It New' encapsulates what the age demanded from art. 'Modernism' is the name that critics use to designate the dramatic shifts in artistic life that accompanied the technological, social and political revolutions that culminated in the early decades of the twentieth century. The term is one of the most complex and intimidating critical categories that readers will encounter. Not only are many modernist works self-consciously difficult, but there is no consensus as to how modernism might be theorised.

The nature of the relationship between modernism and the material conditions of modernity has been the focus of intense critical debate in recent years. These discussions are ongoing and they are revolutionising the discipline. The foundation of the Modernist Studies Association (1999) marks the formal ordination of this new revisionary phase in criticism. The 'New Modernist Studies' is principally concerned with investigating the cultural, aesthetic, political, national and linguistic boundaries that modernity traverses and has superintended a radical expansion of the concept 'modernist'.[2] Accordingly, most critics now use the term 'modernisms' to comprehend the many different literatures that might fruitfully be described as 'modernist', after Peter Nicholls' *Modernisms: A Literary Guide* (1995, second revised edition 2009), one of the finest surveys of the topic produced to date.[3] The popularity of the term 'modernisms' indicates the scale of the challenges facing readers today.

This Guide is unique. It responds to new directions in modernist studies by providing a fresh, accessible, stimulating overview of essential criticism, attending to poetry, fiction and drama. It aims to impart a lively sense of the diverse literatures that participate in modernism, examining more familiar texts that readers are most likely to encounter in their studies as well as materials that have been more recently recovered and theorised, towards a redefinition of what now constitutes essential criticism in the field.

For ease of reference the Guide is organised in two parts. Part I explores how major currents in modernist thinking developed and the contemporary reception of the literatures that they shaped, introducing the theories, movements, 'isms', schisms, critical terms, traditions and individual talents that no reader can afford to ignore. Part II provides a historical and thematic overview of scholarship on literatures of modernism. It introduces the critical ideas that are now essential for readers to master, from the classic, canon-defining accounts of modernist writing by New Critics right up to the cutting-edge methodologies, discoveries and concerns that are reshaping the field today. It presents classic interpretations of familiar texts alongside fresh approaches to more recently recovered materials, investigating modernist responses to new thinking on gender, sexuality, race, civil rights, the rise of the masses, psychology and psychoanalysis, the body, technology, international politics, the First World War, mass media, marketing, popular culture and cinema, furnishing readers with the knowledge and insight to evaluate different viewpoints and make their own interventions in critical debates.

As the Guide addresses an Anglophone audience, its primary focus is modernist literatures in English. While the Guide concentrates on British, Irish and American modernisms, it recognises that modernism thrived on transcultural exchange, not least because the foreign is one category that reliably delivers the shock of the new. The Guide therefore takes particular note of key European developments in literature and art that influenced Anglophone writers in order to enable readers to make productive connections between the different modernisms of authors across the globe.

The Name of Modernism

'Surely no literary term has raised more controversy and misunderstanding than the modest little word *modernism*', wrote Marjorie Perloff in her 1992 account of the discipline.[4] Perry Anderson is one of several critics to argue that the label 'modernism' is void:

> ■ Modernism as a notion is the emptiest of all cultural categories. [...] In fact, [...] what is concealed beneath the label is a wide variety of

very diverse – indeed incompatible – aesthetic practices: symbolism, constructivism, expressionism, surrealism. These, which do spell out specific programmes, were unified post hoc in a portmanteau concept whose only referent is the blank passage of time itself.[5] □

Anderson objects to the name 'modernism' on the basis that it was coined after the fact and it elides importance differences between many schools and movements. The term 'modernism' does in fact have historical pedigree. In the early years of the twentieth century, 'modernism' and 'modernist' were widely used to describe the progressive, relativist movement within the Roman Catholic Church, which was condemned in two papal encyclicals: 'On the Doctrine of the Modernists' (1907) and 'The Oath Against Modernism' (1910). It was less common for the terms 'modernism' and 'modernist' to appear in literary writing. More often, contemporary critics spoke of 'the modern movement'.[6] However, significant literary usages of 'modernism' and 'modernist' do appear from the first decade of the twentieth century onwards, for instance T.E. Hulme (1883–1971) made a declaration of 'extreme modernism' in his 'Lecture on Modern Poetry' (1908).[7] Modernism is not therefore entirely a retrospective critical construction. Its origins as an artistic category can ultimately be traced to writers working at the time.

The Nature of Modernism

From an English-speaking perspective, T.S. Eliot (1888–1965), Ezra Pound and James Joyce (1882–1941) were among the first to be canonised for their daring, formal experimentation. They are celebrated as the architects of 'high modernism', the technically imposing, ambitiously symbolic literature produced in the years directly before, during and after the First World War. Notably all three men left the country of their birth. Americans Eliot and Pound both felt the pull of European culture, while Joyce left his native Dublin to live in Trieste, Zürich and Paris. Among British writers, Virginia Woolf (1882–1941) and the Bloomsbury Group are particularly fêted. Celebrated American writers include Gertrude Stein (1874–1946), Marianne Moore (1887–1972), William Carlos Williams (1883–1963), Wallace Stevens (1879–1955), Ernest Hemingway (1899–1961) and William Faulkner (1897–1962).

The institutionalisation of modernism as a defined field of study forms an important line of enquiry in this Guide. The Guide aims to account for and expose what Raymond Williams calls 'the machinery of selective tradition', whereby a 'highly selected version of the modern', inhering in the ideals of a set of elite artists who chose to exile themselves from bourgeois society and its values, achieved 'comfortable integration' to the extent that men like Pound, Joyce and Eliot came to stand in 'for the whole of modernity'.[8] A particular focus is therefore the criticism of recent decades that successfully contests predominantly white, male canons and brings to the fore the achievements of figures such as Djuna Barnes (1892–1982), Langston Hughes (1902–67), Zora Neale Hurston (1891–1960), Mina Loy (1882–1966) and Claude McKay (1889–1948), to name but a few.

Although the word 'modernism' is in wide use, it is telling that critics often avoid defining the term, relying instead on a notional common understanding of its meaning. As Michael Levenson notes:

■ Vague terms still signify. Such is the case with 'modernism': it is at once vague and unavoidable. Anything more precise would exclude too much too soon; anything more general would be folly. [...] As a rough way of locating our attention, 'modernism' will do.[9] □

In 1992, Marjorie Perloff compiled an indicative list of the formal characteristics that were seen to define modernism as it was codified from the mid-1960s onwards, balancing the general and the precise:

■ (1) the replacement of representation of the external world by the imaginative construction of the poet's inner world via the mysterious symbol; (2) the superiority of art to nature; (3) the concept of the artist as a hero; (4) the autonomy of art and its divorce from truth or morality; (5) the depersonalization and 'objectivity' of art, or what Joseph Frank called 'spatial form'; (6) alogical structure [...]; (7) the concrete as opposed to the abstract, the particular as opposed to the general, the perceptual as opposed to the conceptual; (8) verbal ambiguity and complexity: 'good' writing as inherently arcane; (9) the fluidity of consciousness [...]; (10) the increasing importance attached to the Freudian unconscious and to the dream work; (11) the use of myth as organizing structure [...]; (12) the emphasis on the divided self [...]; (13) the malaise of the individual in the 'lonely crowd', the alienated self in the urban world [...]; and finally, (14) the *internationalism* of modernism...[10] □

The fifth point refers to Joseph Frank's influential essay 'Spatial Form in Modern Literature' (1945), in which he argued that modernists characteristically aimed to replace temporal forms with spatial forms by undermining 'the inherent consecutiveness of language, frustrating the reader's normal expectation of a sequence and forcing him to perceive the elements of the poem as juxtaposed in space rather than unrolling in time'.[11] Perloff's retrospective inventory imparts a lively sense of the qualities that one might expect to see in canonical modernist texts, but also renders the revolutionary literatures of modernism formulaic and uniform. Readers will find it interesting to return to the list as they progress through the Guide and to consider which points might be supplemented or modified in the light of recent scholarship.

Attempts to identify exemplary formal or stylistic qualities only are reductive by definition. As Malcolm Bradbury and James McFarlane note in *Modernism: A Guide to European Literature 1890–1930* (1972) – a superbly wide-ranging essay collection that remains useful today – 'few ages have been more multiple, more promiscuous in artistic style; to distil from the multiplicity an overall style or mannerism is a difficult, perhaps even an impossible, task'.[12] Bradbury and McFarlane therefore tread very carefully, discerning in modernism 'a certain loose but distinguishable group of assumptions, founded on a broadly symbolist aesthetic', marked by 'high aesthetic self-consciousness and non-representationalism, in which art turns from realism and humanistic representation towards style, technique, and spatial form in pursuit of a deeper penetration of life'.[13]

The Age of Modernism

Not only do critics struggle to define modernism succinctly, they also find it hard to agree on its most active years. Raymond Williams's question 'When was modernism?' is deceptively difficult to answer.[14] Bradbury and McFarlane suggest 1890–1930 in their survey of European modernism, whereas Christopher Wilks associates modernism with the period between the two world wars in *Modernism: Designing a New World 1914–1939* (2006), the catalogue produced to accompany a recent international exhibition of American and European visual arts.[15] Other critics focus on different periods. For instance, Jane Goldman's book *Modernism 1910–1945: Image to Apocalypse* (2004) takes in developments from the beginnings of Imagism to the end of the Second World War.

As a global, multidisciplinary phenomenon, modernism spread surely but unevenly, touching poetry, prose, drama, dance, painting, sculpture, music, design and architecture at different times and in different ways. For instance, the vibrant culture of independent theatre companies provided the right conditions for drama to take a starring role in the rise of European modernism, while legal constraints dampened the development of that tradition in America. In Britain and America, modernism in poetry and fiction was kindled by the revolutions in European visual arts. As Peter Nicholls appreciates, there was no singular moment of rupture: 'The beginnings of modernism, like its endings, are largely indeterminate, a matter of traces rather than of clearly defined historical moments'.[16] While there is a broad consensus that the 1910s and 1920s are crucial to British, Irish and American modernisms, not everything produced in these decades was formally innovative. There is, after all, a strong realist tradition in twentieth-century literature that has little to do with the experimental impulses of modernism.

For clarity, this Guide uses 'modernism' to refer to the epochal shift that art underwent in the abstract and also as a way of designating works by groups of writers with a common identity, for instance 'lesbian modernism'. It retains the adjective 'modernist' as a descriptor of stylistic or thematic daring. It uses 'modernisms' to refer to the recent theoretical expansion of the field to include the many different schools and practices that modernity summoned forth and 'modernist literatures' to identify the diverse works which partake of modernism. The Guide also looks forward to postmodernism: the cultural formation that comes after, reacts to, goes beyond and is yet contiguous with modernism.

The term 'avant-garde' is used in the sense defined by Peter Bürger in *The Theory of the Avant-Garde* (1974, English translation 1984) to describe progressive art movements such as Dada or Surrealism that seek to repoliticise the bourgeois institution of art. The avant-garde aggressively reintegrates life and art with a view to making art practical once again and thus seeks to address as wide an audience as possible. Good examples include the use of mass-produced items such as *Fountain* (1917), the porcelain urinal that Marcel Duchamp (1887–1968) bought from a plumbing supply shop and signed R. Mutt, and the Futurist performances where audiences were encouraged to throw vegetables and to riot. The Guide treats modernism and the avant-garde not as antithetical categories but overlapping developments. Complex interchanges between the avant-garde and modernism are explored in the chapters that follow.

Modernism and Modernity

This Guide concentrates purposely on literatures produced between 1890 and 1939 (the outbreak of the Second World War), as this timeframe corresponds to most critics' sense of modernism's most active years. However, it sets essential critical statements on modernist literatures in the context of the intellectual and material conditions of modernity, and the technological, social and historical ferment from which they emerged.

The era of modernity was marked by profound and rapid transition. From the late eighteenth century onwards, huge technological advances were made in the fields of agriculture, mining and manufacturing. The Industrial Revolution spread from European cities to North America, and then further afield, accelerated by late nineteenth-century developments in telecommunication and transport. It brought profound socio-economic and cultural changes, as the old agrarian order gave way to mass production, increased urbanisation, new labour markets and the rise of masses.

An early and enduring analysis of the material conditions of modernity is the *Communist Manifesto* (1848, English translation 1888) by Karl Marx (1818–83) and Friedrich Engels (1820–95), which outlines how changes in the mode of production effect changes in the whole relations of society. They noted that the capitalists in charge of the means of production reaped the benefit of more efficient, profitable industrial systems while the labouring classes endured greater misery and impoverishment, with the result that 'Society as a whole is more and more splitting up into two great hostile camps, into two great classes directly facing each other: Bourgeoisie and Proletariat'.[17] They perceived that as industrial development takes hold, 'the proletariat not only increases in number; it becomes concentrated in greater masses, its strength grows, and it feels that strength more' and rises against the bourgeois social order.[18]

The fear that the rise of the masses engendered in the ruling class is recorded in *The Crowd: A Study of the Popular Mind* (1895, English translation 1896) by Gustave Le Bon (1841–1931):

■ The entry of the popular classes into political life [...] is one of the most striking characteristics of our epoch of transition. [...] The masses are founding syndicates before which the authorities capitulate one after the other; they are also founding labour unions [...]. To-day the claims of the masses are becoming more and more sharply defined, and amount to nothing less than a determination to utterly destroy society as it now exists [...].[19] □

The transference of political power was further consolidated by the campaigns for universal suffrage that were gathering momentum in the world's democracies during the nineteenth century and issuing successive challenges to the restriction of voting rights to property-owning white adult men.

Contemplating the social and political ferment set in motion by industrialisation and the rise of the masses led Marx and Engels to an exhilarating vision of modernity:

■ Constant revolutionizing of production, uninterrupted disturbance of all social conditions, everlasting uncertainty and agitation distinguish the bourgeois epoch from all earlier ones. All fixed, fast-frozen relations, with their train of ancient and venerable prejudices and opinions, are swept away, all new-formed ones become antiquated before they can ossify. All that is solid melts into air, all that is holy is profaned, and man is at last compelled to face with sober senses, his real conditions of life, and his relations with his kind.[20] □

Progress brings crisis and transition, precipitating a revolutionary questioning of class structures as well as sexual and racial hierarchies that compels humanity to conceive the conditions of life anew in thought and art.

Meanwhile, advances in science and philosophy destroyed old certainties and transformed conceptions of human nature and physical reality itself. New technologies of transport and communication changed the experience of distance, while notions of matter, space and time were revolutionised by particle- and astro-physics, relativity and quantum theory, unsettling people's perceptions of the solidity of the material world. Scientific discoveries impelled intense questioning of man's place in the world. Charles Darwin's proposal that animals evolved from simple to complex forms positioned humankind within an evolutionary progression, a view that challenged divine accounts of creation. Philosophers, sociologists and psychiatrists sought to account for human behaviour in terms of anthropology and the unconscious, challenging the assumption that humanity is inherently rational and moral by nature.

These epochal shifts in thinking were accompanied by massive political upheaval and widespread conflict. The most significant for the purposes of this Guide is the First World War (1914–18). In June 1914, a Yugoslav nationalist assassinated the heir to the throne of the Austro-Hungarian Empire, leading Austria-Hungary to declare war on Serbia. The affair quickly escalated into full-scale war between the Central Powers – Germany, the Austro-Hungarian Empire and the Ottoman Empire – and the Allied powers – Britain (with assistance from her Empire), France, Russia (until 1917, the year of the Russian Revolution), and the United States (after 1917). Italy switched allegiance and joined the Allies in 1915. The development of devastating new technologies of warfare, including poison gases, fighter aircraft, tanks and precision artillery brought destruction on a hitherto unimaginable scale.

Overview

Part I of the Guide provides an overview of key critical statements by modernist writers and contemporary commentators in the years before

English literature was institutionalised as an academic discipline. It surveys the criticism written by the most innovative novelists, poets, playwrights and directors, who busily issued manifestos and aesthetic pronouncements, composed essays, book-length studies, letters, prefaces, introductions and reviews, compiled anthologies, staged live performances and held debates in magazines and national newspapers, with a view to readjusting literary taste and creating informed, appreciative audiences for difficult or daring works. It also investigates how their artistic experiments were received by other modernist contemporaries and broader audiences, in journalistic reviews, feature articles, critical analyses in literary quarterlies and periodicals, and even courts of law. It acknowledges that criticism can be directed at specific authors or texts or at literary culture itself.

Part II of the Guide provides a critical survey of modernist studies as an academic discipline. Chapter 4 concerns the construction of modernist reputations and the canonisation of particular strains of modernist writing in the period 1930–80. It examines the critical traditions that modernism hatched, paying particular attention to the ways in which later critics develop lines of thinking already evident in modernist writers' conceptualisation of their own work. The remaining chapters open the discussion out to examine modernisms in their variety, inviting readers to further rethink the highly restrictive, exclusionary modernist canon and overturn old orthodoxies. They set select, thought-provoking critical studies of modernism from recent decades in their intellectual context to produce a lively and informative overview of key issues at stake for modernist studies today. Chapter 5 examines modernist explorations of gender and sexuality. Chapter 6 explores new geographies of modernism, investigating themes of space, place and race. Chapter 7 explores how key developments in cultural studies have impacted on the critical construction of literary modernisms in recent decades, from its relations with mass culture and the marketplace to popular forms such as jazz, music hall and cinema. The Conclusion summarises the Guide.

Of course, there are many ways to tell the story of modernist criticism. Indeed, because New Modernist Studies fruitfully decentres modernism in its institutionalised form, the concept *essential criticism* is not unproblematic. The Guide responds to this challenge by providing multiple, overlapping narratives and emphasising differences of opinion. The two-part structure integrates formalist and historicist approaches. It investigates how aesthetic and technical innovations arise out of culture, while acknowledging that writers took an active role in understanding and shaping their historical moment and also contemplating the institutional factors that have shaped how the movement has been understood and canonised. The Guide is designed to enable readers to: compare and contrast the literary theories of different regional and national artists, schools and movements; find out about the contemporary reception of landmark works; appreciate the ways in which the modernists' own critical writings have guided the course of scholarly enquiry; and make informed judgments about appropriate critical and conceptual frameworks.

PART I

Critical Declarations and Contemporary Responses

CHAPTER ONE

Modernist Beginnings

Charles Baudelaire

'Modernity is the transient, the fleeting, the contingent' declared the French poet Charles Baudelaire (1821–67) in 'The Painter of Modern Life' (1863), an essay often cited as a foundational modernist document.[1] The crowded city is the environment where the flux that characterises modernity is at its most intense. Baudelaire's painter of modern life is 'a singular man' who is by nature 'a great traveller and very cosmopolitan'.[2] He is a *flâneur* who strolls the city streets at his leisure:

> ■ [He] moves into the crowd as though into an enormous reservoir of electricity. He [...] may also be compared to a mirror as vast as this crowd; to a kaleidoscope endowed with consciousness, which with every one of its movements presents a pattern of life, in all its multiplicity, and the flowing grace of all the elements that go to compose life. It is an ego athirst for the non-ego, and reflecting it at every moment in energies more vivid than life itself, always inconstant and fleeting.[3] □

Baudelaire's painter is ambulant and ambivalent. He is the archetypal artist of modernism in its institutionalised form: he observes life and serves as a conductor for the energies that surround him, intensifying what he sees, mindful of himself and his distance from the masses, recording impersonally a multiplicity of fleeting perspectives, from which (as the kaleidoscope metaphor implies) his consciousness constructs a pattern, imposing form on the formless.

According to Baudelaire, immersion in a hyper-stimulating metropolitan environment summons innovative, irregular and discontinuous forms into being, opening up literature to multiple, fragmented perspectives and chronologies:

> ■ Who among us has not dreamed, in his ambitious moments, of the miracle of a poetic prose, musical, yet without rhythm and without rhyme,

supple and resistant enough to adapt to the sudden lyrical stirrings of the soul, the undulations of reverie, and all the sudden leaps of consciousness? This obsessive ideal is born, above all, from the experience of giant cities, from the intersecting of their myriad relations.[4] □

Baudelaire's insights accord with the influential theories set out by the German sociologist Georg Simmel (1858–1918) in 'The Metropolis and Modern Life' (1903), where he considers the psychology of the individual in the crowd. Simmel reasoned that rural existence, with its slow, familiar, rhythms and cohesive community, consumed less mental energy than the metropolis:

■ The psychological foundation, upon which metropolitan individuality is erected, is the intensification of emotional life due to the swift and continuous shift of external and internal stimuli.[5] □

Simmel proposed that the overstimulated metropolitan subject reacts rationally rather than emotionally, cultivating indifference to the people that surround him, treating them as an indistinguishable mass or crowd. The populous cities of modernity are thus paradoxical spaces: they engender mass activity and also feelings of alienation and resistance, which manifest themselves in the intensification of individual subjectivity at the expense of communality.

Baudelaire's most influential volume of poetry, *Les Fleurs du Mal* (*The Flowers of Evil*, 1857), contained wry, lyrical ruminations on urban life and vice; the feelings of anonymity and estrangement engendered by modern Paris; the unsung beggars, prostitutes and gamblers who roam the streets; the scope for erotic encounters; and meditations on sexuality, ennui and death. The first edition was seized by the public prosecutor on grounds of indecency and a suit was issued against Baudelaire and his publisher, resulting in a fine and an order banning the publication of the six poems judged most obscene.

As Victor Hugo (1802–85) immediately perceived, Baudelaire's poems had introduced 'un frisson nouveau' ['a new shudder'] into literature.[6] The early literatures of modernism registered this seismic shift. They defiantly resolved to treat the actuality of modern life, however sordid, and evolved new forms to comprehend and communicate the experience of modernity, breaking with polite conventions of representation and often running into legal difficulties as a consequence. Baudelaire's example would prove hugely influential. As T.S. Eliot stated in 1930: 'It is not merely in the use of imagery of the sordid life of a great metropolis, but in the elevation of such imagery to the *first intensity* [...] that Baudelaire has created a mode of release and expression for other men'.[7]

The following sections explore the beginnings of modernism by examining the foundational critical statements that informed the literary experiments of key proto-modernist figures and movements as they grappled with new subjects and originated new expressive forms.

Walt Whitman

Although Walt Whitman (1819–92) believed nature to be the art of a divine imagination, his poetry accorded with the revolutionary impulses of modernism. As he explained to his publisher, Leaves of Grass (1855) was written in 'a new style, [...] necessitated by new theories, new themes — or say the treatment of themes, forced upon us for American purposes'.[8] The aim was to 'give something to our literature which will be our own; with neither foreign spirit, nor imagery nor form, but adapted to our case, grown out of our associations, [...] strengthening and intensifying the national soul, and finding the entire fountains of its birth and growth in our own country'.[9] For this reason, Whitman wrote in idiomatic free verse (unrhymed lines of unequal length without regular metre), a style then unknown to American poetry. He justified this innovation in terms of simplicity and directness: 'I will not have in my writing any elegance or effect or originality to hang in the way between me and the rest, like curtains. What I tell, I tell for precisely what it is'.[10]

Contemporary reviewers were scandalised by the form and content of Leaves of Grass. Charles Eliot Norton (1827–1908) complained:

> ■ The poems, twelve in number, are neither in rhyme nor blank verse, but in a sort of excited prose broken into lines without any attempt at measure or regularity, and [...] without any idea of sense or reason. The writer's scorn for the wonted usages of good writing extends to the vocabulary he adopts; words usually banished from polite society are here employed without reserve.[11] □

Other press notices were less favourable still, rebuking Whitman for his treatment of sexual themes. Rufus Griswold (1815–57) described the volume as 'a gathering of muck' and accused Whitman (in Latin) of 'That horrible sin not to be mentioned among Christians' (by which he meant homosexuality), while the Boston Intelligencer denounced the poems as 'a heterogeneous mass of bombast, egotism, vulgarity and nonsense', and recommended that Whitman receive 'the lash for such a violation of decency'.[12]

Whitman conceived of himself as a great national poet, a messianic figure whose sheer force of individuality and vision equipped him to be 'the equalizer of his age and land', whose writing could unify and heal an ethnically diverse nation riven by social inequality, racial tension and slavery.[13] His unabashed Americanism and humanist credo would exert a profound influence on the nation's poets. For instance, Whitman occupied a special place in Langston Hughes's heart because his 'all-embracing words lock arms with workers and farmers, Negroes and whites, Asiatics and Europeans, serfs, and free men, beaming democracy to all'.[14] William Carlos Williams was inspired to seek a 'language modified by our environment, the American environment', and strove to continue the programme Whitman started by forming a specifically American localist branch of modernism.[15]

Decadence and Degeneracy

The preface that Théophile Gautier (1811–72) wrote to accompany the 1868 posthumous edition of *Les Fleurs du Mal* praised Charles Baudelaire's painterly palette of 'the morbidly rich tints of decomposition, [...] the roses of consumption, the pallor of chlorosis, the hateful bilious yellows, the leaden grey of pestilential fogs [...], the bitumens baked and browned in the depths of hell; [...] correspondent to [...] the last hours of civilization'.[16] It firmly associated Baudelaire with Decadence, a literary and artistic movement that emerged in France in the latter half of the nineteenth century. Convinced of man's fallen nature and the omnipresence of evil, the Decadent imagination disdained prevailing bourgeois values and instead consciously revelled in the perverse, debauched, grotesque and unhealthy aspects of metropolitan life. Decadent writers did not seek to cure the sickness afflicting society, but were connoisseurs of corruption who sought to shock and outrage by wringing a certain sensual beauty from decline through exquisite stylisation and artifice. The Decadent movement in literature reached its artistic peak in English in the 1890s. The trend was famously described by Arthur Symons (1865–1945) as 'a new and beautiful and interesting disease'.[17]

Concerns over the perceived sudden deterioration in spiritual and moral standards in European cities intensified in the 1890s with the publication of *Degeneration* (1892, first translated into English 1895), a notorious and intemperate tirade by the physician and writer Max Nordau (1849–1923) on the decadent aspects of the social phenomena modernity had generated. Nordau interpreted supposed increases in criminal activity, anarchism, 'unfeminine' behaviour in women, prostitution, homosexuality, sexual perversion, disease, hysteria, ego-mania, insanity and fatigue as evidence that – far from embodying Darwin's ideas about evolution and the progress of species – modern civilisation was in fact retrogressing.

■ One epoch of our history is unmistakably in its decline, and another is announcing its approach. There is a sound of rendering in every tradition, and it is as though the morrow would not link with today. Things as they are totter and plunge, and they are suffered to reel and fall, because man is weary, and there is no faith that it is worth an effort to uphold them.[18] □

Nordau argued that experimental modern art was itself a symptom of degeneracy, and a product of pathological mental and behavioural processes. 'Degenerates', he declared, 'are not always criminals, prostitutes, anarchists, and pronounced lunatics; they are often authors and artists'.[19] The movements that Nordau singled out for particular scorn were those that delved into degenerate behaviour and psychology and/or refuted any necessary link between art and moral good. Decadence figured prominently, as did Realism, Naturalism, Aestheticism and Symbolism.

Naturalism

By the mid-nineteenth century, the European novel had matured as it evolved through two closely related pre-modernist modes: Realism and Naturalism. Realists insisted on accurate documentation, without partiality or idealism, and aimed to depict the material world through an accumulation of empirical detail. They were determined to show society as it is and were adamant that the life of the lower and middle classes warranted literary attention. Naturalists additionally believed that human behaviour was subject to natural laws, which could be explained through contemporary scientific theories (in particular Darwinian ideas concerning heredity and the impact of the environment on human behaviour), and that bringing these underlying motivations out into the open was for the ultimate betterment of society. The desire to reform rather than refine corruption separates Naturalism from Decadence.

In 1880, Émile Zola (1840–1902) prepared a manifesto, 'Naturalism on the Stage', insisting that the theatre must attain the same level of modernity achieved by the European novel.

■ [The novel] touches on all subjects: writes history; treats of physiology and psychology; rises to the highest flights of poetry; studies the most diverse subjects – politics, social economy, religion and manners. Entire nature is its domain. [...] While the novelists are digging always further forward, producing newer and more exact data, the stage will flounder deeper every day in the midst of its romantic fictions, its worn-out plots, and its skilfulness of handicraft. [...] Either the theatre will be naturalistic or it will not be at all [...].[20] □

At that time, the two most popular theatrical forms on the mid-nineteenth-century stage did not present believable characters. Melodrama was unrealistic, romantic and sensational, while intricately plotted well-made plays used stock devices to resolve mysteries and remove obstructions to characters' happiness.

Zola's call for theatre to embrace realistic presentation and a Naturalist willingness to explore difficult, unsavoury or risqué social issues would be answered by the actor-director André Antoine (1858–1943), who founded the Théâtre Libre in Paris in 1890 because the company he was working for refused to let him dramatise Zola's controversial novel *Thérèse Raquin* (1867). The Théâtre Libre was run on a subscription-only basis in order that it could stage provocative plays without falling foul of the censors. It provided the model for other independent companies such as the Independent Theatre Society (London, 1891), founded by J.T. Grein (1862–1935), and the Freie Bühne (Berlin, 1889), without which avant-garde experiments could not have been staged. Antoine's manifesto for his new venture, 'The Free Theatre' (1890), initiated the effective beginning of modernist theatre by setting out a programme of Naturalist reforms:

■ The art of the actor [...] will gain its life from truth, observation, and the *direct* study of nature [...]. Since the theatrical style of the new plays tends to keep close to daily conversation, the actor must no longer '*speak*' in the classical theatrical sense; he must *talk* [...]. [O]nce the scenery is called back down to the dimensions current in contemporary milieu, the characters will express their emotions in credible settings, without continually concerning themselves to strike pictorial poses and form *tableaux*. The audience will enjoy an intimate drama, with natural and fitting moves, and with unaffected gestures and movements appropriate to a modern man, living our normal daily life.[21] □

Antoine used highly innovative production techniques to achieve naturalistic effects, replacing static, painted backdrops with domestic interiors that were arranged as if there were no missing fourth wall, exchanging footlights with more natural lighting, and even hanging haunches of meat on the stage.

The characters that were depicted on the Naturalist stage were conflicted and complex, as the Swedish playwright August Strindberg (1849–1912) explained in his preface to *Miss Julie: A Naturalistic Tragedy* (1888). Copies of this important manifesto for Naturalism in the theatre were distributed to the audience prior to Antoine's 1893 production of the play:

■ As modern characters, living in an age of transition more urgently hysterical at any rate than the one that preceded it, I have depicted the figures in my play as more split and vacillating, a mixture of the old and the new [...]. My souls (characters) are conglomerates of the past and present stages of culture, bits out of books and newspapers, scraps of humanity, torn shreds of once fine clothing now turned to rags, exactly as the human soul is patched together.[22] □

For this reason, Strindberg's 'characters' brains [...] work irregularly as they do in real life' and 'the dialogue also wanders, providing itself in the opening scenes with material that is later reworked, taken up, repeated, expanded, and developed, like the theme in a musical composition'.[23] Strindberg's description of the modern soul as divided, unstable and constituted from fragments of different cultural discourses, anticipated many later modernist writers' ideas about the human psyche and also the formal strategies that they developed to represent characters' thought processes.

Miss Julie herself is representative of a particular kind of 'modern character' known in English as the 'New Woman', so-called after the bestselling novelist Sarah Grand (1854–1943) used the phrase to denote the early nineteenth-century feminists who 'proclaimed [...] what was wrong with Home-is-the-Women's Sphere, and prescribed the remedy'.[24] New Women pushed for marital, sexual, educational, economic and civic rights, stepping outside the domestic realm to enter public life. They were often caricatured in the press as mannishly unattractive, overeducated, hysterical and either unsexed or oversexed, and were associated with suffrage and socialism. Strindberg considered the New Woman to be 'synonymous with degeneracy'.[25] He described Miss Julie as a 'man-hating half-woman', who has become the 'Victim of a superstition [...] that woman, this stunted form of human being who stands between man, the lord of creation, the creator of culture, is meant to be the equal of man or ever could be'.[26] He presented her tragic rebellion against the expected codes of behaviour for a woman of her class as 'the spectacle of a desperate struggle against nature'.[27]

Unlike Strindberg, Henrik Ibsen (1828–1906), the great Norwegian exponent of Naturalism, was sympathetic to the plight of women in a patriarchal society, as his preparatory notes for *A Doll's House* (1879) attest:

■ A woman cannot be herself in the society of the present day, which is an exclusively masculine society, with laws framed by men and with a judicial system that judges feminine conduct from a masculine point of view.[28] □

A Doll's House subverts the formula of the well-made play by depicting the painful breakdown of a marriage. Notoriously, it ends with the protagonist Nora leaving the family home, rejecting her role as a wife and mother: a conclusion that scandalised contemporary audiences.

When the first professional production of *A Doll's House* finally reached the London stage in June 1889, it was a *succès de scandale*, generating fierce debate in the press as to whether, in the words of the leading theatre critic Clement Scott (1841–1904), 'it could ever be possible for any woman with maternal instinct fully developed to desert her children', and how far the play constituted a dangerous attack on the institution of marriage.[29] The critic and translator William Archer (1856–1924) noted 'If we may measure fame by mileage of newspaper comment, Henrik Ibsen has for the past month been the most famous man in the English literary world'.[30]

Ibsen's next play *Ghosts* (1881) responded to the furore surrounding *A Doll's House* by examining what could happen if a woman did not leave a bad marriage. His frank treatment of syphilis was met with horror and the play was promptly banned in most of Europe. When a production of Archer's English translation of *Ghosts* was staged by the Independent Theatre Society (1891), the *Daily Telegraph* compared it to 'an open drain, a loathsome sore unbandaged, a dirty act done publicly'.[31] The Examiner of Stage Plays, E.F.S. Piggott, spoke for the morally prurient majority when he concluded that Ibsen's characters were 'morally deranged', explaining to the 1892 Select Committee on Censorship that 'All the heroines are dissatisfied spinsters who look on marriage as a monopoly, or dissatisfied married women in a chronic state of rebellion [...], as for the men, they are all rascals or imbeciles'.[32]

The British playwright George Bernard Shaw (1856–1950) wrote the first English-language study of Ibsen's work. In *The Quintessence of Ibsenism* (1891), Shaw praised Ibsen's 'vigilant open-mindedness' and defended him against charges of immorality and calls for censorship through the Obscene Publications Act (1857).[33] Shaw was sympathetic to Ibsen's socially progressive politics and identified the quintessence of Ibsenism to be that 'the impulse towards greater freedom' is 'sufficient ground for the repudiation of any customary duty, however sacred, that conflicts with it'.[34]

Many of Shaw's own plays responded to Ibsen's work directly, using humour to intervene in political debates. For instance, *The Philanderer* (written in 1893, first professional performance 1907) referred to marriage as a degrading transaction in which a woman sells herself, but featured a second act that ridiculed a group of trouser-wearing New Women who form an Ibsen Club. Another comedy, *Mrs Warren's Profession* (written 1894, but so controversial that it was unlicensed for unexpurgated performance until 1925), probed the limited opportunities available to women and linked advantageous marriage to prostitution. It concerns stock New Woman Vivie Warren's discovery that her mother, Mrs Kitty Warren, paid for her education by running brothels. Shaw was adamant that the play had moral value, explaining that it was written 'to draw attention to the truth that prostitution is caused, not by female depravity and male licentiousness, but simply by underpaying, undervaluing, and overworking women so shamefully that the poorest of them are forced to resort to prostitution to keep body and soul together'.[35] Censorship was evaded by the two private performances of *Mrs Warren's Profession* produced by the Stage Society in London in 1902. J.T. Grein found the performance 'exceedingly uncomfortable' and accused Shaw of having 'merely philandered around a dangerous subject', treating 'it half in earnest, half in that peculiar jesting manner which is all his own'.[36] Years later, the revolutionary Marxist German playwright and director Bertolt Brecht (1898–1956) would praise Shaw for his outspokenness, his 'delight in dislocating our stock associations' and giving 'the theatre as much fun as it can stand'.[37] Brecht declared Shaw to be 'a terrorist', whose transgression was to claim 'a right for every man to act in all circumstances with decency, logic and humour'.[38]

Aesthetic Criticism

Aestheticism is a movement devoted to the appreciation and cultivation of beauty, and the philosophy of 'art for art's sake'. The movement received critical definition in *Studies in the History of the Renaissance* (1873), a collection of eight idiosyncratic essays on key figures of the Italian Renaissance by Walter Pater (1839–94). Pater approached his subjects as an 'aesthetic critic', someone whose primary qualification is the ability to apprehend an artwork's capacity to impart 'a special, unique impression of pleasure'.[39] The aesthetic critic must be 'deeply moved by the presence of beautiful objects' and should aim 'to distinguish, to analyse, and separate from its adjuncts, the virtue by which a picture, a landscape, a fair personality in life or in a book, produces this special impression of beauty or pleasure'.[40]

In the famous Conclusion to *Studies in the History of Renaissance*, Pater extended his aesthetic theories about the emotional and sensory experience of viewing art into everyday life. 'At first sight', Pater explained, 'experience seems to bury us under a flood of external objects, pressing upon us with a sharp importunate reality', but in fact this data is dissipated under the influence of reflection in such a way that 'each object is loosed into a group of impressions, – colour, odour, texture, – in the mind of the observer':[41]

■ To such a tremulous wisp constantly reforming itself on the stream, to a single sharp impression, with a sense in it, a relic more or less fleeting, of such moments gone by, what is *real* in our life fines down. It is with the movement, the passage and dissolution of impressions, images, sensations, that analysis leaves off, – that continual vanishing away, that strange perpetual weaving and unweaving of ourselves.[42] □

Science cannot hope to catalogue the shower of impressions, which are continually adjusted. But what art can do, Pater argued, is to give 'the highest quality' to impressions by arresting them for appreciation, yielding 'a quickened, multiplied consciousness'.[43] In doing so, aesthetic apprehension might facilitate a more intense awareness of lived experience.

As a piece of art criticism the Conclusion proved seminal, promoting ideas and a vocabulary that many British, Irish and American modernist poets and novelists would draw on in their attempts to capture reality and recreate fleeting events, feelings and sensations. Impressions, images, moments: these concepts would be crucial to many modernist literatures.

Henry James

Henry James (1843–1916) answered Walter Pater's call for 'quickened, multiplied consciousness' by recording the myriad shifting impressions that strike the highly receptive and supple minds of his leading characters. In 'The Art of Fiction' (1884), James theorised the novel in Paterian terms, making the impression the basis of aesthetic response:

■ A novel is in its broadest definition a personal, a direct impression of life: that, to begin with, constitutes its value, which is greater or less according to the intensity of the impression.[44] □

James shared this interest in mental processes with his brother, the Harvard psychologist and philosopher William James (1842–1910). In *Principles of Psychology* (1890), William James argued that consciousness 'does not appear to itself chopped up in bits' and influentially proposed we should speak of 'the stream of thought, of consciousness, or of subjective life'.[45] By contrast, the image that Henry James devised for the workings of consciousness was not continuous or linear but radial and atomised:

■ Experience is never limited, and it is never complete; it is an immense sensibility, a kind of huge spiderweb of the finest silken threads suspended in the chamber of consciousness, and catching every airborne particle in its tissue. It is the very atmosphere of the mind; and when the mind is imaginative – much more when it happens to be that of a man of genius – it takes to itself the faintest hints of life, it converts the very pulses of the air into revelations.[46] □

Henry James did not wish to 'minimise the importance of exactness – of truth of detail', but to affirm that the writer's art fundamentally depends on the imagination's ability to seize on the most tremulous impressions and apprehend their larger significance.[47] The author, he explained, is 'someone on whom nothing is lost'.[48]

Like many of the practitioners at the forefront of their craft, Henry James's writing and his literary criticism was finely responsive to the key artistic movements of his time: not just Aestheticism, but also Realism, Naturalism and Symbolism. The prefaces that James wrote for the New York Edition of his fiction (1907–09) are regarded as foundational critical documents for theories of the Anglo-American novel. A high formalist, James believed that art redeemed life by giving it shape and meaning. Throughout the prefaces, he contrasts the 'splendid waste' of life with the 'sublime economy' of art – 'life being all inclusion and confusion, and art being all discrimination and selection'.[49]

James was born in America, but settled in England. His fiction was extensively reviewed in British and American periodicals and newspapers, often to great acclaim. Attention was frequently drawn to his powers of psychological scrutiny, particularly his use of focalised third-person narration to delineate the subtleties of thought and emotion. A reviewer for the *New York Herald* noted that when James's narrators find 'a young lady worthy of their interest they impale her as a naturalist might a butterfly and make a careful and scientific investigation of her nature'.[50] Another reviewer for the *Atlantic Monthly* also singled out this habit for particular praise, drawing attention to the 'masterly passage' in *The Portrait of a Lady* (1881) where the heroine 'enters upon a disclosure of her changed life, the reader seems to be going down as in a diving-bell into the very secrets of her nature'.[51] Others considered the depths of psychological penetration unseemly. A reviewer of *The Bostonians* (1886) complained that 'To be told not only what his dramatic personae express but what they thought and kept to themselves [...] seems to us a violation of every conceivable rule of literary good breeding'.[52] Reviewers often commented on the high demands that James made on his readers, who were forced to draw inferences and cope with equivocal endings, particularly his propensity to break off 'with the air of saying, "I have furnished all the points and shown you how to proceed. Find the answer for yourselves"'.[53] Some commentators found James's late style exasperating, for instance a reviewer of *The Awkward Age* (1899) complained that 'James has refined refinement, subtilized subtlety, and suggested suggestion to bewilderment'.[54] Others were awed by his techniques. For instance, Edmund Gosse praised *The American Scene* (1904) – a memoir of James's visit to the United States after over two decades' absence – for the 'infinity of minute touches' that were arranged to compose 'a picture which absolutely controls the imagination', achieving the 'most durable surface-portraiture of an unparalleled condition of society which our generation is likely to see'.[55]

Joseph Conrad

Joseph Conrad (1857–1924) was also influenced by Walter Pater's theories. The preface to *The Nigger of the 'Narcissus'* (1897) – the most celebrated statement of Conrad's aesthetic vision – is marbled with references to Pater. Conrad defined his art as 'a single-minded attempt to render the highest kind of justice to the visible universe, by bringing to light the truth, manifold and one, underlying its every aspect':[56]

■ My task which I am trying to achieve is, by the power of the written word to make you hear, to make you feel – it is, before all, to make you see. That – and no more, and it is everything.[57] □

Contemporary reviews of *The Nigger of the 'Narcissus'* emphasised its trueness to life: W.L. Courtney described Conrad as 'an unflinching realist' who 'has no hesitation in giving to his singularly vivid and powerful tale of the sea the ugliest conceivable title', while the *Saturday Review* claimed 'We know nothing else so vivid and so convincing in contemporary fiction as the way in which the reader is forced, along with the crew, to hang on for dear life to the perilously slanting deck'.[58]

In addition to communicating the immediacy of sensory experience, the word '*see*' as Conrad used it in the preface to *The Nigger of the 'Narcissus'* emphatically pertains to insight and truth. He explained: 'To snatch in a moment of courage, from the remorseless rush of time, a passing phase of life, is only the beginning of the task'.[59] That 'rescued fragment' needs to be made to 'reveal the substance of its truth', which is 'the stress and passion within the core of each convincing moment'.[60] He called this truth, 'which binds men to each other and all mankind to the visible world', a 'moment of vision'.[61] For Conrad, success depended on 'unswerving devotion to the perfect blending of form and substance', whereby 'the light of magic suggestiveness may be brought to play for an evanescent instant over the commonplace surface of words: of the old, old words'.[62] His account of the way in which tired language might be rendered suggestive, or even revelatory, has much in common with Symbolist ideas about poetry.

Aesthetic Criticism on Trial:
The Life and Works of Oscar Wilde

The Conclusion to *Studies in the History of the Renaissance* was also inter-preted as a manifesto for hedonism and immorality. Reflecting on 'the splendour of our experience', 'its awful brevity' and the 'desperate effort' required to gather it all up, Walter Pater perceived that there was 'hardly [...] time to make theories about the things we see and touch'.[63] The remedy he proposed was to view and live life as if it were art, and 'be for ever curiously testing new opinions and courting new impressions' and 'great passions' in order to 'burn always with this hard, gem-like flame'.[64] Pater was moved to omit the Conclusion from the second edi-tion, as he 'conceived it might possibly mislead some of those young men into whose hands it might fall'.[65]

Many artists of the younger generation were only too eager to be misled by Pater's sensuous prose exhorting them to court experience for experience's sake. W.B. Yeats (1865–1939), looking back on the early years of modernism (and the so-called 'tragic generation' of 1890s Decadents of whom he was practically the sole survivor), reflected 'we consciously looked to Pater for our philosophy'.[66] Pater's most famous student, Oscar Wilde (1854–1900), would later describe *The Renais-sance* as 'that book which had such a strange influence over my life'.[67] His activities as a critic, writer and public persona, would bring the homosexual subtext to Pater's Conclusion to the fore of debates about Aestheticism and the moral function of art.

Wilde was sensationally tried for gross indecency in 1895, following the unsuccessful libel action that he brought against the Marquess of Queensbury (the father of his lover, Lord Alfred Douglas), who had left him a provocative calling-card accusing him of being a sodomite. Edward Carson QC cross-examined Wilde on his personal life and aesthetic philosophy. He enquired whether the substantial revisions that Wilde had made to the text of the book edition of *The Picture of Dorian Gray* (1891) – in which a portrait which takes on the apparition of the pro-tagonist's sins – were in response to the scathing criticism that followed its first publication in *Lippincott's Monthly Magazine* (1890). For instance, the *Scots Observer* had complained that *Dorian* was concerned 'with matters only fitted for the Criminal Investigation Department' and that it was suitable for 'none but outlawed noblemen and perverted telegraphy boys', while the *Daily Chronicle* described it as 'a tale spawned from the leprous literature of the French *Décadents* – a poisonous book [...] – a gloating study of the mental and physical corruption of a fresh, fair and golden youth, which might be horrible and fascinating but for its effeminate frivolity'.[68] At the time, Wilde defended his work boldly, explaining that 'What Dorian's Gray's sins are no one knows. He who finds them has brought them', and further insisting that 'The sphere of art and the sphere of ethics are absolutely distinct and separate'.[69]

In the wake of the Wilde trials, the most forward-thinking writers began to articulate more enlightened approaches to same-sex desire. For instance, *Sexual Inversion* (1897), the first volume in *Studies in the Psychology of Sex* (1897–1928), a seven-volume series by the British sexologist (Henry) Havelock Ellis (1859–1930), argued that same-sex desire was a naturally arising 'congenital abnormality' which should be treated sympathetically and not criminalised.[70]

Wilde considered the coarseness of Realism at length in 'The Decay of Lying' (1891), in which he articulated a 'new aesthetics' in the form of a mock-dialogue.[71] The core principle is that 'Art never expresses anything but itself': it is self-referential and autonomous.[72] For this reason, Émile Zola is denounced as 'entirely wrong from beginning to end, and wrong not on the grounds of morals, but on the ground of art [...]. The author is perfectly truthful, and describes things exactly as they are'.[73] The Realist slavishly copies Nature as it is, whereas the true artist protests against Nature, which encompasses not only the natural world and its laws, but also 'natural simple instinct as opposed to self-conscious culture':[74]

■ Art takes life as part of her rough material, recreates it, and refashions it in fresh forms, is absolutely indifferent to fact, invents, imagines, dreams, and keeps between herself and reality the impenetrable barrier of beautiful style, of decorative or ideal treatment.[75] □

The artist must draw on personal powers of invention. Art is consciously stylised, not only so that it fulfils its goal of being beautiful, but also to emphasise its separation from nature. In theory, then, the Aesthete retreats from reality into subjective reverie and the pursuit of beauty. However, the conclusion that 'Lying, the telling of beautiful untrue things, is the proper aim of Art' does not preclude the self-conscious artist from intervening in life by challenging the 'simple' social customs that merely pose as natural and instinctive by imagining more sophisticated alternatives.[76] After all, as Wilde insisted, 'Life imitates Art far more than Art imitates Life'.[77]

The Symbolist Movement in Literature and Drama

The theatrical avant-garde were quick to reject Realist and Naturalist conventions, recognising that their power was fatally undermined by the framing context of performance. The most visionary playwrights moved beyond the limits of Naturalism towards Expressionism and Symbolism. Expressionist theatre shattered Realist conventions in order to dramatise interior emotions, making use of symbols, archetypes, abstraction, visions and dream states, but retained Naturalism's determination to examine uncomfortable truths. August Strindberg's *A Dream Play* (1901) was one of the first intimations of this new theatrical mode, which he described in the preface:

■ In this dream play the author has [...] attempted to imitate the inconsequent yet apparently logical form of a dream. Everything can happen, everything is possible and probable. Time and place do not exist; on an insignificant basis of reality the imagination spins and weaves new patterns: a blend of memories, experiences, spontaneous ideas, absurdities, and improvisations. The characters split, double, multiply, evaporate, condense, disperse, and converge. But one consciousness holds sway over them all, that of the dreamer [...]. He neither acquits nor condemns, but merely relates [...].[78] □

Violently anti-mimetic, Expressionism was particularly popular in Germany and remained so into the 1920s. The foreword to the first issue of *Der Sturm* (*The Storm*, 1910) encapsulated the Expressionists' loathing for bourgeois values: 'We want insidiously to demolish their comfortable serious-sublime image of society'.[79]

Of course, the symbol is one of art's basic techniques and is as old as literature itself. Symbolism as a movement was concerned with the more profound use of symbols as a means to reveal truths that cannot be apprehended in the ordinary course of things. As Jean Moréas (1856–1910) explained in his manifesto 'Le Symbolisme' (1886), the aim was to 'clothe the Idea in a perceptible form'.[80] Whereas Naturalists presumed that literature could attain the condition of science, Symbolists held that the function of literature is to comprehend that which cannot be articulated through scientific methods, as per Charles Baudelaire's theory of 'correspondences':

■ In certain, almost supernatural, spiritual states, the profundity of life is revealed in all its fullness in the thing, however banal, which one is looking at. It becomes the symbol of that profundity.[81] □

French Symbolism was first introduced to an English-speaking audience by Arthur Symons in *The Symbolist Movement in Literature* (1899). The first edition contained chapters on Gérard de Nerval (1808–55), Villiers de L'Isle Adam (1838–39), Arthur Rimbaud (1854–91), Paul Verlaine (1844–96), Jules Laforgue (1860–87), Stéphane Mallarmé (1842–98),

Joris-Karl Huysmans (1848–1907) and Maurice Maeterlinck (1862–1949). Symons drew heavily on the ideas that Mallarmé advanced in his seminal critical essay 'Crisis in Poetry' (1896), in which he examined the 'fascinating and fundamental crisis' that literature had reached following 'an almost century-long period of poetic orgy and excess'.[82]

Mallarmé was acutely aware of the rickety relationship between words and their referents and resolved to make the obliqueness of language his ultimate subject. He recognised that 'no one can utter words which would bear the miraculous stamp of Truth Herself Incarnate', but argued that poetic form could redeem language by setting words in intricate arrangements of rhyme and internal rhyme and imbuing them with the magic suggestiveness of music (which communicates in abstract terms).[83] He insisted that this effect depended on the withdrawal of the poet:

■ If the poem is to be pure, the poet's voice must be stilled and the initiative taken by the words themselves, which will be set in motion as they meet unequally in collision. And in an exchange of gleams they will flame out like some glittering swath of fire sweeping over precious stones, and thus replace the audible breathing in lyric poetry of old – replace the poet's own personal and passionate control of verse.[84] □

In the poet's absence, the initiative for orchestrating meaning comes from the words themselves, which reverberate within an autonomous, self-referential structure. The musical arrangement instigates spatial readings, linking 'motifs of like pattern' so that for each theme 'a given harmony will be born somewhere in the parts of the total poem'.[85] Mallarmé praised Decadent poets for retaining only 'the suggestiveness of things' and using music to establish 'a careful relationship between two images, from which a third element, clear and fusible, will be distilled and caught by our imagination'.[86] 'To *name* an object is to suppress three-quarters of the enjoyment of the poem', Mallarmé explained in interview, adding, 'It is the perfect use of this mystery that constitutes the symbol'.[87]

Symons followed Mallarmé, and other French poets and playwrights, by defining 'Symbolism in literature' as 'a form of expression, at best but approximate, essentially but arbitrary, […] for an unseen reality apprehended by the consciousness'.[88] Rejecting realistic standards of exterior description, Symons explained that the Symbolists endeavoured to isolate 'the ultimate essence, the soul, of whatever exists and can be realised by the consciousness'.[89]

■ It is all an attempt to spiritualise literature, to evade the old bondage of rhetoric, the old bondage of exteriority. Description is banished that beautiful things may be evoked, magically; the regular beat of verse is broken in order that words may fly, upon subtler wings.[90] □

The success of this subtle art of evocation – comparable to the mysteries of religion – depends on careful elaboration of form and the abstract, musical and referential qualities of language, which is why Symons insisted that the poet must be released from 'the old bondage' of rhetoric and regular metre.

Translating the critical principles underlying Symbolism from poetry to the stage was challenging, as the physical presence of real actors compromised the sense of mystery that the Symbolists wished to convey. As Maurice Maeterlinck stated, 'the symbol can never support the active presence of man'.[91] His solution was to write three plays for marionettes: *Alladine et Palomides*, *L'Intérieur* and *La Mort de Tintagiles* (1894).

One of the most striking manifestations of Symbolism on the nineteenth-century stage was the production of the surreal, scatological, anti-theatrical *Ubu Roi* (*King Ubu*) by the French writer Alfred Jarry (1873–1907), which the visionary director Aurélien Lugné-Poë (1869–1940) arranged at his daringly innovative Théâtre l'Œuvre (Paris, 1896). Jarry's play usurped theatrical conventions to attack the very premises of theatricality and performance. He railed against all the things 'that encumber the stage uselessly: above all the *scenery* and the *actors*' in his essay 'On the Uselessness of Theatre in the Theatre' (1896). He explained the stage-setting for *Ubu Roi* in the preface he read before the curtain lifted at the first performance on 10 December 1896 to the assembled audience of avant-garde artists and critics:

■ [H]ere you must accept doors that open out on plains covered with snow falling from a clear sky, chimneys adorned with clocks splitting open to serve as doors, and palm-trees growing at the foot of bedsteads for little elephants sitting on shelves to munch on. As to our orchestra that isn't here, we'll miss only its brilliance and tone. The themes for Ubu will be performed offstage by various pianos and drums.[92] □

This madcap introduction set the scene for an anarchic and savage farce concerning the Macbethian exploits of the grotesquely obese tyrant Père Ubu. The play was performed by 'actors pretending to be puppets'.[93] They wore conical costumes and masks so that they might represent depersonalised types. Many of the spectators left after the first word was uttered (a barely disguised profanity). The remainder jeered, screamed and shook their fists in response to what they saw.

W.B. Yeats and Arthur Symons attended the premiere of *Ubu Roi* together. Symons understood the play to represent 'the brutality out of which we have achieved our civilisation'.[94] Although Yeats shouted out for the play, on returning to his hotel, he was sufficiently perturbed to imagine the artistic future it presaged in the pejorative language of degeneracy:

■ The players are supposed to be dolls, toys, marionettes, and now they are all hopping like wooden frogs, and I can see for myself that the chief personage, who is some kind of King, carries for Sceptre a brush of the kind that we use to clean a closet. Feeling bound to support the most spirited party, we have shouted for the play, but that night at the Hôtel Corneille I am very sad, for comedy, objectivity, has displayed its growing power once more. I say: 'After Stéphane Mallarmé, after Paul Verlaine, after Gustave Moreau, after Puvis des Chavannes, after our own verse, after all our subtle colour and nervous rhythm, after the faint mixed tints of Conder, what more is possible? After us the Savage God'.[95] □

(Gustave Moreau (1826–98), Pierre-Cécile Puvis de Chavannes (1824–98) and Charles Conder (1868–1909) were all pioneering modern painters). By Yeats's reckoning Symbolism had reached an artistic peak that could only be succeeded by its opposite: anarchic parody that was alarmingly primitive and destructive, in short, a distinctive modernist sensibility.

The Theatre Criticism of Edward Gordon Craig

The theatre practitioner and theorist Edward Gordon Craig (1872–1966) repeated many of Alfred Jarry's ideas a decade later, rejecting the fussy realism of nineteenth-century theatre in favour of abstraction. In the very early years of the twentieth century, Craig's productions had been notable for their highly inventive staging. He abolished foot-lights for electric lighting, which he used to illuminate his dynamic and emblematic, non-naturalistic scenes (as opposed to the standard painted backdrops). W.B. Yeats saw two of the plays that Craig staged at the Coronet Theatre in 1901 and wrote a letter to the editor of the *Saturday Review* defending what he considered to be 'the only admirable stage scenery of our time':

■ Realistic scenery takes the imagination captive and is at best bad landscape painting, but Mr Gordon Craig's scenery is a new and distinct art. It is something that can only exist in theatre. It cannot even be sep-arated from the figures that move before it.[96] □

Craig's ambition was to achieve the perfect integration of music, art, dance and drama on the stage. Convinced that a single intelligence needed to be in complete control of all aspects of a production, he rejected the role assumed by late nineteenth-century 'actor-managers' like Henry Irving (1838–1905) and George Alexander (1858–1918), who took centre stage and also arranged the performance around themselves. Instead Craig retreated to the auditorium to oversee all elements of the action, holding that it was the director, not the playwright, who was the true theatrical artist.

Craig relocated to Italy in 1907 and founded his own journal, the *Mask* (1908–29). It was dedicated to exploring the art of theatre as performance rather than simply a branch of literature, in the belief that 'A drama is not to be read, but to be seen upon the stage'.[97] Craig was responsible for many of the contributions, but he masked this fact with a series of impersonal pseudonyms. The journal contained polemical essays on stage design, theatre's social function, the world's great theatrical traditions and appraisals of innovative contemporaries across the globe. Its international outlook reflected the ease with which theatrical productions were able to tour the world's major cities, helped by the fact that performance can communicate extra-linguistically, as was the case for the Eastern non-representational dance-dramas that rendered human form abstract and in which Craig discerned great potential.

Craig's most controversial and influential critical essay was 'The Actor and the *Über-marionette*' (1907, reprinted in Craig's seminal book *On the Art of Theatre* (1911), which was widely translated). Having established that the actor's art is imitative, not originally creative, and that the precise nature of any human performance cannot be calculated beforehand, he proposed:

■ The actor must go, and in his place comes the inanimate figure – the *Über-marionette* we may call him, until he has won for himself a better name.[98] □

The notion of the *Über-marionette* that exists beyond the human dimension brought Craig further towards his goal of achieving a theatre of *pure form* that reduced everything to its essence and so brought the theatre closer to the condition of abstract art.

Craig sent copies of the first issue of the *Mask* to every significant European director in the belief that the publication 'might in time come to change the whole theatre – not plays alone, but playing sceneries, construction of theatres'.[99] The influence of his criticism can be traced in many different developments in twentieth-century European theatre, including Futurist scenography and the theatre of W.B. Yeats.

The Abbey Theatre

W.B. Yeats co-founded the Abbey Theatre, Dublin, together with Lady Augusta Gregory (1852–1932) in 1904. They succeeded in their mission to 'bring upon the stage the deeper thoughts and emotions of Ireland' by nurturing the work of some of Ireland's greatest playwrights, including John Millington Synge (1871–1909), Seán O'Casey (1880–1964) and of course Yeats himself.[100] Under Yeats's aegis new impulses in European theatre filtered into many of the Abbey's productions, particularly the work of Gordon Craig. Not only did Yeats use a system of foldable screens designed by Craig to stage three of his own plays at the Abbey in 1911, but he also joined a London-based committee 'to promote the Art of the Theatre as interpreted by Gordon Craig' the following year.[101]

In keeping with other independent European theatres such as the Freie Bühne and Théâtre Libre, productions at the Abbey were often aesthetically or politically challenging. The Abbey became a focus for the Celtic Revival (the movement promoting Irish literary culture). The most notorious production staged by the Abbey was Synge's *The Playboy of the Western World* (1907). Lady Gregory reported what happened in her famous telegram: 'Audience broke up in disorder at the word shift [an item of ladies' underwear]'.[102] Synge had undermined the Revivalists' romantic notion that rural life was the repository of authentic Irish values by depicting a peasant society that condoned murder, drunkenness and coarse language. The nationalist subtext of the play is clear: the son celebrated as a hero for overthrowing and killing his tyrannical father is an example to those who would challenge the oppressive patriarchal and colonial structures holding Ireland back. The performance provoked a riot. Synge defended the play in his preface, arguing that the 'joyless and pallid' language of the kind used by Henrik Ibsen was unequal to communicating the 'rich and living' imagination of the Irish people.[103] And Yeats supported Synge wholeheartedly, making a powerful declaration of artistic liberty to the press:

■ We have claimed for our writers the freedom to find in their own land every expression of good and evil necessary to their art.[104] □

The Abbey continued to defend this freedom in subsequent years, staging George Bernard Shaw's play *The Shewing-Up of Blanco Posnet* in 1910 even though it had been banned by censors in England. It later risked the withdrawal of a recently awarded government subsidy to stage O'Casey's controversial play *The Plough and the Stars* (1926), which depicted the events of the 1916 Easter Rising (in which Irish republicans rebelled against British rule, resulting in a week of bloody fighting, and – following the execution of rebel leaders – great sympathy for the nationalist cause). The Abbey Theatre's influence extended beyond Ireland. *The Playboy of the Western World* was one of the productions that the Abbey Theatre Players performed during their highly successful tour of America in 1911. The development of a truly modern theatrical culture in America had been inhibited by the formation of the highly conservative Theatrical Syndicate (1896), which held a monopoly over America's commercial theatres and controlled bookings for touring productions until 1910. Inspired by the example of the Abbey Players, and independent groups such as the Hull-House Dramatic Association (an arts centre founded in 1896 by Jane Addams (1860–1935) and Ellen Gates Starr (1859–1940) to serve the deprived, largely immigrant community in Chicago), Maurice Browne (1881–1955) founded the Chicago Little Theatre as a venue for staging avant-garde European dramas. The so-called 'Little Theatre Movement' was born. According to the first history of this phenomenon, Constance D'Arcy Mackay's *The Little Theatre in the United States* (1917), sixty-three organisations calling themselves Little Theatres sprang up across America's major cities between 1912 and 1916, modernising the American stage.[105]

Conclusion

The latter half of the nineteenth century witnessed striking developments in the way that literature and drama were written and theorised, as successive schools and movements questioned the sufficiency of established conventions. The experimental impulses of these literatures, formulated in literary criticism, prefaces and manifestos, pointed the way for the next generation of writers. The self-conscious, often extravagant, focus on literary form and technique, the intense concern with subjective experience, and the interest in sexual deviancy that distinguish the Decadent sensibility percolated through the works of later modernist writers, such as T.S. Eliot, James Joyce and Djuna Barnes. The tension between the scientific aspirations of Realism and Naturalism and the urge to communicate higher truths and aesthetic pleasure through Symbolism, relational formal structures and abstraction, informed modernist novelists' attempts to capture the commonplace actuality of experience and imbue it with significance.

The strategies that nineteenth-century writers devised to confront the mounting sense of crisis concerning the adequacy of language were also of prime interest to the next generation of Anglo-American writers. Conrad's efforts to make the 'rescued fragment' speak for the absent whole would become a key modernist technique for communicating truths that resist straightforward explication.[106] The French Symbolists' efforts to render language suggestive did much to spread the use of free verse and registers previously considered unpoetic. They also established three key concepts that would become crucial to high modernist aesthetics: impersonality, the musical immediacy of poetry and the idea that meaning is dependent on the interactions of words themselves rather than the poet's intention. Eliot, for one, read Symons's book in 1908 and later credited it with changing 'the course of his whole life'.[107] It was through Symons that he first encountered the poet Jules Laforgue, whom he credited as 'the first to teach me how to speak, to teach me the poetic possibilities of my own idiom of speech'.[108] Meanwhile, drama had been transformed by the political and moral dimensions of Naturalism, and then the anarchy of anti-theatricalism. By 1910, the stage was set for the consolidation of this growing modern movement and the coming of high modernism.

CHAPTER TWO

High Modernism

On or about December 1910

The year 1910 is often cited as a watershed in the advent of modernism by British critics. The primary reference point is Woolf's famous assertion that 'on or about December 1910, human character changed':

> ■ The change was not sudden and definite like that. But a change there was, nevertheless; and since one must be arbitrary, let us date it about the year 1910. The first signs of it are recorded in the books of Samuel Butler, in *The Way of All Flesh* in particular; the plays of Bernard Shaw continue to record it. In life one can see the change [...] in the character of one's cook. The Victorian cook lived like a leviathan in the lower depths, formidable, silent, obscure, inscrutable; the Georgian cook is a creature of sunshine and fresh air; in and out of the drawing room, now to borrow the *Daily Herald*, and now to ask advice about a hat. [...] All human relations have shifted – those between masters and servants, husbands and wives, parents and children. And when human relations change there is at the same time a change in religion, conduct, politics and literature.[1] □

Woolf's playfully precise declaration in 'Character and Fiction' (1924) belies the fact that *The Way of All Flesh* was published posthumously in 1903 (and written between 1873 and 1884) and that George Bernard Shaw started his career as a playwright in 1892. Both men were highly critical of the Victorian social mores that perpetuated inequality. Radical politics of the kind espoused by Butler and Shaw contributed to the epic shift in human relations, hierarchies of class and gender that meant that Georgian cooks might not only be literate, but sufficiently politicised to take an interest in the *Daily Herald*, a successful newspaper that had its origins in the strike bulletins published by London printers (who were engaged in industrial disputes in December 1910). The sense of a new era would have been compounded that year by the death of King Edward VII, succeeded by George V (May) and two General Elections (January and December). On closer inspection, what first seemed like a frivolous joke at the expense of historians and their compulsion to date what is ineffable with precision actually has some substance to it. It is no coincidence that T.S. Eliot also dated an epochal cultural shift to that year: 'The *point de repère* usually and conveniently taken, as the starting-point of modern poetry, is the group denominated "imagists" in London about 1910'.[2]

As Woolf commented in 'Character in Fiction', 'the prevailing sound of the Georgian age', heard 'in poems and novels and biographies, even in newspaper articles and essays', was 'the sound of breaking and falling, crashing and destruction'.[3] From the rubble, writers strove to construct new literary modes that might represent a reality transformed by the forces of modernity and reconceived through recent developments in science, philosophy and psychology. Some writers also dramatised (and even satirised) the unending quest for styles that might more closely approach the truth of life as it now stood.

The modern movement in London gathered inspiration and momentum from the artistic revolutions of Europe's avant-garde. When Woolf dated the change to December 1910, she was also alluding to 'Manet and the Post-Impressionists', the exhibition curated by her friend, the artist and critic Roger Fry (1866–1934), which ran from 8 November 1910 to 15 January 1911 and introduced contemporary European art to England. It featured work by painters such as Édouard Manet (1832–83), Paul Cézanne (1839–1906), Paul Gauguin (1848–1903) and Vincent van Gogh (1853–90), who used vigorous brushstrokes to communicate their subjective vision and pioneered new modes of representation that would be highly stimulating for literary writers.

The advent of American modernism is likewise often linked to exposure to the European avant-garde, particularly the International Exhibition of Modern Art (1913), held in the vast premises of the 69th Regiment Armory in New York. This event, commonly known as the 'Armory Show', was the first major exhibition to introduce contemporary European art to America. Home-grown art and literature seemed timid by comparison. William Carlos Williams recalled that when he first saw Marcel Duchamp's *Nude Descending a Staircase, No. 2* (1912) – which combined Cubist geometry and Futurist dynamism to depict the descent of a mechanistic figure using a series of superimposed images – he 'burst out laughing from the relief it brought'.[4]

Concurrent developments in music and dance also made their mark on experimental Anglo-American writing. The pivotal event was the first performance of *The Rite of Spring*, an orchestral work by the Russian composer Igor Stravinsky (1882–1971), performed by the Ballets Russes in June 1913. The avant-gardism of Stravinsky's dissonant score and the provocative, atavistic and primitivist choreography of Vaslav Nijinsky

(1889–1950), who eliminated classical grace with jagged gestures, nearly provoked a riot, as the American writer and photographer Carl Van Vechten (1880–1964) recalled:

■ Cat-calls and hisses succeeded the playing of the first few bars, and then ensued a battery of screams, countered by a foil of applause. [...] Some forty of the protestants were forced out of the theatre but that did not quell the disturbance. The lights in the auditorium were fully turned on but the noise continued and I remember Mlle. Piltz executing her strange dance of religious hysteria on a stage dimmed by the blazing light in the auditorium, seemingly to the accompaniment of the disjointed ravings of a mob of angry men and women.[5] □

When T.S. Eliot first heard *The Rite of Spring* he wrote that it seemed to 'transform the rhythm of the steppes into the scream of the motor-horn, the rattle of machinery, the grind of wheels, the beating of iron and steel, the roar of the underground railway, and the other barbaric noises of modern life'; sounds which would inform his own poetry and that of his contemporaries.[6]

This chapter examines how revolutionary literatures and performances between 1910 and 1922 were conceptualised in British and American critical documents, including manifestos, essays and reviews in newspapers and little magazines. It also takes into account contemporary developments in the European avant-garde as critical contexts for the experiments of high modernism, exploring the distinctive but interconnected schools and traditions that unfolded in Britain, Ireland and America during these years.

Literary Impressionism: Ford Madox Ford and Virginia Woolf

Joseph Conrad and Ford Madox Ford (1873–1939) agreed that the business of the modern novel was to produce 'an effect of life' and therefore insisted that one 'must not narrate, but render impressions'.[7] However, they disagreed on the liberties that an author might take with the literal truth. Ford boasted that his book *Memories and Impressions* (1911) was 'full of inaccuracies as to facts, but its accuracy as to impressions is absolute', whereas Conrad felt that such freedom with detail undermined sincerity.[8] In 'On Impressionism' (1913), Ford's extended meditation on his own writing practice, he declared that 'The Impressionist must always exaggerate', on the basis that the particular qualities that strike the author's subjective perception of events must be heightened so as to make a vivid impression on the reader that enhances interest and pleasure.[9] Ford's statement points to an unresolved tension at the heart of much modernist experimentation: the realist impulse to capture the commonplace actuality of experience versus the exaggeration that consists in abstraction, where the artist intensifies elements to represent the true essence of his or her subject.

These issues are foremost in Woolf's mind in her landmark essay 'Modern Fiction' (1925), a significantly revised version of 'Modern Novels' (1919):

■ Examine for a moment an ordinary mind on an ordinary day. The mind receives a myriad impressions – trivial, fantastic, evanescent, or engraved with the sharpness of steel. From all sides they come, an incessant shower of innumerable atoms; and as they fall, as they shape themselves into the life of Monday or Tuesday, the accent falls differently from of old; the moment of importance came not here but there; so that, if a writer were a free man and not a slave, if he could write what he chose, not what he must, if he could base his work upon his feeling and not upon convention, there would be no plot, no comedy, no tragedy, no love interest or catastrophe in the accepted style [...]. Life is not a series of gig-lamps symmetrically arranged; life is a luminous halo, a semi-transparent envelope surrounding us from the beginning of consciousness to the end. Is it not the task of the novelist to convey this varying, this unknown and uncircumscribed spirit, whatever the aberration or complexity it may display, with as little mixture of the alien and external as possible? We [...] are suggesting that the proper stuff of fiction is a little other than custom would have us believe it.[10] □

This famous passage ties together many strands in Woolf's thinking and repays careful analysis. Only if writers free themselves from stifling conventions and disregard considerations of plot or genre might they be able to capture the atomised and fundamentally impressionistic nature of experience. Life is not something material or tangible, and so novelists need not concern themselves with such trivial material objects as buttons. Gig-lamps on the sides of horse-drawn two-wheel carriages are inadequate symbols for the light by which we see modern life. Instead, conscious impressions gather to a hazy radiance. To come closer to life, the writer of modern fiction must escape the tyrannical conventions that novelists customarily obey. '[N]othing – no "method", no experiment, even of the wildest – is forbidden', Woolf advised, 'but only falsity and pretence'.[11] The allusion to *Monday or Tuesday* (1921), a collection of boldly experimental early short fiction, indicated the kinds of literary forms that were particularly fit for this revolutionary purpose.

Short Fiction and Epiphany: Virginia Woolf, Katherine Mansfield, James Joyce and Sherwood Anderson

'The short story is a young art: as we now know it, it is the child of this century', wrote Elizabeth Bowen (1899–1973) in 1937.[12] Shorter fiction released writers from the formal burdens of intricate plotting and in-depth explanation, emboldening them to innovate new ways to communicate moments, phases of life and consciousness, or abstract impressions, and capture the disjointed, elusive and open-ended nature of experience. As Henry James stated in 1909, the merit of reduced length is that it demands writers 'do the complicated thing with a strong brevity and lucidity'.[13]

In *Monday or Tuesday* (1921), Virginia Woolf made full use of the advantages brevity conferred, disrupting expected unities of time and space and experimenting with effects that might bring literature closer to abstract arts such as music and painting (particularly the self-consciously figural style pioneered by Post-Impressionist painters such as her sister Vanessa Bell (1879–1961), who provided illustrative woodcuts to accompany the text of the first edition). In the fragment that gives the collection its name, a day's events are viewed impressionistically from different perspectives, distances and times. Another fragment, 'Blue and Green', attempts to paint with language, comprising two prose poems that plunge the reader's imagination into the different sensations and hues of coloured pools of water. Woolf later dismissed these two pieces as 'wild outbursts of freedom, inarticulate, ridiculous, unprintable mere outcries'.[14]

Several of the experiments collected in *Monday or Tuesday* were extremely fruitful. Woolf's diary entry for 26 January 1920 records her delight at arriving at 'some idea of a new form for a new novel', which she envisioned as the '"Mark on the Wall", "K.G." and "Unwritten Novel" taking hands and dancing in unity'.[15] 'The Mark on the Wall' (1919) follows the thoughts of a narrator pursuing different explanations for an indeterminate blotch that lies just beyond the focal range. 'Kew Gardens' (1917) intercuts snatches of thought and conversation from four groups of people with the reflections of a snail. Winifred Holtby (1898–1935), an English novelist and journalist, and the author of the first book-length critical study of Woolf (1932), commented admiringly:

■ To let the perspective shift from high to low, from huge to microscopic, to let figures of people, insects, aeroplanes, flowers pass across the vision and melt away – these are devices common enough to another form of art. They are the tricks of the cinema.[16] □

'The Unwritten Novel' is narrated by a train passenger who constructs a convincingly rich psychological profile of the woman sitting opposite, only to realise that she has got it all wrong.

The importance of Woolf's brief experiments with perspective was not lost on her contemporaries. T.S. Eliot, for one, commented on Woolf's 'remarkable success' in bridging the gap between the 'experimental prose of *Monday and Tuesday*' and longer fiction in her next novel – *Jacob's Room* (1922) – in which readers are invited to assemble a picture of the eponymous figure's adult life from the fragmented viewpoints of those who knew him and snapshots of the spaces he inhabited.[17] As an exemplary modernist genre in its own right, the short story played a decisive role in modernism's transformation of fiction writing, both in terms of the genesis of longer works and also at the level of technique and form.

Many of the notices received by *Jacob's Room* emphasised the cleverness and originality of Woolf's impressionist methods. The *Times Literary Supplement* praised the way that the 'stream of incidents, persons, and their momentary thoughts and feelings [...] is arrested and decanted [...] into little phials of crystal vividness', relishing Woolf's 'subtle, slyly mocking and yet poignant vision' and above all her 'adventurousness'.[18] Several reviewers admired how deftly Woolf caught and conveyed the impression of a scene, but nonetheless regretted the lack of a story.[19] The journalist, author and critic Rebecca West (1892–1983) answered this criticism by recommending an alternative way of seeing things, advising readers to 'take the book not as a novel but as a portfolio' and adjusting expectations of what a novel should be by aligning *Jacob's Room* with the 'pictorial arts'.[20] The commercially successful novelist Arnold Bennett (1867–1931) commented: 'I have seldom read a cleverer book than Virginia Woolf's *Jacob's Room*, a novel which has made a great stir in a small world. It is packed and bursting with originality, and it is exquisitely written'.[21] However, his observation that her 'characters do not survive vitally in the mind because the author has been obsessed with originality and cleverness' stung Woolf deeply.[22] She took her antagonist to task in 'Mr Bennett and Mrs Brown' (1923), for what she saw as his crassly materialistic approach to rendering character, complaining that the Edwardian novelists' 'books are already a little chill, and must steadily grow more distant, for "the foundation of good fiction is character-creating, and nothing else", as Mr Bennett says; and in none of them are we given a man or woman whom we know'.[23]

Another significant pioneer of shorter fiction was Katherine Mansfield (1888–1923), whose story *Prelude* (1918) was one of the earliest works chosen by Virginia and Leonard Woolf (1880–1969) for publication by their Hogarth Press. *Prelude* explores the difficult emotions that arise from social, familial and sexual relations, and the vissicitudes of colonial life, by constellating select naturalistic details and fleeting impressions. The aim was to make Mansfield's native New Zealand 'leap into the eyes of the Old World' and to tell all 'with a sense of mystery, a radiance, an afterglow'.[24]

Mansfield held that creativity inhered in intense, direct empathetic identification, reflecting: 'I've *been* this man, *been* this woman [...]. It isn't as though one sits and watches the spectacle. [...] But one *is* the spectacle for the time'.[25] Following this surrender to another's inner life, she believed it was for the writer to bring form to the material. It was a culminating glimpse of climactic revelation that provided Mansfield with the formal principle she needed to give her stories coherence and meaning without recourse to the exigencies of plot:

■ What is to prevent each [spiritual event from] being unrelated – complete in itself – if the gradual unfolding in growing, gaining light is not to be followed by one blazing moment?[26] □

These rare moments of sudden lucidity temporarily still the flux of everyday life, creating a 'moment of suspension' in which 'the whole life of the soul is contained. One is flung up – out of life – one is "held" and then, down, bright, broken, glittering on the rocks, tossed back, part of the ebb and flow'.[27] Mansfield's critical vocabulary for describing these suspended moments of psychological revelation is not dissimilar to Woolf's, whose essays likewise give special prominence to 'moments of being'.[28]

Critics tend to refer to the revelatory moments that punctuate modernist narratives as epiphanies, despite the fact that James Joyce was the only author to use that particular terminology and he used it idiosyncratically. In *Stephen Hero* (a fragmentary draft of *A Portrait of the Artist as a Young Man* (1916)), Joyce defined the epiphany as 'a sudden spiritual manifestation, whether in the vulgarity of speech or of gesture or in memorable phrase of the mind', and insisted that it is 'for the man of letters to record these epiphanies with extreme care, seeing that they themselves are the most delicate and evanescent of moments'.[29] In a theological context, the term 'epiphany' pertains to the manifestation of the divine in human form, but Joyce uses it in a secular sense to refer to moments when something trivial is suddenly transfigured, or shown forth, and appears in a different light. In Joyce's definition, epiphanies arise because a subject's language (or body language) is particularly telling, either to a discerning observer or to a sensitive subject's mind.

Dubliners (1914) is given shape by the species of epiphany that depends on implication. The series of fifteen short stories detailing the drab and difficult reality of life for Dublin's lower-middle class hinges on the premise (learned from Henrik Ibsen) that 'out of the dreary sameness of existence, a measure of dramatic life can be drawn'.[30] Joyce explained that the stories present Dublin society 'under four of its aspects: childhood, adolescence, maturity and public life' and that they 'are arranged in this order'.[31] The final story, 'The Dead', completes the city's life-cycle. The stories are written 'in a style of scrupulous meanness', so as to leave gaps in the narrative record for readers to fill with their own conjectures and ponder the potentially far-reaching ramifications of unmistakeable but finally indeterminate revelations.[32] Joyce's spare realism was very well received. Pound, for one, extolled the virtues of Joyce's 'clear hard prose', and likened him to the French master Gustave Flaubert (1821–80), noting that Joyce 'deals with subjective things, but he presents them with such clarity of outline that he might be dealing with locomotives or with builder's specifications'.[33]

Sherwood Anderson (1876–1941) also used the episodic form of the short story cycle to assemble a composite picture of the life of a particular town using fragmentary vignettes in *Winesburg, Ohio* (1919). In a letter to Waldo Frank (1889–1967), Anderson explained he was writing a 'series of intensive studies of people of my home town, Clyde, Ohio', in the hope 'they will suggest the real environment out of which present-day American youth is coming'.[34] Of Winesburg's population of eighteen hundred, readers are fleetingly introduced to over one hundred and twenty people, of whom over thirty appear two or more times. Many are lost souls, who have been spiritually and psychologically warped by the alienation, loneliness, yearning, and emotional and sexual frustration that defined provincial existence in a rapidly modernising world. Anderson described *Winesburg* as 'something like a novel, a complete story', a statement that he then modified with the observation that 'the novel form does not fit an American writer [...] in *Winesburg* I had made my own form'.[35] Although he was evidently at a loss for the appropriate technical vocabulary to describe this episodic fictional work, Anderson was nonetheless conscious that he was creating a new form which American writers might imitate after him. The book was internationally acclaimed: the poet Hart Crane (1899–1932) stated that 'America should read this book on her knees. It constitutes an important chapter in the Bible of her consciousness'; the influential critic H.L. Mencken (1880–1956) asserted that Anderson belonged to 'a small group that has somehow emancipated itself from the prevailing imitativeness and banality of the national letters'; Rebecca West declared that 'it contains two of the half dozen most remarkable stories written this century'.[36]

Consciousness in Fiction

Modernists developed their own critical vocabulary to describe the narrative techniques that they used to convey reality as it is experienced and imbue fragmentary impressions or snatches of consciousness, speech or action with significance. Joseph Conrad and Ford Madox Ford's shared search for 'a new form for the novel' is recorded in Ford's essay 'Techniques' (1935):

■ We evolved then a convention for the novel and one that I think still stands. The novel must be put into the mouth of a narrator – who must be limited by probability as to what he can know of the affair that he is adumbrating.[37] □

Narratologists today would describe the use of a speaker or writer whose knowledge or account of events is inconsistent or ultimately misleading as unreliable first-person narration.

The other narrative technique that Ford and Conrad explored was the omniscient third-person narrator, who, 'being almost omnipotent, may, so long as he limits himself to presenting without comment or moralisation, allow himself to be considered to know almost everything that there is to know'.[38] They insisted that the author should not judge what he presented in order to preserve 'the illusion that he has attempted to build up'.[39]

One of the most striking techniques that modernist authors developed was 'interior monologue'. The term first appeared in English in T.S. Eliot's review the *Criterion*, in a translation of an essay by the French writer Valery Larbaud (1881–1957) that disseminated James Joyce's own private comments on his novel *Ulysses*.[40] In Joyce's definition, 'interior monologue' describes the occasions when 'the reader finds himself established' in the 'uninterrupted rolling' of a character's thought, which 'conveys to us what this personage is doing and what is happening to him' in lieu of third-person narration.[41]

'Interior monologue' is often referred to as 'stream of consciousness' after May Sinclair (1863–1946), who reached for William James's phrase to describe the way that the novelist Dorothy Richardson (1873–1957) plunges into the mind of Miriam Henderson, the principal character in *Pointed Roofs* (1915), the first instalment of *Pilgrimage* (1915–35):

■ In this series there is no drama, no situation, no set scene. Nothing happens. It is just life going on and on. It is Miriam Henderson's stream of consciousness going on and on. [...] In identifying herself with this life, which is Miriam's stream of consciousness, Miss Richardson produces her effect of being the first, of getting closer to reality than any of our novelists who are trying so desperately to get close. [...] The moments of Miriam's consciousness pass one by one, or overlapping; moments tense with vibration, moments drawn out fine, almost to snapping-point.[42] □

For Sinclair, 'The novelist who would be close to reality must confine himself to [...] knowledge at first hand'.[43] Sustained immersion in the experiences of others becomes proof of modernity: 'The more modern the novelist the longer his capacity to stay under'.[44]

While the terms 'interior monologue' and 'stream of consciousness' appear frequently in critical studies of modernism, these techniques are thin on the ground in their pure form. The 'Penelope' episode of *Ulysses* is the most famous example, being an unpunctuated transcript of the uncensored succession of thoughts that enter Molly Bloom's mind as she lies in bed. With respect to *Pointed Roofs* – and many other modernist novels besides – it would be more correct to speak of a variable combination of straightforward third-person narration, interior monologue and free indirect discourse. This last technique flexibly draws on characters' distinctive ways of thinking or speaking, including their markers of time and place, but without necessarily offering any explanation or comment (the narrator does not use tags such as 'he felt' or 'she said').

Sinclair's review of *Pointed Roofs* is attentive to the fluctuations in Richardson's narrative technique and the suddenness with which interior monologue gives way to third-person narration:

■ The first-hand, intimate and intense reality of the happening is in Miriam's mind, and [...] seizes reality alive. The intense rapidity of the seizure defies you to distinguish between what is objective and what is subjective.[45] □

As Sinclair noted, the melding of different narrative techniques blurred the boundaries between interiority and exteriority, and opened narratives to split chronologies, as characters' thoughts were able to flit between memories of times past, hopes for the future and immediate responses to present stimuli:

■ On one page Miss Richardson seems to be accounting for every minute of Miriam's time. On another she passes over events that might be considered decisive with the merest slur of reference. She is not concerned with the strict order of events in time.[46] □

Combining different narrative modes in this way enabled novelists to overcome what Virginia Woolf called 'this appalling narrative business of the realist: getting on from lunch to dinner: it is false, unreal, merely conventional' and provided a crucial technique for addressing Ford Madox Ford and Joseph Conrad's critique 'that what was the matter with the Novel, and the British novel in particular, was that it went straight forward'.[47]

Many critics and authors considered narrative techniques that present the stream of a character's consciousness to be particularly suitable for depicting the workings of the female psyche. The style and form of *Pilgrimage* was dictated by Richardson's belief that the 'womanly woman' has a 'completely self-centred consciousness', 'she is one with life' so that 'past, present, and future are together in her, unbroken', 'she thinks flowingly, with her feelings' and is 'relatively indifferent to the fashions of men, to the momentary arts, religions, philosophies and sciences'.[48] To convey 'womanly' consciousness, Richardson created what Woolf famously praised as 'the psychological sentence of the feminine gender. It is of a more elastic fibre than the old, capable of stretching to the extreme, of suspending the frailest particles, of enveloping the vaguest shapes'.[49] Richardson singled out Joyce as a male author who intuitively understood that 'Feminine prose [...] should be properly unpunctuated, moving from point to point without formal obstruction'.[50] Arnold Bennett too praised Joyce's presentation of a female mind in 'Penelope', arguing that it 'might in its utterly convincing realism be an actual document, the magical record of inmost thoughts by a woman that existed'.[51]

Psychoanalysis and Sex: Sigmund Freud and D.H. Lawrence

The modernist interest in what Virginia Woolf called 'the dark places of psychology' extended beyond the presentation of subjective experience to the workings of the unconscious mind.[52] In this respect, writers were strongly influenced by psychoanalysis. Its founding father and most influential theorist, the Austrian physician Sigmund Freud (1856–1939), believed that neurosis and hysteria are caused by traumatic experiences that are repressed by the conscious mind but linger on in the unconscious as powerful motivating forces, and that reconstructing these experiences so that they become comprehensible would provide therapeutic relief. *The Interpretation of Dreams* (1900, English translation 1913) brought Freud and psychoanalysis to an international audience. It proposed that dreams enact repressed desires seeking fulfilment unachievable in waking life and that their significance is not in their manifest content, but the way in which they disguise latent wishes as symbols. Freud's most contentious proposition was that neuroses were largely traceable to the traumas associated with infantile sexual experience, particularly children's anxious fascination with sexual difference and physical gratification. He interpreted the legend of Oedipus (who inadvertently kills his father and marries his mother) as confirmation of this universal pattern of infantile incestuous sexual desire and repression.

Freud subsequently divided the mind into three mutually affective categories in *The Ego and the Id* (1923), providing a model for the relations of conscious and unconscious thought and a vocabulary to describe how the taboo fantasies and phobias that children repress and carry into adulthood are processed. The psyche of the new-born child is pure id, which is instinctive, unreasoned, unconscious and governed by the pleasure principle (the urge to satisfy every wishful impulse immediately, without regard to consequence). The ego (reason) develops in infancy to enable the individual to master the chaotic impulses of the id and strives to work out realistic ways to delay the desired gratification until it can be achieved appropriately. The super ego is the part of the ego that develops as the result of the defensive efforts to repress Oedipal impulses. Morality is therefore not innate to humankind, but only achievable by suppressing the primitive passions that preoccupy the id.

Freud's controversial ideas were extensively debated in medical and intellectual circles in the 1910s and 1920s, most notably the Bloomsbury group, which included practising psychoanalysts. (The Woolfs' Hogarth Press became the English-language publisher of Freud's works in 1924). As Leonard Woolf perceived, psychoanalysis used methods not dissimilar to those employed by literary writers and critics, including striving to decode symbols, placing resonant details in relation and reading between the lines:

■ Whether one believes in his [Freud's] theories or not, one is forced to admit that he writes with great subtlety of mind, a broad and sweeping imagination more characteristic of the poet than the scientist or medical practitioner.[53] □

Freud's most compelling case histories, such as 'Dora' (1905), 'Little Hans' (1909), 'Rat Man' (1907–09) and 'Wolf Man' (1918) interpret fragmented narratives so as to unravel intricate plots that explain his patients' psychopathologies by tracing neurotic and hysterical symptoms to sexual desires, extrapolating universal models for human behaviour based on readings of mythic and literary figures.

Freud's theories profoundly changed the popular understanding of the roles of memory, language, sex and gender in the construction of the individual psyche. May Sinclair was one novelist who consciously employed psychoanalytic models to explore women's experiences of infancy, particularly the eroticism of close contact with the maternal body, subjugation of desire and aspirations beyond the domestic. Despite her unorthodox focus on female subjectivity, she was nonetheless criticised for slavishly adhering to the discipline. Of her novel *The Life and Death of Harriett Frean* (1922), T.S. Eliot churlishly complained 'because the material is so clearly defined (the soul of man under psychoanalysis) there is no possibility of tapping the atmosphere of unknown terror and mystery in which our life is passed and which psychoanalysis has not yet analysed'.[54]

D.H. Lawrence (1885–1930) was also notable for his direct challenges to psychoanalytic models of sexuality, although it has to be said that he engaged with the detail of Freud's writings fitfully and idiosyncratically. *Sons and Lovers* (1913), Lawrence's third novel, boldly linked Paul Morel's early relationships with his parents, particularly his overbearing mother, to his adult sexual relationships. However, Lawrence hated the article '*Sons and Lovers*: A Freudian Appreciation' (*Psychoanalytic Review*, 1916), which read the novel in terms of incestuous desire for the mother. He was adamant that the mother-complex 'is not simply a sex-relation: far from it'.[55] Lawrence responded by adumbrating his own theories in *Psychoanalysis and the Unconscious* (1921) and *Fantasia and the Unconscious* (1922), which aimed to provide an alternative to the 'huge slimy serpent of sex, and heaps of excrement, and a myriad repulsive little horrors spawned between sex and excrement' he found in Freud.[56] In distinction to Freud's abject model, Lawrence proposed that 'there is another seat of consciousness than the brain and the nerve system: there is a blood-consciousness which exists in us independently of the ordinary mental consciousness, which depends on the eye as its source or connector'.[57] In its purest, most life-affirming and passionate form 'blood-consciousness', the bodily seat of powerful feeling, is the sexual connection between man and woman, who inhabit separate mutually incomprehensible spheres. 'Women will *never* understand the depth of the spirit of purpose in man', Lawrence declared, 'And men will never understand the sacredness of feeling to woman'.[58]

Lawrence's frank explorations of the workings of sexual desire aimed to reform a society that he considered to be damaged by its collective reticence:

■ I do so break my heart over England [...] And I am so sure that only through a readjustment between men and women, and a making free and healthy of the sex, will she get out of her present atrophy.[59] □

However, the courts saw matters differently and banned his novel *The Rainbow* (1915) for its frank portrayal of the sexual desires of three generations of the Brangwen family (including a lesbian passion), following negative reviews in the largely prurient popular press. Robert Lynd found the book 'windy, tedious, and even in its excitements nauseating' and judged it to be 'a monotonous wilderness of phallicism'.[60] James Douglas (1867–1940) complained that 'the subtlety of phrase is enormous, but it is used to express the unspeakable and to hint at the unutterable'.[61] The strength of moral outrage was such that Catherine Carswell (1879–1946) lost her job at the *Glasgow Herald* for writing a largely sympathetic review in praise of Lawrence's powers of characterisation. She interpreted *The Rainbow* as an 'impassioned declaration' that the 'modern world, according to Lawrence, is mad and sick and sad because it knows not how to love'.[62]

The pattern of engaged resistance to psychoanalysis seen in many writers' works (too easily reducible to repression) reflects the ways in which literature, literary criticism and psychoanalysis were complimentary but also competing discourses, probing similar issues, myths and texts.

Criticism of Stream of Consciousness

Not everyone was convinced by the new psychological novel. D.H. Lawrence's distance from his peers can be measured by his vituperative comments in 'Surgery for the Novel – Or a Bomb' (1923, now known as 'The Future of the Novel'), where he criticised contemporary authors for paying minute attention to the fluctuations of the mind and indulging in the kind of self-absorption and childish self-interest that, in his view, was killing the serious novel:

> ■ It is self-consciousness, picked into such fine bits that the bits are most of them invisible, and you have to go by the smell. Through thousands and thousands of pages Mr Joyce and Miss Richardson tear themselves into pieces, strip their smallest emotions to the finest threads, till you feel you are sewed inside a wool mattress that is being slowly shaken up, and you are turning to wool along with the rest of the woollyness [sic].[63] □

Unfounded as this criticism is (it conflates characters with their creators), it is indicative of Lawrence's own priorities as a writer. So far as Lawrence was concerned, excoriating the self to the point that it disintegrates misses the vital function of art, which is 'to reveal the relation between man and his circumambient universe, at the living moment'.[64] According to Lawrence, novels only come alive when they display this fundamental interrelatedness in all its dynamic and shifting complexity, a circumstance which obliges the novelist to break beyond the confines of the single mind and show characters in their changing social relations.

Another notable opponent of narrative focalised within an individual consciousness was Wyndham Lewis (1882–1957). In *Time and Western Man* (1927), Lewis upbraided modernism for failing in its avant-garde aim of formenting revolutionary action. In no small part, he attributed this failure to modernist writers' adherence to the fashionable 'time-cult' produced by the '"timelessness" of einsteinian [sic] physics, and the time-obsessed flux of Bergson'.[65] Henri Bergson (1859–1941) influentially proposed that the way time is experienced is relative, as consciousness is not divided into discrete moments, but consists in a continuous succession of interpenetrating impressions, which are conditioned by previous experiences and have the potential to colour future perception. He termed this rolling, multi-layered quality of consciousness 'real duration', by which he meant interior time as it is experienced subjectively and intuitively rather than as it is measured on the clock.[66]

Lewis singled out James Joyce as the time-cult's leader in literature, scorning his representation of the flow of characters' thoughts. Lewis complained that the method of *Ulysses* 'lands the reader inside an Aladdin's cave of incredible bric-à-brac in which a dense mass of dead stuff is collected', imposing 'a softness, flabbiness and vagueness everywhere in its bergsonian [sic] fluidity'.[67] Unselective, retrospective, feminine in its softness, 'telling from the inside' lacked the order, hardness and masculine vigour that Lewis associated with righteous antagonism and resistance, and so he dismissed it as a faux-revolutionary technique.[68] Both Lawrence and Lewis were influenced by Futurism, which opposed formless subjectivity and valorised the non-human.

Futurism

The first avant-garde movement to shake European society in the new century was Italian Futurism, which aimed to sever the arts from their agrarian past and fasten them to the age of the machine. Filippo Tommaso Marinetti (1876–1944) launched the movement with his 'Foundation and Manifesto of Futurism', which blazed across the front page of the Parisian newspaper *Le Figaro* on 20 February 1909 and brought Marinetti and his new school to international attention. Italian Futurists sought to revolutionise all art forms, but had a particular interest in performance; an arena where they put the ideas of Alfred Jarry and Gordon Craig into practice.

'Foundation and Manifesto of Futurism' is perhaps the archetypal avant-garde pronouncement: a systematic programme linking aesthetic proposals to the changing world. It begins with an enthralled first-person description of a high-speed car crash, where a group of once jaded Decadents are revitalised by a dip in an amniotic ditch of industrial effluent. Marinetti exalted the motor car and 'the man at the wheel, who hurls the lance of his spirit across the Earth along the circle of its orbit'.[69] Having test-driven an artistic renaissance for the machine age, Marinetti sets out his agenda for the art of the future:

■ Up to now literature has exalted a pensive immobility, ecstasy, and sleep. We intend to exalt aggressive action, a feverish insomnia, the racer's stride, the mortal leap, the punch and the slap.[70] □

He takes the principle that 'No work without an aggressive character can be a masterpiece' to its extreme conclusion: [71]

■ We will glorify war – the world's only hygiene – militarism, patriotism, the destructive gesture of freedom-bringers, beautiful ideas worth dying for, and scorn for women.[72] □

The pronoun 'we' was merely rhetorical, as Marinetti launched this great publicity exercise alone. However, the force of his manifesto was such that visual artists, playwrights, architects and poets soon gathered to the movement, pioneering new techniques to communicate dynamism even in static media.

Marinetti's professed 'scorn for women' was provocative, but it was essentially metaphorical. As he explained in the preface to the 1910 Italian version of the manifesto: 'I wasn't talking about the worth of women as biological entities but of the sentimental importance that is generally attributed to them'.[73] For Marinetti, femininity stood for passivity, nurturing and natural reproduction, whereas masculinity stood for potency, dynamism and self-determination, and thus functioned as a metaphor for modern industrial production.

Futurism proved attractive to women who were keen to escape traditional gender roles. The British-born visual artist and poet Mina Loy urged readers to 'ACCEPT the tremendous truth of Futurism' in 'Aphorisms on Futurism' (1914).[74] However, in her 'Feminist Manifesto' (written in 1914, but unpublished in her lifetime), she imitated Marinetti's declamatory style to criticise the Futurist discourse that divides 'women into two classes the mistress & the mother', and also the feminist movement, which she considers 'Inadequate' for focusing on equal rights and placing 'confidence in economic legislation' and 'reform', as opposed to enforcing 'Absolute Demolition' of the present system (Loy's emphases).[75] She made the radical proposition that feminists should acknowledge biological difference, but resist adapting themselves to 'a theoretical valuation of their sex' by vanquishing 'the man made bogey of [women's] virtue' through 'the unconditional surgical destruction of virginity through-out the female population at puberty'.[76]

In the years leading up to the First World War, Marinetti and others published further manifestos in national newspapers and literary journals, specifying the qualities expected of Futurist works. In 'Technical Manifesto of Futurist Literature' (1912), a 'whirring propeller' performs the role of the Muse and inspires Marinetti to shred old sentence structures:[77]

■ [O]ne must destroy syntax and scatter one's nouns at random [...] One must abolish the adjective, to allow the naked noun to preserve its essential colour [...] One must abolish the adverb [...and] even the punctuation.[78] □

These measures were calculated to produce 'an uninterrupted sequence of new images' that would 'destroy the *I* in literature' and with it individual subjectivity.[79]

Heavily policed 'Futurist Evenings' featured performers aggressively declaiming their manifestos, improvising speeches, playing disturbing, noisy music, insulting their audiences and starting brawls. The idea, as Marinetti explained in 'The Variety Theatre' (1913), was to amplify the boisterous irreverence of the music hall.

■ *Futurism exalts the Variety Theatre because:*
1 The Variety Theatre, born as we are from electricity, is lucky in having no tradition, no masters, no dogma, and it is fed by swift actuality.
2 The Variety Theatre is absolutely practical, because it proposes to distract and amuse the public with comic effects, erotic stimulation or imaginative astonishment.[80] □

Idle spectatorship was to be abolished by co-opting the audience as part of the performance, for instance by using 'powerful glue on the seats', 'dust to make people itch and sneeze', or selling the same seat ten times.[81] Between 1915 and 1916, Italian Futurists also staged '*Sintesi*', short dramatic works that compress 'into a few minutes, into a few words and gestures, innumerable situations, sensibilities, ideas, sensations, facts, symbols' in a way that is '*dynamic, simultaneous*', 'improvised (hours, minutes, seconds), not extensively prepared (months, years, centuries)' and '*autonomous, alogical, unreal*'.[82]

The activities of Marinetti and his followers were hotly debated in the commercial press. For instance, 'The Variety Theatre' reached a wide English-speaking audience when it was published in what was then the world's largest mass-circulation newspaper, the *Daily Mail*.[83] Many of England's most forward-looking literary figures identified with Futurism's revolutionary impulses, but modified them for their own purposes. For instance, Harold Monro (1879–1932), poet, editor and proprietor of the Poetry Bookshop in London, devoted the largest part of the September 1913 issue *Poetry and Drama* to the Futurists, and staked his claim to kinship:

> ■ Futurism, indeed, *is* at war with tradition; but its activities, in our conception, are confined neither to Italy nor to Sackville Street [the location of a recent exhibition]; it is represented neither by rebel thought nor ragged verse; it is an attitude of the mind – a condition of the soul.[84] □

D.H. Lawrence also saw affinities between his own developing artistic credo circa 1914 and Marinetti's pronouncements, as he explained in a famous letter to Edward Garnett (1868–1937), written as he was drafting the text that would eventually be split into *The Rainbow* (1915) and *Women in Love* (1920):

> ■ But when I read Marinetti – "the profound intuitions of life added one to the other, word by word, according to their illogical conceptions, will give us the general lines of an intuitive physiology of matter" – I see something of what I am after [...] – that which is physic – non-human, in humanity, is more interesting to me than the old-fashioned human element – which causes one to conceive a character in a certain moral scheme and make him consistent. [...] You mustn't look in my novel for the old stable ego of the character. There is another ego, according to whose action the individual is unrecognisable, and passes through, as it were, allotropic states which it needs a deeper sense than any we've been used to exercise, to discover are states of the same single radically-unchanged element. (Like as diamond and coal are the same pure single element of carbon).[85] □

Futurism also made a deep impression on Ezra Pound and Wyndham Lawis, who would launch their own pseudo-Futurist movement, Vorticism. As Pound wrote in the *Egoist* (1914), 'The modern artist must live by craft and violence'.[86] This declaration represented an abrupt departure from the classicist poise of Imagism, the poetic school Pound had launched just two years earlier together with other leading London-based writers.

Modernist Classicism

T.E. Hulme was instrumental in persuading Ezra Pound that romanticism had run its course.

> ■ This period of exhaustion seems to me to have been reached in romanticism. We shall not get any new efflorescence of verse until we get a new technique, a new convention, to turn ourselves loose in.[87] □

In his essay 'Romanticism and Classicism' (c. 1911–12), Hulme proposed that 'dry and hard' classical poetry that conformed to standards of unsentimental 'accurate, precise and definite description' was the necessary corrective to slushy, insipid romanticism.[88] He argued that these respective manners arose out of fundamentally opposed attitudes to human nature. For Hulme, romanticism proceeded from the basis that 'the individual, is an infinite reservoir of possibilities', whereas classicism maintained humanity to be 'an extraordinarily fixed and limited animal whose nature is absolutely constant. It is only by tradition and organisation that anything decent can be got out of him.'[89] In this definition – which, as Hulme points out, is indebted to the far-right, royalist, anti-Semitic French political movement Action Française – classicism stands for authoritarianism.

Hulme's new classicism decisively shaped the anti-romantic idiom of the modernist mainstream. In the first issue of *Poetry Review* (1912), Pound predicted that the poetry written during the coming decade would 'move against poppy-cock, it will be harder and saner, [...] "nearer the bone" [...], austere, direct, free from emotional slither'.[90] Over the course of his career, T.S. Eliot also had great success promoting a classicism which went beyond matters of style. In 'The Reaction against Romanticism' (1916), he explained that the new century had witnessed 'a return to the ideals of classicism': '*form* and *restraint* in art, *discipline* and *authority* in religion, *centralization* in government'.[91]

For other writers in Pound and Hulme's circle, classicism meant renewed interest in the writers of antiquity. Hilda Doolittle (1886–1961) and Richard Aldington (1892–1962) launched the Poets' Translation Series in 1915 to rescue a literature 'more alive, more essential, more human than anything we can find in contemporary English' from the deadening 'wranglings of grammarians' and the 'hands of clumsy metrists'.[92] They produced six inexpensive pamphlets 'by poets whose interest in their authors will be neither conventional nor frigid' without 'glosses, notes, or any of the apparatus with which learning smothers beauty'.[93] Their free-handed approach to translation was typical of modernist engagements with literature from distant times or cultures.

Imagism

The first coherent movement in Anglo-American modernist poetry had its origins in the meetings of the Secession Club in London (1909–10), which gathered figures such as T.E. Hulme, Ezra Pound and F.S. Flint (1885–1960). The Club mainly discussed French *vers libre*, Japanese poetry and what they called 'the Image', a concept that derived from

Henri Bergson, who argued for intuition and sensory experience as valid means to grasp those things that lie beyond rational comprehension. In 'An Introduction to Metaphysics' (1903), Bergson argued that the real duration of consciousness resisted straightforward description, as it is constantly shifting and not restricted to a single moment in time, but theorised that it might be expressed through images, which are the closest we can get to an intuitive language.

While Hulme's English translation of Bergson's essay was published in 1913, the impact of Bergson on Hulme's own critical prose was evident from as early as 1909:

■ Poetry [...] is not a counter language, but a visual concrete one. It is a compromise for a language of intuition which would hand over sensations bodily. It always endeavours to arrest you, and to make you continuously see a physical thing, to prevent you gliding through an abstract process. It chooses fresh epithets and fresh metaphors [...]. Images in verse are not mere decoration, but the very essence of an intuitive language.[94] □

Pound saw that Hulme's ideas had the makings of a movement that could be used to generate interest in the poetry of his circle. The Imagist(e) brand was a brilliant marketing strategy: it helped to get H.D.'s poems published and it resulted in wide press coverage for the poems and pronouncements published in little magazines such as *Poetry: A Magazine of Verse* (Chicago) and the *New Freewoman*, later the *Egoist* (London).

Pound publicised the ground rules in 'Imagisme', a note signed by Flint that appeared in the March 1913 issue of *Poetry*:

■ 1 Direct treatment of the 'thing', whether subjective or objective.
   2 To use absolutely no word that does not contribute to the presentation.
   3 As regarding rhythm: to compose in sequence of the musical phrase, not in sequence of a metronome.[95] □

Written in free verse, so that language is not subject to any distorting formal constraints, Imagist poetry was to embody the classical values of precision, directness and economy, as per Pound's sales pitch for H.D.'s first Imagist poems: 'Objective – no slither; direct – no excessive use of adjectives; no metaphors that won't permit examination. It's straight talk, straight as the Greek!'[96]

To clarify what Pound meant by 'direct treatment of the "thing" whether subjective or objective', it is helpful to refer to his account of how he wrote 'In a Station of the Metro' (1913), 'a one image poem' that seeks to capture the precise emotion Pound felt on seeing a succession of beautiful faces in a crowd as he alighted from an underground train.[97] He translated the experience into a succession of discrete visual units (separated by innovative spacing), setting the objective phenomenon that struck his intellect on top of the subjective impression it produced, a technique he called 'super-position'.[98] In doing so, he communicated his intuition of the event with a fresh metaphor that recorded 'the precise instant when a thing outward and objective transforms itself, or darts into a thing inward and subjective'.[99] He would later distil this interchange into the famous definition: 'An "Image" is that which presents an intellectual and emotional complex in an instant of time'.[100]

T.S. Eliot developed his own version of the image in 'Hamlet and His Problems' (1919):

■ The only way of expressing emotion in the form of art is by finding an 'objective correlative'; in other words, a set of objects, a situation, a chain of events which shall be the formula of that *particular* emotion; such that when the external facts, which must terminate in sensory experience, are given, the emotion is immediately evoked.[101] □

Pound was alive to Eliot's use of this technique and praised his use of 'two sorts of metaphor: his wholly unrealizable, always apt, half ironic suggestion, and his precise realizable picture', paying tribute to 'his method of conveying a whole situation and half a character by three words of a quoted phrase; his constant aliveness, his mingling of very subtle observation with the unexpectedness of a backhanded cliché'.[102]

Pound gathered poems by himself, Flint, H.D., Richard Aldington, William Carlos Williams, Amy Lowell (1874–1925), Skipwith Cannell (1887–1957), John Cournos (1881–1966), James Joyce, Ford Madox Ford and D.H. Lawrence, into an anthology, *Des Imagistes* (1914). However, very few of the submissions fully conformed to all three of the Imagist principles that Pound and Flint specified. The British novelist and journalist Storm Jameson (1891–1986) quipped:

■ They sign one manifesto: they should have signed twenty, for whatever common aims they think to have, their ends are as far apart as might have been expected.[103] □

Amy Lowell intensely identified with the new school and used her wealth to publish three further Imagist anthologies (*Some Imagist Poets* (1915, 1916, 1917)), to Pound's annoyance. Pound judged Lowell's poetry to be insufficiently hard and clear and cruelly renamed her version of the movement 'Amygism'.

Vorticism

Ezra Pound quickly abandoned Imagism for Vorticism, an adversarial new school publicising developments in English painting, sculpture and literature. 'The Vortex' was Pound's invention; he used the phrase in a letter to William Carlos Williams to mean the dynamic centre of artistic production.[104] At the heart of the vortex was the short-lived Rebel Arts Centre, founded by Wyndham Lewis in March 1914 to rival Roger Fry's Post-Impressionist Omega workshops. The Vorticists' organ was *BLAST* (1914–15), a little magazine edited by Lewis, with the assistance of Pound. The iconographic first issue, with its shocking pink cover and shouting typography, sought both to engage with and to change the modern world. Contents included manifestos, non-representational Cubist-*cum*-Futurist artwork and Lewis's play 'Enemy of the Stars'. The first Vorticist manifesto famously doled out blasts and blesses to professions, mannerisms, movements, places and objects, after the manner of the '*merde à*' and '*rose à*' columns in the Futurist magazine *Lacerba* (1913). The spirit of the magazine is summarised in the maxim: 'BLAST years 1837 to 1900'.[105] For all that Vorticism mocked the sentimental aestheticism of Marinetti's love affair with the motorcar, the emphasis on industrialism, dynamism, immediacy and abstraction had clear affinities with Futurism.

Literary Vorticism, as Pound defined it in *BLAST*, was but another name for Imagism. H.D. remained the exemplary poet. He announced that 'Every concept, every emotion, presents itself to the vivid consciousness in some primary form' (its most highly energised and concentrated state) and that the 'primary pigment' in poetry is the image.[106] The second and final issue of *BLAST* (July 1915) was a 'War Number', focusing on the Europe-wide conflict and the damaging repercussions for art.

After Imagism

Imagism had an enduring influence on modern poetry, helping to get rid of verbiage, inversion and forced rhyme. As of 1918, *Poetry: A Magazine of Verse* could confidently state: 'Free verse is now accepted in good society, where rhymed verse is even considered a little shabby and old-fashioned.'[107]

The proliferation of careless free verse, written without regard for musical effects, was attacked by Ezra Pound and T.S. Eliot, who agreed that 'no *vers* is *libre* for the man who wants to do a good job'.[108] The liberties taken by unskilled versifiers did not sit well with their classicist desire for order. The two men briefly reacted against the 'dilution of *vers libre'* and 'Amygism' by instigating a 'counter-current' predicated on 'Rhyme and regular strophes'; an experiment that resulted in 'Poems in Mr Eliot's *second* volume not contained in his first (*Prufrock*, Egoist 1917), also "H. S. Mauberley"'.[109]

The notion of the image as an intuitive language was enriched by contact with the ideas of Ernest Fenollosa (1853–1908), a respected (if eccentric) American orientalist, whose papers Pound began to edit in December 1913. Fenollosa's critical writings introduced Pound to the 'ideogram': the picture formed by Chinese characters. The theory Fenollosa and Pound followed (now discredited by sinologists) is that the characters are stylised pictorial representations of the thing or concept they signify and so they are more concrete, direct and poetic than alphabetic script:

■ It speaks at once with the vividness of painting [...]. In reading Chinese we do not seem to be juggling mental counters, but to be watching *things* work out their own fate.[110] □

From Fenollosa's explanation of the composite nature of ideograms, Pound developed the 'ideogrammic method', a 'process of compounding, [whereby] two things added together do not produce a third thing but suggest some fundamental relation between them'.[111] The classic example is the Chinese character for 'red', which he broke into four separate characters: 'rose', 'iron-rust', 'cherry' and 'flamingo'.[112] This method enabled diverse fragments of different kinds of poetry – dramatic monologues, elegies, satires, songs and moments of Imagist luminosity and compression – to be placed in apposition without discursive links, a technique that would be crucial to Pound's *Cantos* (1917–68) and also Eliot's poem *The Waste Land* (1922), which owed its shape to Pound's visionary editorial interventions.

Noh Theatre

Between 1913 and 1916, Ezra Pound worked closely with W.B. Yeats, spending the winter months with him at Stone Cottage. Gordon Craig's criticism had awakened Yeats to the dramatic potential of the highly ritualised, ancient theatres of Asia. Pound's work on Ernest Fenollosa's English translations of Japanese Noh drama consolidated this interest. Noh was striking for its elegant unity of form. As Fenollosa observed:

■ All elements – costume, motion, verse and music – unite to produce a single clarified impression [...], elevated to the plane of universality by the intensity and purity of treatment.[113] □

In Noh theatre Yeats discovered the anti-mimeticism, spiritualism, symbolism and total integration of dance, music and composition he had been searching for, and set about applying these principles to his own art.

Yeats reflected on the influence of Noh on his own development as a playwright in his introduction to Pound's *Certain Noble Plays of Japan: From the Manuscripts of Ernest Fenollosa* (1916). He discussed his own play *At the Hawk's Well* (1916), which transposed the conventions of Noh to depict the story of Cuchulain, a heroic figure in Irish mythology:

■ There will be no scenery, for three musicians [...] can describe place and weather, and at moments action, and accompany it all by drum and gong or flute and dulcimer. Instead of the player working themselves into a violence of passion indecorous in our sitting-room, the music, the beauty of form and voice all come to climax in pantomime dance. In fact with the help of these plays 'translated by Ernest Fenollosa and finished by Ezra Pound' I have invented a form of drama, distinguished, indirect and symbolic, and having no need of the mob or press to pay its way – an aristocratic form.[114] □

Three further Noh plays followed, published, together with *At the Hawk's Well*, in *Four Plays for Dancers* (1921). Envisaged as private productions to be funded by a small, select audience, Yeats's Noh plays could not be further from the spirit of the Abbey Theatre, which was founded to serve as a national forum.

Gertrude Stein

Meanwhile, the push to modernise literature received fresh impetus in America in 1913 with the exhibition of American and Post-Impressionist European art at the New York Armory Show. The new European modern movements such as Fauvism (a wild non-naturalistic style characterised by expressive brushstrokes and vivid colour), Cubism (where objects and figures are constructed from the fragmented juxtaposition of planes and facets drawn from multiple perspectives) and Futurism (which celebrated the dynamic age of the machine) provoked controversy in a nation steeped in the realist tradition. The Armory Show marked a decisive moment of rupture in the form of American art, prompting a period of intense literary experimentation as writers explored verbal equivalents for new modes of visualisation.

Gertrude Stein was the first of her compatriots to see the literary potential of the new trends in European art. Promoted as the literary counterpart to the Cubists, Stein was the only non-visual artist to be exhibited at the Armory Show. Her verbal 'Portrait of Mabel Dodge at the Villa Curonia' was sketched in a flat, highly restricted vocabulary that was given depth through repetition. It was distributed together with 'Speculations, or Post-Impressionism in Prose' (1913), an article by Mabel Dodge Luhan (1879–1962), a notable arts patron, who explained that 'Stein is doing with words what Picasso is doing with paint'.[115] Extensive press coverage of the Show brought Stein instant fame.

Stein had encountered Cubism when she relocated from America to Paris in 1903, where she immersed herself in the community of avant-garde painters who gathered in bohemian Montparnasse and befriended Pablo Picasso (1881–1973). Stein's first book, *Three Lives* (privately published in 1909), was written under the influence of Paul Cézanne's idea that 'Each part is as important as the whole'.[116] The *Faux-naïf* technique Stein developed to decentre *Three Lives* was a highly stylised form of free indirect discourse. She confined herself to the narrowly restricted language of the three lower-class, racially displaced, uneducated women she profiled: two German immigrants, Anna and Lena, and Melanctha, a black, bisexual woman.

Stein considered 'Melanctha', the longest of the three stories to be 'the first definite step away from the nineteenth century and into the twentieth century in literature'.[117] It was written in a version of the black patois that she encountered in Baltimore. When *Three Lives* was reprinted by a commercial publisher in 1920 it was widely acclaimed by critics, with 'Melanctha' singled out for particular praise. Carl Van Vechten promoted 'Melanctha' as 'The first American story in which the Negro is regarded as a human being and not as an object for condescending compassion or derision' and included *Three Lives* in the list of the ten most important books published since 1900 that he produced for the *Literary Digest International Book Review* (1923).[118] Other figures who would later be associated with the Harlem Renaissance also took note of 'Melanctha', for good or ill. Nella Larsen (1891–1964) wrote to Stein, praising her for her realistic portrayal and wondering 'just why you and not some one of us should so accurately have caught the spirit of this race of mine'; Richard Wright (1908–60) reported that 'Melanctha' enthralled the 'group of semi-literate Negro stockyard workers' who heard him read it aloud; whereas Claude McKay shrugged 'I found nothing striking and informative about Negro life'.[119]

In 'Melanctha', Stein began to hone what would become her signature technique, 'insistence', whereby information is time and again retold but with variations in its delivery. Since no single retelling can be considered dominant, each part becomes integral. As Luhan recognised, this technique of insistent repetition served to render prose poetic, activating the musical qualities of words to give them an existence beyond linguistic reference:

> ■ In Gertrude Stein's writing every word lives and, apart from concept, it is so exquisitely rhythmical and cadenced that if we read it aloud and receive it as pure sound, it is like a kind of sensuous music [...], listening to Gertrude Stein's words and forgetting to try to understand what they mean, one submits to their gradual charm.[120] □

As Mina Loy explained in her perceptive essay 'Gertrude Stein' (1924), Stein used the 'process of reiteration' to round out her subjects 'gradually, progressively':[121]

> ■ For Gertrude Stein obtains the *belle matière* of her unsheathing of the fundamental with a most dexterous discretion in the placement and replacement of her phrases, of inversion of the same phrase sequences that are so closely matched in level, as the fractional tones in primitive music or the imperceptible modelling of early egyptian [sic] sculpture'.[122] □

While Loy was evidently enthralled by Stein's writing, she did acknowledge that 'it is not easy for the average reader to "get" Gertrude Stein' because 'a goodly amount of incoherent debris gets littered around the radium that she crushes out of phrased consciousness'.[123]

Insistent repetition operated not only to reimagine words and their relations to the things of the world but to disrupt temporal sequence, an effect Stein heightened by describing past events and actions as if they were ongoing. She reflected on the development of this technique in her lecture 'Composition as Explanation' (1926):

> ■ So then I as a contemporary creating the composition in the beginning was groping toward a continuous present, a using everything a beginning again and again and then everything being alike then everything very simply everything was naturally simply different and so I as a contemporary was creating everything being alike was creating everything naturally being naturally simple different, everything being alike.[124] □

The 'continuous present' (marked by heavy use of gerunds and present participles) became Stein's stylistic calling card: it was the medium for her long psychological novel *The Making of Americans: Being a History of a Family's Progress* (1925); her gossipy memoir of her Paris years, *The Autobiography of Alice B. Toklas* (1933); and her literary criticism. Much has been made of the fact that Stein was a student of William James, but her eddying prose is not directly analogous to a stream of consciousness because Stein's relentless circularity impedes causal thinking.

Stein's work alerted American writers to language as language by activating the world-creating power of the word. Throughout her career, Stein sought to renew the force of worn out words, and increase their variety, by making them conjure material realities unconnected to their usual referents:

■ Poetry is concerned with using with abusing, with losing with wanting, with denying with avoiding with adoring with replacing the noun.[125] □

Nowhere is this principle more evident than in *Tender Buttons* (1914), a whimsical sequence of prose poems apparently depicting domestic objects – a carafe, an umbrella, a chair, sugar, potatoes – after the manner of the Cubist still life. Once named, objects are then described 'by suggestion' after the manner of an abstract painter, rendered not as they appear directly to the eye, but as certain facets of their being are perceived in the mind, thus replacing the noun with Stein's idiosyncratic vision of 'the thing itself'.[126] Used thus, words become abstract counters or buttons; they are tender because they yield and because their denominational value can be exchanged.

Contemporary reviewers of *Tender Buttons* noted Stein's closeness to Cubism, but rarely meant it as a compliment. Many columnists expressed bewilderment or mocked Stein's linguistic experiment as nonsense. As Sherwood Anderson remarked in his introduction to Stein's 1922 collection, *Geography and Plays*, there was 'a good deal of fuss and fun being made over it in American newspapers', all of which further helped to establish Stein as a household name.[127] Even writers who counted themselves as participants in the modern movement were sometimes unsure quite what to make of *Tender Buttons*. Alfred Kreymborg (1883–1966) edited two little magazines – *Glebe* (1913–14) and *Others* (1915–19) – that promoted innovative poetry, including Imagist verse. Nonetheless, he was thoroughly perplexed by Stein's poetry and wrote a review entitled 'Gertrude Stein – Hoax and Hoaxtress: A Study of the Woman Whose "Tender Buttons" Has Furnished New York with a New Kind of Amusement'.[128] By contrast, H.L. Mencken persevered with *Tender Buttons*, remarking that 'the emotions aroused by a first reading of Miss Stein are "something like terror", but as one proceeds the beauty of these super-sentences begins to caress the refined mind, and in the end the effect is almost electrical'.[129]

Stein's *Faux-naïf* strategies for rendering language non-meaningful anticipated the eruptions of the next significant movement in Europe's avant-garde, Dadaism, winning her the popular sobriquet 'The Mama of Dada'.

Dada

Dada was launched at the Cabaret Voltaire in Zürich in 1916 by a group of German and Romanian artists who had sought refuge from the First World War by relocating to neutral Switzerland. Hugo Ball (1886–1927), Richard Huelsenbeck (1892–1974), Tristan Tzara (1896–1963), Marcel Janco (1895–1974) and Hans Arp (1886–1966), staged Futurist-inspired variety shows featuring poems (read in different languages simultaneously), comic songs and dances, Cubist collages and Bruitism ('noise music'). The flavour of their evenings is recorded by Arp:

■ On the stage of a gaudy, motley, overcrowded tavern there are several weird and peculiar figures [...]. Total pandemonium. The people around us are shouting, laughing and gesticulating. Our replies are sighs of love, volleys of hiccups, poems, moos and meowing of medieval Bruitists. Tzara is wiggling his behind like the belly of an Oriental dancer. Janco is playing an invisible violin and bowing and scraping. [...]. Huelsenbeck is banging away nonstop on the great drum, with Ball accompanying him on the piano, pale as a chalky ghost. We were given the honorary title of Nihilists.[130] □

The group documented their antics in a single-issue magazine, *Cabaret Voltaire* (1916), which was succeeded shortly after by Tzara's publication *Dada* (1917–18). Tzara's relentless promotion of Dada helped to bring the group's activities to international notice.

Dadaism combined Futurist strategies of performance and provocation with satire and buffoonery to articulate disgust at a European culture mired in deathly conflict, bafflement at the absurdity of the human condition and hostility to the bourgeois valuation of commodities over art. It was avowedly anti-authoritarian to the extent that it had no coherent aesthetic programme. As Tzara explained in 'Dada Manifesto 1918', 'We recognize no theory':[131]

■ Every product of disgust capable of becoming a negation of the family is Dada; a protest with the fists of its whole being engaged in destructive action: *Dada; knowledge of all the means rejected up until now by the shamefaced sex of comfortable compromise and good manners: Dada; abolition of logic, which is the dance of those impotent to create: Dada; of every social hierarchy and equation set up for the sake of values by our valets: [...].* Freedom: *Dada Dada Dada*, a roaring of tense colors, and interlacing of opposites and of all contradictions, grotesques, inconsistencies: LIFE.[132] □

The desired liberty, spontaneity, folly and contradiction was realised through the destruction of conventional logic, language and syntax (for instance in Ball's phonetic poems) and the non-hierarchical juxtapositions of collage. Tzara insisted that the term Dada was both meaningless and suggestive. He claimed 'DADA MEANS NOTHING', before informing readers that the word variously denoted 'the tail of the holy cow' in Kru (a West African language), 'the cube and the mother in a certain district of Italy', a 'hobby horse, a nurse both in Russian and Rumanian', and was regarded by 'some learned journalists [...] as an art for babies, [...] a relapse into a dry and noisy, noisy and monotonous primitivism'.[133] Tzara's 'Dada Manifesto 1918' can be read as a manifesto against manifestos and programmatic movements, using negation and unsystematic thinking to parody and criticise the form of the genre itself.

In 1920, Tzara took Dada to Paris and gathered many artists to his cause, including André Breton (1896–1966). In 1922, Breton broke decisively with Tzara and set about clearing the way for Surrealism. 'Dada, thank goodness, is no longer an issue', Breton sneered in 'After Dada' (1922), 'and its funeral in around May 1921 engendered no brawls'.[134]

Ulysses (1922)

Although James Joyce intended that *Ulysses* should 'give such a picture of Dublin so complete that if the city one day suddenly disappeared from the earth it could be reconstructed', his ambitions were far from provincial.[135] Not only was the novel written in Trieste, Zürich and Paris, but Joyce's irrepressible experimental narrative techniques belonged to the insurgent activities of the European avant-garde. *Ulysses* concerns the meeting of Stephen Dedalus (an aspiring artist), and Leopold Bloom (a middle-aged Jewish advertising canvasser), on the day that Bloom's wife, Molly, takes a lover. It is loosely based on the adventures of Homer's wily Greek mythic hero Odysseus (known as Ulysses to the Romans). In the Homeric scheme of things, Bloom is a modern-day Ulysses, Stephen is Ulysses's son, Telemachus, and Molly is Ulysses's wife, Penelope. Joyce's intention was to 'transpose the myth [of the *Odyssey*] *sub specie temporis nostri*' [in the light of our own times], so that 'Each adventure (that is, every hour, every organ, every art being interconnected and interrelated in the structural scheme of the whole) should not only condition but even create its own technique'.[136] The result was a book written 'from eighteen different points of view and in as many different styles, all apparently unknown or undiscovered by [...] fellow tradesmen', each in some way suggested by the Homeric adventure in question.[137]

As Joyce wrote *Ulysses*, his prose evolved beyond a flexible combination of interior monologue and free indirect discourse (which he referred to as 'the initial style') to a radical point where the narrative idiom no longer had any necessary grounding in character.[138] For instance: the 'Aeolus' episode is intercut with newspaper headlines; 'Sirens' is written in a language that aspires to the condition of music, structured, Joyce confided, as a *'fuga per canonem'* (a fugue by way of a canon); 'Cyclops' is a first-person narrative interrupted by a series of inflated parodies, corresponding to the Homeric themes of monocularism and 'gigantism'; 'Circe' is written as a hallucinatory play-script; 'Eumaeus' is written in clichés; and 'Ithaca' is written in the question-and-answer 'form of a mathematical catechism'.[139] The stylistic odyssey endowed the novel with adventure and epic proportion.

The book publication of *Ulysses* was an international event, not least because serial publication in the *Little Review* (March 1918–August 1920) had been brought to a halt after the Secretary of the New York Society for the Suppression of Vice took exception to the 'Nausicaa' episode (in which Bloom masturbates as he gazes at a young woman, who, at least on a cursory reading, appears to be encouraging him). The successful prosecution of the magazine's two editors, Margaret Anderson (1886–1973) and Jane Heap (1883–1964), for obscenity generated enormous publicity, but prevented further publication in the United States, with the result that the book was first published in France by Sylvia Beach (1887–1962), the proprietor of the Parisian bookshop Shakespeare and Company.

Valery Larbaud introduced Joyce to the French literary world in a landmark lecture (7 December 1921), expanded for publication in *La Nouvelle Revue Française* (1922), and abridged and translated into English for the *Criterion* (1922), where he announced that with *Ulysses* 'Ireland makes a sensational re-entrance into high European tradition'.[140] (This view, supported by Ezra Pound – who promoted Joyce as the successor to Gustave Flaubert, Cervantes and Rabelais – was challenged by Ernest Boyd, who asserted that Joyce was emphatically an Irish writer whose work developed from within the context of the Irish Revival, providing a foretaste of the tension that still exists between critics who emphasise Joyce's internationalism and those who emphasise his Irishness).[141] Larbaud provided a chapter-by-chapter analysis of symbols, styles and Homeric correspondences, based on a schema Joyce had prepared to assist readers and impress them with his ingenuity.

T.S. Eliot hailed Joyce's creation to be the 'most important expression which the present age has found' in '*Ulysses*, Order, and Myth' (1923).[142] The essay was intended as a rebuttal of a hostile review of *Ulysses* by Richard Aldington, who treated Joyce 'as a prophet of chaos; and wailed at the flood of Dadaism which his prescient eye saw bursting forth at the tap of the magician's rod'.[143] Eliot's view was that if *Ulysses* 'is not a novel, that is simply because the novel is a form which will no longer serve'.[144] His essay took account of the complex structural schemata Joyce prepared to make the Homeric correspondences apparent:

■ In using the myth, in manipulating a continuous parallel between contemporaneity and antiquity, Mr. Joyce is pursuing a method which others must pursue after him. [...] It is simply a way of controlling, of ordering, of giving a shape and a significance to the immense panorama of futility and anarchy that is contemporary history. [...] Psychology [...], ethnology, and *The Golden Bough* have concurred to make possible what was impossible even a few years ago. Instead of narrative method, we may now use the mythical method.[145] □

So far as Eliot was concerned, myth brought order to a chaotic present. However, Eliot overlooked Joyce's whimsical interpretation of episodes from the *Odyssey*, his unwieldy encyclopaedism, the anarchy of style, the mock-epic comedy he brought to bear on his reinterpretation of Homer's myth, his substantial structural use of other intertexts (most notably *Hamlet*) and the welter of autonomous symbolism that is peculiar to *Ulysses*. In fact, Eliot's commentary on 'mythical method' as a means to control the 'anarchy of contemporary history' is better taken as a statement of his own practice in *The Waste Land*, especially in the light of the reference to *The Golden Bough: A Study in Magic and Religion* (1890–1915), a weighty account of primitive myths and rituals by Sir James George Frazer (1854–1941), which was an important source for the poem.

Many contemporary reviewers of *Ulysses* simply could not get past the obfuscatory styles or the unabashed treatment of sexual desire and the human body. The anonymous correspondent for Dublin's *Sporting Times* complained that *Ulysses* 'appears to have been written by a perverted lunatic who has made a speciality of the literature of the latrine'.[146] Even D.H. Lawrence denounced *Ulysses*, calling it 'the dirtiest, most indecent, obscene thing ever written'.[147] (His objection stemmed from the idea that the sexual and the excremental are opposing forces that should remain separate).

Censorship of *Ulysses* in English-speaking countries did not prevent this notorious book from having a revolutionary impact on Anglo-American literature. During the 1920s, sophisticates smuggled cheap European copies through customs. From 1930 onwards, interested readers who were unable to buy the book could consult *James Joyce's 'Ulysses': A Study*, a richly instructive chapter-by-chapter guide to the novel and its Homeric dimensions, with lengthy excerpts, written by Stuart Gilbert (1883–1969), with assistance from Joyce.[148] The ban was overturned in America in 1933, after the judge ruled that Joyce 'did not write *Ulysses* with what is commonly called pornographic intent' and that if anything its effect was 'emetic' rather than 'aphrodisiac'.[149]

The New York Avant-Garde: The Provincetown Players and New York Dada

Exposure to revolutionary European art movements ignited the growth of a distinctively American avant-garde. The lack of new significant writing by American playwrights was remedied by the formation of the Provincetown Players (1915–22), a small but highly influential non-commercial theatre company that relocated to Greenwich Village in 1916. Participants included Djuna Barnes, Mina Loy, William Carlos Williams, Wallace Stevens, Marianne Moore and Edna St Vincent Millay (1892–1950), poet-painters such as Marguerite and William Zorach (1887–1968 and 1887–1966) and the two Pulitzer Prize-winning playwrights whose careers were launched by Provincetown, Susan Glaspell (1876–1948) and Eugene O'Neill (1888–1953). William Archer recognised Provincetown's revolutionary significance as early as 1921, hailing it to be 'the real birthplace of the American drama'.[150]

The Players' first modernist play was *Lima Beans* (1916) by Alfred Kreymborg, about a woman who breaks with the nightly tradition of serving her husband lima beans for dinner. Kreymborg conceived the play 'as a pantomime dance of automatons to an accompaniment of rhythmic words, in place of music' and directed the actors Loy, Williams and Zorach to behave as if they were marionettes, dictating the tempo of their lines as if conducting an orchestra.[151] The stage was designed by Zorach, based 'on the screens of Gordon Craig', producing the effect of 'colors in planes and angles with patterns of remarkable vegetables'.[152] This anti-mimetic drama, in which characters, abstracted into types, spoke stylised poetic dialogue in front of symbolic sets, achieved an autonomous synthesis of aural and visual elements, and prepared the ground for further experimentation.

It is a measure of how socially progressive the Provincetown Players were that their greatest commercial and critical success was O'Neill's boldly Expressionist play *Emperor Jones* (1920), the first production by a white company to star an African-American actor – Charles Gilpin (1878–1930) – in the lead role. *Emperor Jones* interrogated the brutality of colonialism and enslavement, presenting the stricken conscience of an African-American escaped convict who sets himself up as the despotic ruler of a Caribbean island and is forced to escape when the native population revolts. From the first scene onwards, a tom-tom drum is hit at the pace of a human pulse. It then gets faster and faster to convey Jones's mounting panic, with the aim of synchronising the audience's hearts with the pounding primal beat. Leading black American writers recognised that although Jones is himself a brutal imperialist, he is also haunted by nightmarish visions of the torments white masters inflicted on black subjects, and praised O'Neill for his portrayal of a collective black unconsciousness. Jean Toomer (1894–1967) commended the play as 'a section of Negro psychology presented in significant dramatic form' in 1921, noting that 'Jones lives through sections of an unconscious which is peculiar to the Negro. Slave ships, whipping posts, and so on'.[153] James Weldon Johnson (1871–1938) applauded O'Neill for using 'the Negro and Negro life as pure dramatic material'.[154]

Another hub for avant-garde activity was the New York salon of art collectors Louise and Walter Arensberg (1879–1953 and 1878–1954). Here, expatriates who fled war-ravaged Europe, such as the radical French producers of anti-art Marcel Duchamp and Francis Picabia (1879–1953), the former Futurist Mina Loy (who arrived in 1916), and the German artist and personality Baroness Elsa von Freytag-Loringhoven (1874–1927), socialised with American artists, such as the photographer Man Ray (1890–1976) and the writers Marianne Moore, William Carlos Williams and Wallace Stevens. Many of the Arensburgs' circle had an interest in Dada. Jane Heap described Freytag-Loringhoven as one 'who dresses Dada, loves Dada, lives Dada'.[155] Members of the group briefly adopted the label New York Dada in 1921.

American Modernism: Mina Loy, Marianne Moore and Wallace Stevens

The New York art scene provided the crucible in which a specifically American branch of modernism was forged. It made the techniques of European art serve American purposes, resisting the old-world values and the classicist trends of London-centred modernism to seek stimulus from the material and social fabric of contemporary American culture. A key statement in the formation of this self-consciously American brand modernism was articulated by Van Wyck Brooks (1886–1963) in *America's Coming-of-Age* (1915). He argued that 'Human nature itself in America exists on two irreconcilable planes, the plane of stark intellectuality and the plane of stark business', a duality 'resulting in the final unreality of most of American culture', and posited literature (specifically poetry) as the potentially redemptive intermediary that might overcome this damaging split between the Highbrow (the superficially refined, genteel tradition of American thought) and the Lowbrow (rampant entrepreneurialism).[156] He praised Walt Whitman as a poet who was in contact with actuality and who 'laid the cornerstone of a national ideal capable [...] of releasing personality and of retrieving for our civilization, [...] bled and flattened out by the "machine process", the only sort of "place in the sun" that is really worth having'.[157] Brooks's call for literature to overcome the contradictions dividing American cultural life and achieve a revolutionary synthesis between the material and the spiritual is paradigmatic of American modernism.

In 'The Great American Billposter' (1922), a critical essay-*cum*-manifesto published in *Broom: An International Magazine of the Arts*, Matthew Josephson (1899–1978) argued that if contemporary writers wanted to create truly indigenous art they should forsake French Symbolism and British romanticism and instead take fresh stimulus from the 'daring and ingenious literature' that copywriters produced to advertise the consumer products, the automobiles, motion pictures, food and sports fixtures through which one really knows a country's culture:

■ The terse vivid slang of the people has been swiftly transmitted to this class of writers, along with a willingness to depart from syntax, to venture sentence forms and word constructions which are at times breath-taking, if anything, and in all cases far more arresting and provocative than 99 per cent of the stuff that passes for poetry in our specialized magazines.[158] □

Making creative use of the vivid language spoken by the people and used in daily life would further help to distinguish this new, distinctively American movement in art from Eurocentric modernism.

Mina Loy was among the many writers who were struck by the vitality of modern American speech, particularly the way that it had been enriched and variegated by many waves of immigration. Looking back from the vantage point of 1925, she asserted that this quality made it inevitable that 'the renaissance of poetry should proceed out of America':[159]

■ You may think it impossible to conjure up the relationship of expression between the high browest modern poets and an adolescent Slav who has speculated in a wholesale job-lot of mandarines and is trying to sell them in a retail market on First Avenue. But [...] both have had to become adapted to a country where the mind has to put on its verbal clothes at terrific speed if it would speak in time; where no one will listen if you attack him twice with the same missile of argument. And, that the ear that has listened to the greatest number of sounds will have the most to choose from when it comes to self-expression, each has been liberally educated in the flexibility of phrases.[160] □

Loy herself made brilliant use of this newly flexible, variegated tongue in her own work.

Loy's 'Love Songs' appeared in the first issue of *Others: A Magazine of New Verse* (1915). These poems offered frank examinations of women's psycho-sexual experience. They mixed linguistic curios with common idioms, breaking the rules of grammar and syntax by using intuitive blank spaces, dashes and capitals in lieu of more formal punctuation. Their sonorous qualities conform to her definition of poetry as 'prose bewitched, a music made of visual thoughts, the sound of an idea'.[161] Kreymborg recalled that 'Detractors shuddered at Mina Loy's subject-matter and derided her elimination of punctuation marks and the audacious spacing of her lines'.[162] However, Ezra Pound considered her wayward free verse and her sardonic mix of high, low and technical registers to be a finely judged assault on literary decorum. He highlighted this quality in one of the earliest notices of her work, in which he praised Loy and her fellow *Others* contributor Marianne Moore for their 'arid clarity' and striking use of '*logopoeia*' (which Pound later defined as employing words 'not only for their direct meaning' but also taking 'count in a special way of habits of usage, of the context we *expect* to find with the word, its usual concomitants, of its known acceptances and of ironical play').[163] While Pound traced this technique to the unconscious influence of Jules Laforgue (in line with his own enthusiasm), he nonetheless acknowledged that the poetry produced by Loy and Moore was 'a distinctly national product, [...] which would not have come out of any other country'.[164]

Marianne Moore wrote pithy free verse that was austere yet idiomatically American. In 'Poetry' (1919), her most famous reflection on her practice, Moore stated 'nor is it valid / to discriminate against "business documents and / school books"; all these phenomena are important' (the embedded quotation is from Tolstoy's diaries).[165] Skilled in the 'science of assorting and the art of investing that assortment with dignity', Moore constructed textual patchworks that tease connotations from words, showing how profoundly reality is mediated through language.[166] Aspiring to create 'imaginary gardens with real toads in them', Moore brought the subjects that she patiently observed and studied to a new and singular clarity, renewing the idea of the thing by discarding the associations which have accrued through casual viewing and time-worn description.[167] In this way, her poetry found a 'place for the genuine'.[168] Wallace Stevens celebrated Moore's talent for establishing what he called 'a reality of her own particulars' to achieve 'an aesthetic integration', while William Carlos Williams praised her ability to show the vastness of the particular, 'So that in looking at some apparently small object, one feels the swirl of great events'.[169] In his introduction to Moore's *Selected Poems* (1935), T.S. Eliot praised her work for forming 'part of the small body of durable poetry written in our time [...] in which an original sensibility and alert intelligence and deep feeling have been engaged in maintaining the life of the English language'.[170]

Like Moore, Wallace Stevens also asserted the primacy of the imagination and its relation to reality. Whereas Pound had been concerned with the problem of how to use language to convey objective 'things' and fix a given experience in words, Stevens saw language as immanent to the way that experience is conceived, and so he regarded the poet's imagination as an active force that engages in *constituting* the world. While Pound aspired to classical decorum, Stevens believed that 'The whole effort of the imagination is toward the production of the romantic'.[171] In his later critical writing, Stevens cast the poet as a high priest of the imagination, a 'potent figure' who 'creates the world to which we turn incessantly and without knowing it' and 'gives to life the supreme fictions without which we are unable to conceive of it'.[172] By contrast with the nineteenth-century romantics, Stevens held that the poet's revelations are not spiritual in the religious sense but verbal: 'Poetry is a revelation in words by means of the words'.[173] To answer that 'deepening need for words to express our thoughts and feelings which, we are sure, are all the truth that we shall ever experience', the sounds of words must be probed 'for a finality, a perfection, an unalterable vibration, which it is only within the power of the acutest poet to achieve'.[174]

The poems collected in Stevens's first book *Harmonium* (1923) dated from as early as 1915. Several had previously appeared in little magazines. Reviewers were alert to the melodious qualities of his verse. Matthew Josephson noted 'the music of his words' and Harriet Monroe expressed her delight at the 'sheer beauty of sound, phrase, rhythm'.[175] Edmund Wilson (1895–1972) praised Stevens as 'the master of a style' and complimented 'the richness of his verbal imagination', but also commented on his whimsical titles, opacity, and emotional detachment:

■ His gift for combining words is fantastic but sure: even when you do not know what he is saying, you know he is saying it well. [...] Emotion seems to emerge only furtively in the cryptic images of his poetry, as if it had been [...] disposed of by being dexterously turned into exquisite amusing words.[176] □

'The Dandyism of Wallace Stevens' (1925), an influential essay by the Greenwich Village-based literary critic Gorham Munson (1896–1969), consolidated the view that Stevens' persona was aloof and devoted to 'elegance', 'fastidious vocabulary' and 'impeccable form'.[177] When a revised edition of *Harmonium* appeared in 1931, leftist critics disparaged what they saw as sensuous aestheticism and dissociation. R.P. Blackmur (1904–65) defended the poet from these accusations in an extended essay, 'Examples of Wallace Stevens' (1932), in which he advanced Stevens's reputation by drawing attention to his exacting use of esoteric diction to balance sound and sense, to the extent that he can convey ambiguities, feelings and thoughts with precision: 'Somewhere between the realms of ornamental sound and representative statement, the words pause and balance, dissolve and resolve'.[178]

Tradition and the Individual Talent

Like their female peers, Pound and Eliot were writing poetry that thrived on *logopoeic* contrasts between high literary and low idiomatic diction. However, the two men's strategies of allusion and quotation were of a different character to Mina Loy's democratisation of art or Marianne Moore's unshowy gatherings of cultural knowledge. Pound and Eliot shared an explicit aim: to position their work as the culmination of (European) literary tradition.

'Tradition and the Individual Talent' (1919), first published in two parts in the *Egoist* and then in *The Sacred Wood* (1920), is widely seen as the key to Eliot's own 'programme for the *métier* of poetry'.[179] Eliot proposed that 'what makes a writer most acutely conscious of his place in time, of his contemporaneity' is 'the historical sense'.

■ [T]he historical sense involves a perception, not only of the pastness of the past, but of its presence; the historical sense compels a man to write not merely with his own generation in his bones, but with a feeling that the whole of the literature of Europe from Homer and within it the whole of the literature of his own country has a simultaneous existence and composes a simultaneous order'.[180] □

Because good art transcends history and remains enduringly relevant, the poet needs a detailed knowledge of past literatures if he is to produce truly new work of lasting value, hence the conviction that 'the most individual parts of his work may be those in which the dead poets, his ancestors, assert their immortality most vigorously'.[181]

'Tradition and the Individual Talent' also sets out to establish an 'Impersonal theory of poetry' that debunks the authenticity of the lyric 'I'.[182] It attempts to deflect attention from the individual poet's personality by setting poems firmly within their literary context. Eliot begins with the observation that highly innovative art can reshape tradition itself:

■ The existing monuments form an ideal order among themselves, which is modified by the introduction of the new (the really new) work of art among them.[183] □

Next, Eliot proposes a thoroughly anti-romantic model for poetic composition using a complex scientific analogy. Oxygen and sulphur dioxide mixed in the presence of platinum form sulphurous acid. The shred of platinum acts as a catalyst: it is itself 'inert, neutral, and unchanged', but its presence is what transforms the two gases into a new combination.[184] Ideally, Eliot argues, the poet's mind acts as the platinum does, being distinct from and unaffected by the elements it fuses and transforms. By analogy, the poet need not have personal experience of the emotions he depicts because past literature provides a store of feeling from which contemporaries with 'historical sense' can select impersonally. Eliot explains, 'the more perfect the artist, the more completely separate in him will be the man who suffers and the mind which creates'.[185] 'Poetry', Eliot concludes, 'is not a turning loose of emotion, but an escape from emotion; it is not the expression of personality, but an escape from personality.'[186]

Eliot's passive model for 'the poet's mind' as 'a receptacle for seizing and storing up numberless feelings, phrases and images, which remain there until all the particles which can unite to form a new compound are present together' avoids grasping the nettle that is authorial intention or accounting for the institutions that shape the canon.[187] It is necessary to look to elsewhere to understand how Eliot saw the elements of a poem interacting to produce something new. A celebrated statement appears in Eliot's essay 'Philip Massinger' (1920):

> ■ Immature poets imitate; mature poets steal; bad poets deface what they take, and good poets make it into something better, or at least something different. The good poet welds his theft into a whole of feeling which is unique, utterly different from that from which it was torn; the bad poet throws it into something which has no cohesion. A good poet will usually borrow from authors remote in time, or alien in language, or diverse in interest.[188] □

The financial metaphors imply that literary capital can be amassed by poets when they add value to the material they steal. 'The whole point' of unacknowledged quotation, Eliot explained (defending himself against charges of plagiarism), is 'that the reader should recognise where it came from and contrast it with the spirit and meaning of my own poem'.[189] Mature adaptation is therefore to be distinguished from immature cribbing in terms of how successfully it orientates the new work in relation to tradition.

The Waste Land (1922)

Eliot's vocabulary of order, cohesion and wholeness presents a seemingly harmonious vision of the relation of the individual talent to tradition. In practice, however, the number, density and obscurity of the works Eliot fleetingly referenced in his poetry left plenty of room for confusion and doubt. Ezra Pound hailed *The Waste Land* as 'the justification of the "movement", of our modern experiment, since 1900'.[190] However, many readers simply did not know what to make of Eliot's experiment when it first appeared in the *Criterion* (Eliot's own periodical) in October 1922 and then in America in the November issue of *Dial*. J.C. Squire (1884–1958), the editor of the staunchly conservative *London Mercury*, confessed he was 'unable to make head nor tail' of *The Waste Land* and suggested that 'A grunt would serve equally well', while Louis Untermeyer (1885–1977), who was genuinely knowledgeable about modern poetry, dismissed the poem as a 'pompous parade of erudition' that was 'cryptic in intention and even more dismal in effect'.[191]

Eliot defended difficult poetry in 'The Metaphysical Poets' (1921):

■ We can only say that it appears likely that poets in our civilization, as it exists at present, must be *difficult*. Our civilization comprehends great variety and complexity, and this variety and complexity, playing upon a refined sensibility, must produce various and complex results. The poet must become more and more comprehensive, more allusive, more indirect, in order to force, to dislocate, if necessary, language into his meaning.[192] □

The 'Notes' that Eliot supplied for the first book edition of *The Waste Land* (published by Boni and Liveright in December 1922) guided readers to select sources and provided brief explanatory comments, which helped to demystify the poem. The headnote stated that 'Not only the title, but the plan and a good deal of the incidental symbolism of the poem were suggested by Miss Jessie L. Weston's book on the Grail legend: *From Ritual to Romance* (Macmillan)' and further recommended the anthropological work which inspired her and which influenced Eliot's generation 'profoundly': James George Frazer's *The Golden Bough: A Study in Magic and Religion*.[193]

Frazer's encyclopaedic account of primitive myths and rituals emphasised the continuities between ancient societies and modern civilisation, discerning in present-day customs the relics of the past cultures from which European society had evolved and advanced. Comparing themes of god, king and tree-worship, royal and priestly taboos, the killing of divine kings, cycles of purgation and regeneration, fertility rituals and the idea of the eternal soul in peasant customs, myths and ancient world religions, Frazer revealed 'the essential similarity with which, under many superficial differences, the human mind has elaborated its first crude philosophy of life'.[194] These similarities are shown to persist in cultural institutions throughout history, appearing in different forms as man's thinking progressed 'from magic through religion to science'.[195] In other words, myths encode the unchanging realities of human experience.

Frazer's fine style and comparative approach to myth, interweaving many different stories from diverse cultures, found favour with literary writers interested in examining the historical impulses underlying modern belief and behaviour. His ethnographical thinking is mirrored in modernist theories of history like Eliot's that assert the presence of the past.

Edmund Wilson, the editor of the *Dial*, was the first reviewer to take account of Eliot's notes and penetrate some of the poem's mystery in 'The Poetry of Drouth [drought]', published in that magazine in December 1922. Packed with fruitful insights, his short review set the agenda for subsequent appreciation. He was the first to explore the *leitmotifs* that give Eliot's cryptic poem thematic coherence with reference to the Arthurian myth of the waste land (the desolate, sterile territory ruled by an impotent king, that is only returned to health and fertility when a knight succeeds in his quest for the Holy Grail), which Weston linked to analogous fertility rituals in other pre-Christian cultures that address seasonal cycles of dearth and renewal:

■ Mr. Eliot uses the Waste Land as the concrete image of a spiritual drouth. His poem takes place half in the real world – the world of contemporary London, and half in a haunted wilderness – the Waste Land of the mediaeval legend; [...] the hero's arid soul [...] exists not only upon these two planes, but as if throughout the whole of human history. [...] So Mr. Eliot hears in his own parched cry the voices of all the thirsty men of the past. In the centre of his poem he places the weary figure of the blind immortal prophet Tiresias, who, having been woman as well as man, has exhausted all human experience and [...] knows exactly what will happen in the London flat between the typist and the house-agent's clerk; [...] Not only is life sterile and futile, but men have tasted its sterility and futility a thousand times before. T.S. Eliot, walking the desert of London, feels profoundly that the desert has always been there. [...] In the end the dry-rotted world is crumbling about him – his own soul is falling apart. There is nothing left to prop it up but some dry stoic Sanskrit maxims and the broken sighs from the past, of singers exiled or oppressed.[196] □

Wilson also drew attention to the haunting 'strains of an unfading music' and memories that provide fleeting remission from the dryness, as well as the triumph of Eliot's mastery of the forms of English verse.[197] Although Wilson admitted that his account reduced the poem's rich complexity, he nonetheless argued that 'for all its complicated correspondences and recondite references and quotations, *The Waste Land* is intelligible at first reading' as 'the very images and sounds of the words [...] are charged with a strange poignancy' and that it bespeaks 'our whole world of strained nerves and shattered institutions' where the 'pursuit of grace and beauty is something which is felt to be obsolete'.[198] As Wilson perceived, what coherence *The Waste Land* achieves inheres in its 'historical sense', the way it draws on the store of human experience concentrated in myth and literature and brings this to bear on the present.

Conclusion

The critical principles that sculpted the revolutionary upheaval in artistic practice between 1910 and 1922 were developed in reaction to a series of contrary impulses. There was no consensus as to whether modern art should be subjective and impressionistic or impersonal and hard (perhaps even non-human), whether it should engage directly with the specific conditions of its own historical moment, view the present through the prism of the past, imagine a future society or pursue pure form as an aesthetic end in itself, or indeed how far abstraction and symbolism might convey a higher realism. The reception of the most experimental literatures was typically split between initiates, who vaunted bold innovations, rival artists, who promoted alternative aesthetic agendas, conservative commentators, who took a dim view of avant-garde work and dismissed it as nonsensical or obscure, and zealous censors, who sought to prohibit the production of art that they deemed dangerous to public morality. Time would tell which modernist works and critical ideas would make the transition from the cultural margins to the fashionable mainstream to be taken up by future generations of writers, theorists, readers and critics.

CHAPTER THREE

Modernism after 1922

Formal Experimentation and Social Commentary

The modernist revolution in the arts continued in the years after the War, but its character changed. While modernists still appealed to form as an arena where aesthetic, epistemological and ideological battles could be fought, their critical writings became more explicitly concerned with social, regional and national issues, the global political and economic situation, and literature's role in shaping the future of society. This chapter examines this overtly politicised sensibility, exploring innovative writers' attempts to formulate national and international modernisms, harness the anarchic irruptions of the unconscious mind and use experimental modernist techniques to intervene in debates concerning race, gender and class.

Localism and American Modernism: William Carlos Williams and William Faulkner

■ It wiped out our world as if an atom bomb had been dropped upon it [...]. Critically Eliot returned us to the classroom just at the moment when I felt that we were on the point of escape to matters much closer to the essence of a new art form itself – rooted in the locality which should give it fruit. I knew at once that in certain ways I was most defeated.[1] □

William Carlos Williams was speaking personally about the shock that *The Waste Land* delivered to New York's avant-garde. T.S. Eliot, an expatriate American living in London, had won overnight celebrity for a self-consciously erudite poem that positioned itself as the culminating achievement of the ostensibly European literary tradition it redefined. It was a bitter setback to Williams's hopes of continuing the revolutionary programme envisioned by Walt Whitman and enacted by writers such as Sherwood Anderson in *Winesburg, Ohio*: the task of delivering a modern American literature rooted in its native history and culture.

The battle lines had been drawn several years earlier. In 1917, Ezra Pound declared 'Provincialism the enemy'.[2] This high-handed comment was made in response to the political situation in Ireland in the wake of the Easter Rising, registering Pound's irritation with debates focused on local issues rather than civilisation as a whole. Williams rebutted his friend's internationalist position in the pugnacious Prologue to *Kora in Hell* (1920), a series of prose improvisations infused with the spirit of Dada. Williams drew a distinction between Americans like him who stayed at home and expatriate Europhiles like Eliot and Pound, whom he considered to be 'Men content with the connotations of their masters', accusing Eliot of being 'a subtle conformist' and 'an archbishop of procurers to a lecherous antiquity'.[3]

Williams increasingly singled out Eliot as his chief literary antagonist, defining his own resolutely localist poetics against Eliot's expatriate modernism. He seized victory from the jaws of apparent defeat with *Spring and All* (1923), a fertile riposte to *The Waste Land*'s characterisation of April as the cruellest month, consisting of twenty-seven untitled free-form poems interspersed with polemical prose commentaries that makes use of Dadaist strategies of fragmentation, collage, typographical anomalies and incomplete sentences.[4] However, the poems explore local particulars and material objects. 'The Red Wheelbarrow', the most famous poem in *Spring and All*, is often mistakenly classed as an exemplary Imagist poem for its direct and spare precision.[5] Now that Williams had discovered open forms that admitted diverse genres of writing, he felt the structural and conceptual limitations of Imagism. 'The insignificant "image" may be "evoked" never so ably and still mean nothing', he explained in the surrounding commentary.[6] Instead, that poem was a manifesto for precise realisation of the actual thing as it exists – in this case a simple smallholder's tool – rather than a symbol for anything else. It is on this act of artistic materialisation that so much depends. So far as Williams was concerned, 'the imagination is supreme': 'Its unique power is to give created forms reality, actual existence'.[7]

Williams's work only received wide recognition after the publication of *In the American Grain* (1925), which consisted of imaginative reconstructions of key moments in the lives of the nation's founding figures, from the first settlers in Greenland to Christopher Columbus, Hernán Cortés, Benjamin Franklin, George Washington, Edgar Allan Poe and Abraham Lincoln. It was written in the belief that 'Americans have lost the sense [...] that what we are has its origin in what *the nation* in the past has been; that there is a source in AMERICA for everything we think or do'.[8] The idea was to create a usable history by identifying the true American pioneering spirit to be openness to the new, rather than its stultifying opposite, Puritan suspicion, insularity and the imposition of Old World ideals. The most perceptive contemporary review was by D.H. Lawrence, who grasped that Williams's history was not 'ordinary history, which is a complacent record of the civilization and Europizing (if you can allow the word) of the American continent', but 'a sensuous record of the Americanization of white men in America' as they came into contact with local culture and soil.[9] Lawrence summarised Williams's attempt to bring his fellow countrymen into a new consciousness of what the land itself wants men to be: 'The great continent, its bitterness, its brackish quality, its vast glamour, its strange cruelty. Find this, Americans, and get it into your bones.'[10]

After 1925, reviews of Williams's poems and stories tended to note his mission to give utterance to a live American tradition and his post-Imagist techniques. For instance, Alfred Kreymborg hailed Williams as 'the most indigenous of modern American poets'.[11] Philip Blair Rice (1904–56), the editor of the *Kenyon Review*, compared the immediacy, sensuality, gaiety and lack of constraint that Williams admired in the 'pioneers at their best' (and himself strove to emulate) with 'the qualities that the post-impressionists sought in primitive art, and Lawrence in his peasants'.[12] Rice also commented on Williams's search for 'immediate presentation, his passion for "objectivity"', noting that the word had become the slogan of a new post-Imagist school that made use of techniques Williams had developed.[13]

Spring and All was one of the texts that Louis Zukofsky (1904–78) deemed essential reading for understanding the orientation of the 'Objectivist' poets – chiefly Zukofsky, Charles Reznikoff (1894–1976), George Oppen (1908–84), Carl Rakosi (1903–2004) and Basil Bunting (1900–85), mentored by Williams and Pound. 'Objectivist', as Oppen explained, 'meant, not an objective viewpoint, but to objectify the poem, to make the poem an object' by rigorous attention to form and technique.[14] According to Zukofsky, the perfected totality of the poem as an object depends on 'sincerity', in which 'shapes appear concomitants of word combinations, precursors of (if there is continuance) completed sound or structure, melody or form'.[15] The stipulation that writing entails 'thinking with the things as they exist' requires that the author attend to 'historic and contemporary particulars', an obligation which further distinguished 'Objectivist' poetry from Imagism.[16] The desire 'To make a start, / out of particulars / and make them general' would be key to Williams's great five-volume poem *Paterson* (1946–58), an intimate portrait of the life of an industrial city in his native New Jersey.[17]

Zukofsky compiled the Objectivist Press edition of Williams's *Collected Poems 1921–1931* (1934). In the Preface, Wallace Stevens argued that Williams's 'passion for the anti-poetic is a blood passion'.[18] The statement irritated Williams, who insisted that no subject was intrinsically anti-poetic. His protests did not prevent future critics from interpreting Williams's work according to Stevens's suggestion that it struck a balance between the 'anti-poetic' and the 'sentimental' and romantic.

William Faulkner was another American modernist who strongly identified as a provincial writer, locating his work in Mississippi and his fictional Yoknapatawpha country. In the discarded preface to his breakthrough novel *The Sound and the Fury* (1929), Faulkner outlined the necessary impact of his native home on his writing, explaining that southern writers 'try in the simple furious breathing (or writing) span of the individual to draw a savage indictment of the contemporary scene' (by which he meant the racial, familial and gendered conflict that beset the American south) 'or to escape from it into a make-believe region of swords and magnolias and mockingbirds which perhaps never existed anywhere'.[19] *The Sound and the Fury* views the decline of an old aristo-cratic southern family through the unreliable, non-sequential, streams of consciousness of three brothers (Benjy, an 'idiot' who has no grasp of speech or time and whose mental processes are relayed in a lan-guage he himself would be unable to use, Quentin, who is suicidal, and Jason, who lacks self-knowledge) and then an omniscient third-person narrative centred on their old black housemaid Dilsey. A promotional pamphlet, written by the then more established Tennessee writer Evelyn Scott (1893–1963), set the tone for the critical reception of *The Sound and the Fury* by elucidating the method and the plot, noting the influ-ence of James Joyce and insisting that this 'overwhelmingly powerful and even monstrous' story of 'the collapse of a provincial aristocracy in a final debacle of insanity, recklessness, psychological perversion' had the 'noble essence' and proportions of Greek tragedy:[20]

■ Here is beauty sprung from the perfect realization of what a more lim-iting morality would describe as ugliness. Here is a humanity stripped of most of what was claimed for it by the Victorians, and the spectacle is moving as no sugar-coated drama ever could be.[21] □

Even without the benefit of Faulkner's preface, reviewers recognised that here was a 'provincial writer' who modified European techniques for his own use to show, in the words of the *Southwest Review*, 'the unguessed possibilities in the treatment of provincial life without loss of universality'.[22]

A sticking point in many reviews of *The Sound and the Fury* was the success of Faulkner's use of fragmentation and stream of consciousness. For instance, the correspondent for *Times-Picayune* judged that Faulkner simplified Joyce's methods to more poignant and forceful effect in parts (particularly Benjy's narrative), but carried them to an incomprehensible extreme on others, and forecast that 'out of such experimentation [...] will grow fine new impulses in English prose'.[23]

More extreme multi-perspectival, achronological experiments followed. *As I Lay Dying* (1930) braided together fifty-nine first-person monologues by fifteen characters, while *Absalom, Absalom!* (1936) made complex use of multiple conflicting first-person narratives within a third-person frame. When asked why he developed these intricate, unreliable narratives, Faulkner explained:

> ■ I think that no one individual can look at truth. It blinds you. You look at it and you see one phase of it. Someone else looks at it and sees a slightly awry phase of it. But taken all together, the truth is in what they saw though nobody saw the truth intact. [...] It was [...] thirteen ways of looking at a blackbird. But the truth, I would like to think, comes out, when the reader has read all these different ways of looking at a black-bird, the reader has his own his own fourteenth image of that blackbird, which I would like to think is the truth.[24] □

The reference to Wallace Stevens's poem 'Thirteen ways of Looking at a Blackbird' locates Faulkner's work within a wider modernist tradition that proposes that all perspectives are relative, but that truths can none-theless be discerned if readers are prepared to weigh and discriminate.

Surrealism

Meanwhile, European art had been transformed by Surrealism, the first significant avant-garde movement after the War. What differenti-ated Surrealism from Paris Dada was its attitude to psychoanalysis. In 'Dada Manifesto 1918', Tristan Tzara had denounced psychoanalysis as a 'dangerous disease' that 'puts to sleep the anti-objective impulses of man and systematizes the bourgeoisie'.[25] By contrast, as André Breton later explained, 'Surrealism believes Freudian criticism to be the first and only one with a really solid basis'.[26] The Surrealists regarded the anarchic energies of the unconscious as a creative force with the poten-tial to solve the problems produced by a repressive bourgeois culture that is ruled by logic and policed by the censorious and oppressive workings of the super ego.

Breton's 'First Manifesto of Surrealism' (1924) is often taken to be Surrealism's foundational document. However, the movement itself is usually dated to 1922, when Breton published 'The Mediums Enter', an account of his circle's experiments with automatism (spontaneous composition undertaken in a dreamlike or hypnotic state modelled on

Freudian free association).[27] That year, Breton defined the movement 'once and for all':

■ SURREALISM, n. Psychic automatism in its pure state, by which one person proposes to express – verbally, by means of the written word, or in any other manner – the actual functioning of thought. Dictated by thought, in the absence of any control exercised by reason, exempt from any aesthetic or moral concern.

ENCYCLOPAEDIA. *Philosophy.* Surrealism is based on the belief in the superior reality of certain forms of previously neglected associations, in the omnipotence of dream, in the disinterested play of thought. It tends to ruin once and for all other psychic mechanisms and to substitute itself for them in solving all the principal problems of life.[28] □

Because automatic writing does not allow for artistic shaping, it increasingly came to be valued more as a symbol than a fixed technique. By 1924, sufficient interest had already been stirred to gather members for 'The Bureau of Surrealist Research', a collective of writers and artists directed by Antonin Artaud (1896–1948).

The Surrealists strove for the future resolution of 'two states, dream and reality, which are seemingly so contradictory, into a kind of absolute reality, a *surreality*'.[29] Central to their purpose was the Surrealist image, a principle of unexpected juxtaposition perfectly expressed in the line from *Les Chants de Maldoror* (1869), a prose poem by the obscure nineteenth-century poet Comte de Lautréamont (pseud. Isidore Ducasse, 1846–70) that the Surrealists took for their motto: 'the chance meeting on a dissecting-table of a sewing-machine and an umbrella'.[30] Uncanny effects are produced when disparate things are disconnected from their habitual contexts and coupled perversely so as to achieve a strange affinity, making the ordinary marvellous. The technique pointed the way for visual artists, for instance, the traumatic dreamscapes enacting human taboos, desires and fears that Salvador Dalí (1904–89) painted with lurid precision.

In 1926, Artaud was involved in the founding of the short-lived but influential Alfred Jarry Theatre. He was concerned that the 'reflected, filtered and projected images' presented by cinema inculcated passivity, and held that the theatre alone could prompt 'direct, violent action'.[31] He strove to develop an anti-bourgeois theatre that would violently awaken the masses' 'heart and nerves' and so 'rediscover a little of the poetry in the ferment of great, agitated crowds hurled against one another'.[32] Artaud began to expound the idea of the Theatre of Cruelty as early as 1932. He wanted to lacerate the audience with 'truthful distillations of dreams where its taste for crime, its erotic obsessions, its savageness, its fantasies, its utopian sense of life and objects, even its cannibalism, do not gush out on an illusory, make-believe, but on an inner level'.[33] He drew inspiration from the performances of the Balinese theatre company that he saw at the French Colonial Exhibition (1931), where he was struck by what he perceived to be the use of ritualistic 'angular, sudden, jerky postures [...], syncopated inflections formed at the back of the throat [...], musical phrases cut short [...], hollow drum sounds, robot creaking, animated puppets dancing' to communicate spiritual truths in 'a new bodily language' without recourse to words.[34] The experience confirmed Artaud's opinion that theatre is most effective when it is visceral and transcends writing. He therefore advocated the use of 'a revolving show, which instead of making stage and auditorium into two closed worlds without any possible communication between them, will extend its visual and oral outbursts over the whole mass of spectators', integrating the audience and the performance.[35] His theories were only tested in one production, *The Cenci* (Paris, 1935), a violent, surreal adaptation of an 1819 verse-drama by Percy Bysshe Shelley. The play was a commercial and critical failure. However, Artaud's ideas would prove hugely influential for later experimental practitioners following the publication of his essays and manifestos in *The Theatre and its Double* (1938, English translation 1958).

The Fates of 'the Men of 1914'

Wyndham Lewis coined the phrase 'the men of 1914' retrospectively to designate 'the literary band, or group, comprised within the critical fold of Ezra Pound – the young, "New", group of writers assembled in Miss Weaver's *Egoist* just before and during the War'.[36] The epithet made an explicit parallel between the fighting on the frontline and the war that Pound, T.S. Eliot, James Joyce and Lewis had waged against outmoded romantic conventions. In Lewis's view, 'the men of 1914' were thwarted revolutionaries:

■ What has happened – slowly – as a result of the War, is that artistic expression has slipped back again into political propaganda and romance, which go together. [...] *We are the first men of a Future that has not materialized.* We belong to a "great age" that has not "come off" [...] We set too sharp a pace. And, more exhausted by War, Slump, and Revolution, the world has *fallen back*.[37] □

Lewis was right that the War had done much to dissipate insurgent cultural energies, although he minimised the degree to which wider modernist conventions had become dominant in the War years and after, and elided crucial differences that distinguish Joyce's work from his contemporaries. Certainly, the rebarbative, hard, objective, classicist turn that Lewis, Pound and Eliot hoped to inaugurate had been frustrated. The War, the consequent slide towards economic depression and political crisis, and the success of Surrealism's seemingly unstructured anti-bourgeois forays into the irrational workings of the mind, persuaded Pound, Eliot and others that formal innovation was only viable if it could be adapted to engage with urgent social and political concerns.

'The symbolist position, artistic aloofness from world affairs, is no good now', Pound decreed in 1921.[38] He was reviewing a book by A.R. Orage (1873–1934), the editor of the *New Age* (a socialist magazine that was at the forefront of debates about modernism), and Major C.H. Douglas (1879–1952), an economist. Douglas was critical of the way that capitalism funnelled wealth to the already affluent, who then withdrew that money from circulation or invested it in financial industries, leading to under-consumption and economic depression. He advocated that the state should fix prices and pay everyone a national dividend, as the cultural knowledge that underpins the creation of wealth is common property. Pound enthusiastically promoted Douglas's social credit proposals and, from the mid-1930s onwards, a system whereby the value of money depreciates over time to encourage quick spending.

Pound's belief that usury was the ultimate source of all social and cultural problems reinforced his anti-Semitism. He moved to Italy in 1924, finding the fascist regime of Benito Mussolini (1883–1945) congenial to the extent that he promoted Italian fascism in his journalism, in his book *Jefferson and/or Mussolini* (1935), and by lobbying American politicians and issuing radio broadcasts during the Second World War. Pound was indicted for treason against the United States in 1943 and incarcerated by American troops in Pisa in 1945, resulting in extradition, arraignment and disgrace. Judged insane, Pound was admitted to St Elizabeth's Hospital. His release was secured in 1958.

Eliot too became conscious that the world had changed and art must follow. 'Only from about the year 1926 did the features of the post-war world begin clearly to emerge – and not only in the sphere of politics', Eliot reflected in 1939. 'From about that date [the year of the first general strike in Britain] one began slowly to realise that the intellectual and artistic output of the previous seven years had been rather the last efforts of an old world, than the first struggles of a new'.[39] A personal turning point was Eliot's conversion to the Anglican Church in 1927. He recalibrated his literary critical standpoint accordingly, noting in his preface to the 1928 edition of *The Sacred Wood* that he had since 'passed on to another problem not touched upon in this book: that of the relation of poetry to the spiritual and social life of its time and of other times'.[40] Eliot's major poems after his conversion – *Ash Wednesday* (1930) and *Four Quartets* (1943) – probe the mystery of faith and its unyielding nature despite fastidious questioning. His experiments with verse drama – including *Murder in the Cathedral* (1935), a contemporary miracle play on the martyrdom of Archbishop Thomas Becket, and a series of plays for the commercial stage aiming at a wider audience, of which *The Cocktail Party* (1949) was the greatest popular success – reflected his conviction that 'The ideal medium for poetry [...] and the most direct means of social "usefulness" for poetry is the theatre'.[41] Even William Carlos Williams was impressed:

■ *The Cocktail Party* is a very thrilling play which in the reading moved me deeply. [...] To me this would be a very considerable achievement on the part of Mr. Eliot.[42] □

Eliot's reputation had soared stratospherically high by the 1930s on the wings of *The Waste Land* and the critical eminence that he achieved through his literary essays and as editor of the *Criterion* (1922–39), the most distinguished international literary review of its time. His conservative social and religious views consolidated his position as a figure of the establishment. He would remain the most dominant voice in Anglophone literary criticism for the next three decades.

The Jazz Age and the Lost Generation: F. Scott Fitzgerald and Ernest Hemingway

F. Scott Fitzgerald (1896–1940) belonged to the new generation of Americans who were 'tired of Great Causes' in the years after the First World War.[43] In 'Echoes of the Jazz Age' (1931), Fitzgerald looked back with nostalgia on the ten heady years before the Wall Street crash of October 1929: 'It was an age of miracles, it was an age of art, it was an age of excess, and it was an age of satire'.[44] Young people were now 'cynical rather than revolutionary' and so made a 'general decision to be amused', embracing hedonism and consumerism.[45] The rich indulged in wild speculation and spent their money as if there was no tomorrow. The devil-may-care culture of the Jazz Age provided Fitzgerald with the prime subject for his fiction, which satirised 1920s America as a land of opportunity and dissolute opportunism.

Fitzgerald's highly acclaimed first novel, *This Side of Paradise* (1920), recounted the young life of an ambitious Princeton undergraduate with literary tendencies by shifting back and forth between narrative and dramatic dialogue, letters and verses. H.L. Mencken called it 'a truly amazing novel – original in structure, extremely sophisticated in manner, and adorned with a brilliancy that is [...] rare in American writing'.[46] Brisk sales brought Fitzgerald celebrity and helped him to make a good living writing stories for mass-circulation magazines such as the *Saturday Evening Post.*

The reception of Fitzgerald's debut novel contrasted sharply with the tepid first notices that *The Great Gatsby* (1925) received. Several reviewers made comments about its longevity, for instance suggesting that it was 'neither profound nor durable', or that there was nothing in it to make readers think '"here is a great novel" or even that "here is a fine book"'.[47] Critical reservations regarding the moral seriousness of the novel had much to do with Fitzgerald's subject: 'the loss of those illusions that give such colour to the world that you don't care whether things are true or false as long as they partake of the magical glory'.[48] While Fitzgerald aimed to capture the emerging zeitgeist, he also sought to move beyond the well-established conventions of modern American realism by inflecting *The Great Gatsby* with a modernist sense of form as spatial rather than strictly chronological. From the outset, Fitzgerald intended that the novel should be 'something *new* – something extraordinary and beautiful and simple + intricately patterned'.[49] Gatsby's story is told through the multiple impressions of an unreliable first-person narrator, Nick Carraway, forcing readers to discriminate between retellings, infer from omissions and interpret the significance of recurrent motifs and symbols. Whatever the misgivings of the press, leading modernists were enthusiastic from the outset. T.S. Eliot stated 'it has interested and excited me more than any new novel I have seen, either English or American, for a number of years', and suggested that it was 'the first step that American fiction has taken since Henry James', while Gertrude Stein praised Fitzgerald for 'creating the contemporary world much as Thackeray did'.[50] It was only after Fitzgerald's early death that general opinion was turned by obituary tributes and the publication of his last unfinished novel *The Last Tycoon* (1941), securing his reputation as one of America's greatest novelists.

Gertrude Stein's Paris salon attracted many American writers in the post-war years, including Fitzgerald and Ernest Hemingway. Stein dubbed them the 'Lost Generation', after overhearing a car mechanic use that phrase to describe the outlook of the youths who had come of age during the War. The set's fast-living and hard-drinking disillusionment was captured by Hemingway in his best-selling novel *The Sun Also Rises* (1926), which took Stein's epithet for its ironic epigraph.

Hemingway's experiences as a Red Cross ambulance driver on the Italian front in the First World War and then as a fearless war correspondent dispatching ground-breaking reports on the human cost of European conflicts informed the subject and manner of his literary writing:

> ■ A writer's job is to tell the truth. His standard of fidelity to the truth should be so high that his invention, out of his experience, should produce a truer account than anything factual can be. For [...] when a good writer is creating something, he has time and scope to make of it an absolute truth.[51] □

In his fiction, Hemingway strove to confront the truth of violence, danger and death and yet maintain aesthetic mastery. Like the skilled bullfighter facing down his opponent in the ring in *The Sun Also Rises*, Hemingway wanted to hold 'his purity of line through the maximum of exposure'.[52] In interview, Hemingway explained that he achieved the desired purity by writing 'on the principle of the iceberg. There is seven-eighths of it under water for every part that shows. Anything you know you can eliminate and it only strengthens your iceberg.'[53]

Hemingway's work attracted recognition from the outset. Edmund Wilson's review of *in our time* (1924), a short collection of highly compressed vignettes, acclaimed Hemingway as a prose stylist 'of the first distinction' and 'strikingly original':[54]

> ■ [I]ts cool objective manner really constitutes a harrowing record of barbarities: you have not only political executions, but criminal hangings, bull-fights, assassinations by the police, and all the cruelties and enormities of the war.[55] □

Sixteen of these vignettes were used as interchapters between the fourteen short stories Hemingway collected in the American edition of *In Our Time* (1925). The most far-seeing contemporary review was by Paul Rosenfeld, who placed these brusque stories about soldiering, policing and sporting contests alongside Cubist painting and *The Rite of Spring* and other recent works in the 'primitive modern idiom'.[56] He perceived that the work owed something to Sherwood Anderson's simple diction and Stein's use of reiteration. He also analysed Hemingway's controlled style – noting how 'Emphatic, short declarative sentences follow staunchly upon one another', 'spoken prose is characteristically iron, with a lyricism, aliveness and energy tremendously held in check', and 'conflicting principles are established without psychologizing' – to determine how the balance was struck between 'The sheer unfeeling barbarity of life, and the elemental humor and tenderness lying close upon it'.[57] Later critics followed Allen Tate (1899–1979) in describing Hemingway's style as 'hard-boiled'.[58]

The critical consensus is that Hemingway's prose slackened after *A Farewell to Arms* (1929), a study of a disillusioned American ambulance officer and his role as a deserter. For instance, of *Death in the Afternoon* (1932), a non-fictional work about bullfighting, Wilson complained about the 'purple patches which go on spreading for pages on end'.[59] In *Men without Art* (1934), Wyndham Lewis mounted a damaging attack on Hemingway's style, powers of characterisation, intellect and lack of political engagement, foregrounding what was derivative about his manner, complaining that Gertrude Stein had 'strangely hypnotized him with her repeating habits and her *faux-naif* prattle' and that the 'sort of First-person-singular that Hemingway invariably invokes is a dull-witted, bovine, monosyllabic simpleton'.[60] Hemingway's reputation recovered with the publication of *For Whom the Bell Tolls* (1940), a long, ambitious, politically and morally serious novel based on his experiences as a reporter during the Spanish Civil War (1936–39). 'This is a book about love and courage and innocence and strength and decency and glory', Dorothy Parker (1893–1967) enthused, 'It is a book about all those things [...] that are only heightened and deepened by the war [...]. It is written with an understanding that rips the heart with compassion'.[61]

The Harlem Renaissance: W.E.B. Du Bois, Jean Toomer, *The New Negro*, Carl Van Vechten and Zora Neale Hurston

F. Scott Fitzgerald's description of the roaring twenties in 'Echoes of the Jazz Age' overlooked the degree of civil unrest that decade witnessed. It also failed to account for the experiences of the ethnic groups who originated the music that supplied the soundtrack to the era. From an African-American perspective, it was an age of opportunity and mass economic migration, as large numbers of black Americans left the agrarian economies of the south for better prospects in the industrialised cities of the north. But it was also an age of heightened racial consciousness and political activism in the face of segregation, inequality and the resurgence of the Ku Klux Klan.

The 'New Negro' movement for black empowerment had been gathering momentum since the post-Reconstruction era (the period of social, political and legislative adjustments following the Civil War and the abolition of slavery), when the first generation of African and Caribbean Americans to be admitted to higher education and public life agitated for the full equality promised to them in the Thirteenth, Fourteenth and Fifteenth Amendments. The distinguished Harvard-educated intellectual and activist W.E.B. Du Bois (1868–1963) led the way with his impassioned and humane treatise *The Souls of Black Folk* (1903). He declared that 'The problem of the Twentieth Century is the problem of the colour-line', the global social and economic divide enforced by imperial conquest, empire, slavery and segregation, which was powerfully felt in America.[62]

Du Bois advocated 'the ideal of fostering and developing the traits and talents of the Negro, not in opposition to or contempt for other races, but rather in large conformity to the greater [democratic] ideals of the American Republic, in order that some day on American soil two world-races may give each to each those characteristics both so sadly lack'.[63] If this ideal was to be fulfilled, internalised discourses about race had to be overthrown:

■ After the Egyptian and Indian, the Greek and Roman, the Teuton and Mongolian, the Negro is a sort of seventh son, born with a veil, and gifted with second-sight in this American world, – a world which yields him no true self-consciousness, but only lets him see himself through the revelation of the other world. It is a peculiar sensation, this double-consciousness, this sense of always looking at one's self through the eyes of others, of measuring one's soul by the tape of a world that looks on in amused contempt and pity. One ever feels his two-ness, – an American, a Negro; two souls, two thoughts, two unreconciled strivings; two warring ideals in one dark body, whose dogged strength alone keeps it from being torn asunder.[64] □

As Du Bois knew, literature had a crucial role to play in the struggle to tear away the veil that is the dominant perspective imposed by the white supremacist gaze. He called on writers to interrogate the double identity of the split black psyche and aim for truly autonomous self-definition. His cultural mission found expression in the *Crisis: A Record of the Darker Races* (1910–22), the magazine of the National Association for the Advancement of Colored People, which provided an important forum for up-and-coming black literary talent, including Jessie Fauset (1882–1961), Jean Toomer and Langston Hughes.

The campaign for equality intensified in the years immediately after the First World War, when the black soldiers who had risked their lives to secure democratic rights in Europe returned home to a land where they were second-class citizens. It was in this cultural moment, in the migrant communities of the cities of the north, that black pride found its expression in an efflorescence of art articulating a self-determined American identity. The appearance of works such as *Harlem Shadows* (1922), by Claude McKay, and *The Book of American Negro Poetry* (1922), by James Weldon Johnson, affirmed a new spirit in African-American writing. They belong to the intensely creative period in black American history known as the Harlem Renaissance, after the area of New York that was its most crucially productive site.

The perceived need for black writers to please white readers, patrons and publishers is described by Langston Hughes in 'The Negro Artist and the Racial Mountain' (1926):

> ■ The Negro artist works against an undertow of sharp criticism and misunderstanding from his own group and unintentional bribes from the whites. "Oh, be respectable, write about nice people, show how good we are," say the Negroes. "Be stereotyped, don't go too far, don't shatter our illusions about you, don't amuse us too seriously. We will pay you," say the whites. Both would have told Jean Toomer not to write 'Cane'.[65] □

Cane (1923) was perhaps the first masterpiece of the Harlem Renaissance to be unmistakeably modernist in form. It manipulated the techniques of collage to assemble a composite sketch of black and mixed-race America from disparate fragments of impressionistic short fiction, poetry, folk-song and dramatic dialogue. Conceived as a 'swan-song' for the 'folk-spirit [...] walking in to die on the modern desert', the mosaical form of Cane enabled Toomer to project modern black experience and also assert the cultural necessity of retaining an authentic connection to the old Negro culture.[66] In Cane, Toomer fearlessly confronted social taboos. For his frank portrayal of 'Karintha, an innocent prostitute; Becky, a fallen white woman; Carma, a tender Amazon of unbridled desire; Fern, an unconscious wanton; Esther, a woman who looks age and bastardy in the face and flees in despair; Louise, with a white and black lover; Avey, unfeeling and unmoral; and Doris, the cheap chorus girl', Du Bois hailed Toomer as the writer 'who first dared to emancipate the colored world from the conventions of sex'.[67] Certain concessions were nonetheless necessary to get Toomer's vision of mixed-race America to a reading public. He accepted that race was a selling point, but flatly resented the way that the publishers Boni and Liveright ignored the complexity of his racial heritage in their crudely conceived publicity campaign for Cane. Toomer considered himself to be 'French, Dutch, Welsh, Negro, German, Jewish, and Indian'.[68] However, his book was advertised as a depiction of 'negro life whose rhythmic beat, like the primitive tom-tom of the African jungle, you can feel because it is written by a man who has felt it historically, poetically and with deepest understanding'.[69]

The diversity of Harlem Renaissance literatures is evident from The New Negro: An Interpretation (1925), a vibrant compendium of new fiction, poetry and drama showcasing black talent, accompanied by celebratory reflections on 'New Negro' history, society, politics, culture and heritage, folk literature and song, the contemporary Harlem scene and the exemplary Americanism of the democratic aims of the Negro movement, interspersed with drawings, African sculpture and decorative designs, with an extensive bibliography. Edited by the Harvard-educated philosopher Alain Locke (1886–1954), *The New Negro* included contributions from almost every significant black American literary writer, including: romantic poems by Countée Cullen (1903–46) reflecting on black identity and racial injustice; a feisty short story in a richly figurative African dialect by Zora Neale Hurston, an anthropologist and ethnographer who would later become a novelist; impressionistic fragments from *Cane*; urban vignettes by Rudolph Fisher (1897–1934); and free verse by Langston Hughes, who was among the first to adapt the syncopated rhythms and repetitive phrases of blues and jazz music in his writing.

The New Negro was the definitive articulation of black American modernism, promoting a programme of social change through artistic excellence. Its global political mission was twofold: to rehabilitate 'the race in world esteem from that loss of prestige for which the fate and conditions of slavery have so largely been responsible' and to act 'as the advance-guard of the African peoples in their contact with Twentieth Century [sic] civilization'.[70] As Locke explained, 'New Negros' were 'shaking off of the psychology of imitation and implied inferiority' enforced by the 'tyranny of social intimidation', re-evaluating their cultural heritage and showing a mastery of that rich tradition in their own progressive literary work, asserting self-determined racial identity and engaging with present-day social and aesthetic concerns:[71]

■ It has been their achievement also to bring the artistic advance of the Negro sharply into stepping alignment with contemporary artistic thought, mood and style. They are thoroughly modern, some of them ultra-modern [...].[72] □

While Locke perhaps overstated the modernity of certain contributors (Cullen for instance), his anthology established beyond question that a generation of 'New Negro' writers had broken through the colour-line and were writing with verve and panache, having begun 'to evolve from the racial substance something technically distinctive'.[73]

H.L. Mencken hailed *The New Negro* as a 'phenomenon of immense significance': 'For the first time', he commented approvingly, 'one hears clearly the imposing doctrine that, in more than one way, the Negro is superior to the white man'.[74] But for all Mencken contrasted the dignity, intellect and self-possession of the contributors with the 'sound and fury' of white Southern writers who are 'simply romantic wind-jammers', he nonetheless signalled the appalling prejudice that New Negro writers still had to overcome when he suggested that the majority 'of their race are but two or three inches removed from gorillas'.[75] Carl Van Vechten's attitude was entirely different. He used his influence as a white patron to promote African-American art to a wide audience in publications such as *Vanity Fair*, albeit at times presuming to speak for the race. In his review of *The New Negro*, Van Vechten made a point of mentioning as many names connected with the Harlem Renaissance as he could. He praised Locke for gathering so many voices into the one volume: 'He has put not merely the best foot of the new Negro forward; he has put *all* his feet forward'.[76] However, Van Vechten took issue with William Braithwaite (1878–1962), who argued that 'Negro novels must be written by Negroes', by insisting that 'Negroes among themselves [...] behave and react very much as white people, *of the same class*, behave and react'.[77] Van Vechten was defending his forthcoming novel *Nigger Heaven* (1926), which muddied the lines between black art and white authority. Du Bois considered Van Vechten's attempt to write a Negro novel 'a blow in the face' and advised readers to 'drop the book gently into the grate'.[78]

Whereas Locke insisted that 'New Negro' writing was original precisely because it had shaken off the psychology of imitation, Zora Neale Hurston made the opposite case in 'Characteristics of Negro Expression' (1934), insisting that 'Every phase of Negro life is highly dramatised' and their speech is so richly metaphorically vivid that their 'very words are action words', to the extent that 'the art of mimicry is better developed in the Negro man than in other racial groups'.[79] Imitation does not therefore stem from a feeling of inferiority, or a wish 'to be the like one imitated', but is done for the love of the act.[80] In Hurston's view, the originality of Negro expression consisted precisely in creative performance, in transforming derivative material self-consciously and critically:

■ While he lives and moves in the midst of a white civilisation, everything that he touches is re-interpreted for his own use.[81] □

'Mimicry', Hurston explained, 'is an art in itself'.[82] Any attempt by white performers merely to imitate Negro creative expression would necessarily pale by comparison.

Hurston herself was chastised by contemporaries for her cartoonish characters, her examinations of female sexuality, folk superstitions, drinking culture and other vices, and her failure to provide the 'racial uplift' that the Harlem Renaissance promoted. Locke admonished her for creating 'those pseudo-primitives whom the reading public still loves to laugh with, weep over, and envy' in *Their Eyes Were Watching God* (1937), which focuses on the black heroine Janie Crawford's turbulent life and loves as she struggles to find her authentic self.[83] The novel fell into obscurity and Hurston died in poverty. However, Hurston's feisty feminist heroine would inspire later generations of women writers, thanks to the novelist and civil rights campaigner Alice Walker, who is credited with rediscovering her work in the 1980s and bringing it to critical attention. Of *Their Eyes Were Watching God*, Walker wrote 'There is no book more important to me than this one'.[84]

Sexual Politics: Radclyffe Hall and Virginia Woolf

Writers positioned themselves at the forefront of debates concerning gender and sexual behaviour. Although sex was a legitimate topic for discussion in reference works, novelists who treated the subject frankly risked falling foul of obscenity legislation, as the publication histories of *The Rainbow* and *Ulysses* attest. Marguerite Radclyffe Hall (1880–1943) drew on sexological theory and her own personal experience in *The Well of Loneliness* (1928), a *bildungsroman* which became a cause célèbre in Britain and America. The heroine is a masculine girl called Stephen (named so because her father had hoped for a son), who at first feels anguished that her difference sets her apart from society, but grows to assert her right to love women and for sexual inversion to be tolerated and accepted as natural.

Hall hoped that the novel would 'encourage the inverted in general to declare themselves, to face up to a hostile world in their true colours, and this with dignity and courage [...], spurring all classes of inverts to prove that they are capable of being as good and useful citizens as the best of the so-called normal men and women' and bring 'normal men and women [...] to a fuller and more tolerant understanding of the inverted'.[85] She envisioned that the text would be of use to school teachers, welfare workers, parents, doctors and psychologists, and persuaded Havelock Ellis to provide a preface for the book.

Early reviews were mixed, commending the author for her brave choice of material, but dismissing her lumbering style. Leonard Woolf, for instance, praised Hall's 'understanding and frankness', but complained that the book 'fails completely as a work of art'.[86] Six weeks after the novel's publication, a vituperative review in the *Sunday Express* denouncing Hall's lesbian theme brought the novel to the attention of the censors. In 'A Book that Must be Supressed', James Douglas declared, 'I would rather give a healthy boy or a healthy girl a phial of prussic acid than this novel. Poison kills the body, but moral poison kills the soul'.[87] The book sold out.

Fearing prosecution in Britain, the publisher arranged for a second edition to be published in France. Leading authors rallied in support of the book when the Parisian edition was seized by British Customs and both publishers were charged with obscenity. As Rebecca West recorded, 'practically every writer of standing' signed a petition in favour of the publication of *The Well of Loneliness*.[88] E.M. Forster (1879–1970) and Virginia

Woolf protested in a joint letter to the editor of *Nation & Athenaeum*, taunting the Home Secretary with a request for guidance as to whether the subject matter of *The Well of Loneliness* 'recognized by science and recognizable in history' though 'forbidden as a main theme' in fiction may be mentioned incidentally or 'alluded to, or ascribed to subsidiary characters'.[89] 'What of the other subjects known to be more or less unpopular in Whitehall', they enquired, 'such as birth-control, suicide and pacifism? May we mention these? We await our instructions!'[90] Their serious point was that no topic should be off limits for art and that art cannot help but be political. After all, 'The free mind has access to all the knowledge and speculation of its age'.[91] They were, however, sufficiently wary to defend lesbianism as a theme for art in diffident terms, noting that 'It enters personally into very few lives, and is uninteresting or repellent to the majority'.[92]

Virginia Woolf and Forster attended the trial alongside other writers and medical professionals who were prepared to testify. The presiding magistrate was unmoved, deeming Hall's refusal to denounce lesbian love sufficient grounds to find the publishers guilty of obscene libel. Obscenity charges were successfully defeated in America following the publication of a New York edition in 1929.

Forster and Woolf had vested interests in the trial's outcome. The Bloomsbury group was unusually permissive and open regarding sexual matters. Fear of prosecution had prevented Forster from publishing *Maurice* (a semi-autobiographical novel about a young man and his male loves, started in 1913 and published posthumously in 1971), while Woolf's *Orlando: A Biography* (1928), a gala of androgyny and same-sex desire, had been published only weeks before. *Orlando* escaped the notice of the censor through its lightheartedness, literariness, indirection and whimsy. It satirised the solemnities of nineteenth-century life-writing by presenting a fictionalised biography of a man who becomes a woman and lives for over four centuries. Emboldened, Woolf made tentative claims for the inclusivity and confidence of the female author in her feminist manifesto and theory of literary history, *A Room of One's Own* (1929), in which a copy of Mary Carmichael's *Life's Adventure* (a fictitious novel) is inspected:

> ■ Do you promise me that behind that red curtain over there the figure of Sir Chartres Biron is not concealed? We are all women you assure me? Then I may tell you that the very next words I read were these – 'Chloe liked Olivia...' Do not start. Do not blush. Let us admit in the privacy of our own society that these things sometimes happen. Sometimes women do like women.[93] □

(Biron was the presiding magistrate in the trial against *The Well of Loneliness*). The new frankness that Woolf discerned was testament to writers' readiness to defy obscenity legislation and address the taboo subjects that were being theorised by contemporary scientists, sociologists and psychologists, with a view to making radical interventions in the public understanding of sex, sexuality and subjectivity.

In *A Room of One's Own*, Woolf presented women's writing as a transgressive practice that could disrupt the dominant linguistic conventions that underwrite patriarchal power structures. She noted that the female writer inherits a male-dominated tradition where the shape that sentences take 'has been made by men out of their own needs' to the extent that there is 'no common sentence ready for her use'.[94] She suggested that the future of fiction would rest on women's efforts to create linguistic and literary forms for their own purposes: 'whole flights of words would need to wing their way illegitimately into existence' to articulate 'the whole of that extremely complex force of femininity'.[95] In *Three Guineas* (1938), another extended critical essay, Woolf would argue that precisely because women (even in the educated class) have always been positioned as outsiders to the patriarchal state and its legislative, economic and religious institutions, they are in a position to develop a radical political and cultural identity that can challenge the rise of fascism and ultimately stay the advent of war.

Writers Take Sides: The Auden Group

Michael Roberts (1902–48) was the first to introduce the new generation of leftist, socially and politically engaged British writers – principally W.H. Auden (1907–73), Stephen Spender (1909–95) and C. Day-Lewis (1904–72) – as a fresh, coherent movement in his representative anthology *New Signatures* (1932). Roberts neglected the debt that the group owed to the technical prowess (and patronage) of their predecessors, particularly T.S. Eliot, and focused instead on the sharp contrast between these younger writers' desire to 'say something to an audience' and find 'solidarity with others' and the habits of their elders who, to his mind at least, had 'become aloof from ordinary affairs' and produced 'esoteric work which was frivolously decorative or elaborately erudite'.[96]

During the 1930s, failure of liberal capitalism, growing support for communism, the aggressive rise of fascism, the nationalist military uprising against Spain's democratically elected republican government that plunged the country into a bloody civil war and finally the spectre of another world war gave writers increasing cause to confront the relationship between aesthetics and politics and determine the role of art. The Spanish Civil War in particular became a cause célèbre amongst artists and intelligentsia. It marked the first major clash between left and right, the labouring and the land-owning classes, communism and fascism, and made artists aware of the threat that the tyranny of fascism posed to freedom of expression and cultural progress. The writer and campaigner Nancy Cunard (1896–1965) canvassed 148 leading British writers with the heavily weighted question:

■ Are you for, or against, the legal Government and the People of Republican Spain? Are you for, or against, Franco and Fascism? For it is impossible any longer to take no side.[97] □

She published responses in *Authors Take Sides on the Spanish Civil War* (1937), a pamphlet that showed overwhelming support for the Republic. The next year, Day-Lewis made the case that poetry should be evaluated in terms of its political effect, defining 'a good poem' as one that 'enters deep into the stronghold of our emotions', adding 'if it is written by a good revolutionary, it is bound to have a revolutionary effect on our emotions, and therefore to be essentially – though not formally – propaganda'.[98]

By the end of the 1930s, the Auden group were established as Britain's foremost literary coterie. As George Orwell (1903–50) would note in his essay 'Inside the Whale' (1940), 'For the middle and late thirties, Auden, Spender & Co. *are* "the movement", just as Joyce, Eliot, & Co. were for the twenties'.[99] The metaphor of the whale – the creature that swallowed and contained Jonah, enforcing introspection and 'an attitude of completest indifference' to the outside world – is invoked by Orwell to divide the first generation of modernists from the second.[100] Virginia Woolf unravelled a similarly suggestive analogy to identify the difference between the two generations at their height in 'The Leaning Tower' (1940). She suggested that the most representative names in literary writing in Britain in the years from 1910 to 1925 (D.H. Lawrence excepted) enjoyed all the privileges of their moneyed, educated class, secure in their high social station. They sat in their figurative towers and surveyed the masses at an angle below, continuing to write as if the tower were firm beneath them even after the First World War. The Auden generation were also born into the tower class, Woolf noted, but as they were shaken by change, revolution and the rise of communism and fascism, their towers leant more and more to the left. In Woolf's view, the fact that their towers are 'founded upon injustice and tyranny' haunts their writing, producing a literature 'full of discord and bitterness, full of confusion and of compromise', neither the 'rich speech of the aristocrat' nor 'the racy speech of the peasant', but marked by the desire to 'no longer [...] be isolated and exalted in solitary state upon their tower, but to be down on the ground with the mass of human kind'.[101]

For a time, anti-fascist feeling inclined leftist writers towards the communist party, which was apparently fighting on the side of democracy. As Orwell noted, 'it was generally imagined that socialism could preserve and even enlarge the atmosphere of liberalism'.[102] As the Spanish Civil War progressed, it became clear that communist propaganda was hollow. Writers became increasingly uneasy and disillusioned, and the 'Boy Scout atmosphere of bare knees and community singing' that Orwell sensed in the Auden group no longer cut it.[103] Writing after the collapse of the Republican resistance and the outbreak of the Second World War, Orwell expressed widely held fears that 'Almost certainly we are moving into an age of totalitarian dictatorships' in which the 'autonomous individual is going to be stamped out of existence'.[104] At a loss, Orwell recommended that writers:

■ Get inside the whale – or rather, admit you are inside the whale (for you *are* of course). Give yourself over to the world-process, stop fighting against it or pretending that you control it; simply accept it, endure it, record it. [...] A novel on more positive, "constructive" lines, and not emotionally spurious, is at present very difficult to imagine.[105] □

By contrast, Woolf's hopes for literature were premised on the notion of community, where everyone, regardless of class or educational standing, has an equal stake in deciding which books are enduringly valuable:

■ Literature is no one's private ground; literature is common ground. It is not cut up into nations; there are no wars there. Let us trespass freely and fearlessly and find our own way for ourselves. It is thus that English literature will survive this war and cross the gulf – if commoners and outsiders like ourselves make that country our own country, if we teach ourselves how to read and write, how to preserve and create.[106] □

Woolf believed that the cultural work performed by literature was vitally important to the survival of the human race. Not only the modern movement, but the very future of humanity itself hung in the balance.

The Revolution of the Word

The radical journal *transition* was founded in Paris in 1927 by Eugène and Maria Jolas (1894–1952 and 1893–1987), together with Elliot Paul (1891–1958). It became a leading international forum for experimental writing, featuring contributions from an illustrious roster of American and European modernists, including Samuel Beckett (1906–89), André Breton, H.D., Ernest Hemingway, James Joyce, Gertrude Stein and

William Carlos Williams. Early issues also devoted extensive space to English translations of European works, while later issues published submissions in their native tongue. This multilingual melting pot would be the scene for 'The Revolution of the Word'.

So far as Eugène Jolas was concerned, the rise of totalitarian ideologies and the homogeneity of capitalist America threatened the production of new art. He sought refuge in linguistic revolution, calling for the creation of a future 'super-tongue for intercontinental expression' that would be unconstrained by any single nation's laws and provide an antidote to deadening conformity and the political situation in Europe.[107] A 'Proclamation' was launched in a special double issue of *transition* in 1929:

> ■ The Revolution in the English language is an accomplished fact [...].
> Pure poetry [...] seeks an a priori reality within ourselves alone.
> Narrative is [...] the projection of a metamorphosis of reality [...].
> The literary creator has the right to disintegrate the primal matter of words imposed on him by textbooks and dictionaries.
> He has the right to use words of his own fashioning and to disregard existing grammatical and syntactical laws [...].
> The plain reader be damned.[108] □

These Surrealist pronouncements were a manifesto for the pioneering writing by the *transition* contributors who were tapping into the fluid logic of the unconscious to dismantle traditional languages and renovate the word.

The supreme embodiment of the revolution of the word would be *Finnegans Wake* (1939), which was serialised in *transition* from 1927 to 1938 under the title *Work in Progress*. It was a philological fantasia, written in a virtuoso deformation of Anglo-Irish, assembled by collapsing words from many tongues into polyphonic portmanteaus. In defence of what seemed like wilful esotericism, James Joyce offered the following explanation to his perturbed patron: 'One great part of every human existence is passed in a state which cannot be rendered sensible by the use of wideawake language, cutanddry grammar and goahead plot'.[109] *Finnegans Wake* was to be a book of the night, the unconscious and dreams.

The issue of *transition* in which Jolas announced 'The Revolution of the Word' also contained a seminal essay by Beckett, 'Dante... Bruno. Vico.. Joyce' (1929). This essay would be one of the twelve included in *Our Exagmination Round His Factification for Incamination of 'Work in Progress'* (1929), a promotional book designed to defend and explain Joyce's experiment:

> ■ Here form *is* content, content *is* form. You complain that this stuff is not written in English. It is not written at all. It is not to be read – or

rather it is not only to be read. It is to be looked at and listened to. His writing is not *about* something; *it is that something itself*. [...] When the sense is sleep, the words go to sleep. [...] When the sense is dancing, the words dance. The language is drunk. The very words are tilted and effervescent. [...] How can we qualify this general esthetic vigilance without which we cannot hope to snare the sense which is for ever rising to the surface of the form and becoming form itself? [...] Mr Joyce has desophisticated language.[110] □

Joyce's radical conflation of form and content would exert a profound influence on Beckett's own experiments with language. The difference, as Beckett himself perceived, is that Joyce tends 'towards omniscience and omnipotence as an artist', 'making words do the absolute maximum of work' and claiming he can explain every syllable, whereas Beckett works 'with impotence, ignorance', taking failure and the futility of expression as his theme.[111]

Our Exagmination remains one of the most revealing studies of *Work in Progress*, conveying privileged insights into how Joyce conceived the final text would appear. For instance, Elliot Paul's contribution, 'Mr. Joyce's Treatment of Plot' remarked on the circular nature of the work, alighted on recurrent motifs, such as the fall of man, and explained that 'the characters are composed of hundreds of legendary historical figures, as the incidents are derived from countless events'.[112] Joyce's circular understanding of history was inspired by the eighteenth-century Italian philosopher Giambattista Vico, who postulated a fundamental cycle of three ages (the mythic or divine, the heroic, and the human), followed by a *ricorso* (a return to a comparatively primitive condition, albeit more advanced than before), which describes the pattern of rise, development, peak, then decline and fall common to all civilisations. Accordingly, *Finnegans Wake* is divided into four parts, the last of which, a *ricorso*, takes readers back to the book's very beginning. Time is collapsed, identities merge and scenes melt, so that all ages are continuously present as part of the collective unconscious.

Despite the efforts that Joyce and his circle made to prepare the ground for *Finnegans Wake*, the completed work met with bewilderment. Oliver St. John Gogarty (1878–1957), the real-life model for Buck Mulligan, Stephen's adversary in *Ulysses*, suggested that it was 'The most colossal leg-pull in literature since McPherson's Ossian', while Richard Aldington confessed that he was 'unable to explain either the subject or the meaning (if any) of Mr. Joyce's book' and that he had 'no intention of wasting one more minute of precious life over Mr. Joyce's futile inventions, tedious ingenuities, and verbal freaks'.[113] The most critically astute appraisal came from Harry Levin, a literary critic who offered an appealing, coherent commentary on *Finnegans Wake:*

> ■ [I]t envisages the whole course of history, according to Vico's conception. Allegorically, it celebrates the topography and atmosphere of the city of Dublin and its environs. Literally, it records the adventures – or rather the nightmares – of Earwicker, as he and his wife and three children lie sleeping above his pub, and alcoholic slumber rehearses the events of the day before. Morally, it combines all these strands of symbolism into a single theme [...] the problem of evil and original sin.[114] □

Joyce singled out Levin's review for particular praise. But to Joyce's despair, the outbreak of war greatly inhibited the critical reception of his masterwork and stayed the modernist revolution in art.

Conclusion

Modernists working in the 1920s and 1930s remained compelled to justify their innovations to communities of writers and readers, and to debate the function of literature and its role in society at length. Their critics continued to answer them in kind. What comes across most strongly from the survey of critical statements of or on modernist literatures is how remarkably well-informed the modernists were about one another's practices, how voraciously and astutely they read pronouncements and works by their peers, and how receptive they were to developments overseas. Tracing the proliferating connections between fellow modernists and avant-gardists that emerge in reviews and correspondence reveals the value that they placed on being part of a wider global community that was actively debating how to reimagine the modern world through art, literature and criticism.

PART II

Literary Criticism from 1930–Present

CHAPTER FOUR

The Making of Modernist Canons

Literary Reputations

The mechanisms that consolidated literary reputations were various and complex. Many of the writers who were once deemed to be producing lastingly valuable work are now virtually unstudied. For instance, the poets Carl Sandburg (1878–1967), Vachel Lindsay (1879–1931) and Edgar Lee Masters (1868–1950) were published in little magazines alongside Ezra Pound and T.S. Eliot and were once considered heavyweights. At least a third of the poets whom W.B. Yeats selected for inclusion in the *Oxford Book of Modern Verse: 1892–1935* (1936) are now all but forgotten. By contrast, many of the writers whom we think of today as major modernist innovators had already achieved celebrity status by the 1920s and 1930s thanks to frequent mentions in newspaper columns and popular magazines. It is a measure of how successfully modernism had become part of mainstream culture that so many figures associated with the movement graced the front cover of *Time* magazine, notably: Joseph Conrad (1923), Amy Lowell (1925), Gertrude Stein (1933), James Joyce (1934, 1939), Ernest Hemingway (1937), Virginia Woolf (1937), William Faulkner (1939) and T.S. Eliot (1950).

New Criticism

No literature needed systematic analytical procedures more than high modernism. Experimental works wrong-footed established critical approaches, necessitating the development of interpretative practices that could unlock their secrets, make sense of their methods and impart pleasure to readers. The critical method that did most to sculpt English-language modernism in its institutionalised form up to the 1960s was New Criticism, which was in turn contoured by the values of the modernist writers it held to be exemplary. It was developed by a group of

American poet-critics who taught at southern universities during the years following the First World War. John Crowe Ransom (1888–1974), Allen Tate and Robert Penn Warren (1905–89) met through the small clique of poets known as the Fugitive group and founded a little magazine, the *Fugitive* (1922–25), which provided a forum for debates about modernist poetry. The germinal event for Fugitive poetics was the dispute between Ransom, who argued that *The Waste Land* failed because it lacked unity, and Tate, who defended the unity of the poem by claiming Ransom had failed to discover its form.[1] Evaluating modernist poetry by judging the success of its formal properties would become a cornerstone of New Criticism.

The group remained interested in modernist poetry after the *Fugitive* folded and began to articulate the literary theory that would be known as New Criticism. They also developed an anti-modern, anti-capitalist agenda called Southern Agrarianism, which presented the less industrialised south as the last repository of America's cultural life. Their reactionary standpoint was articulated in *I'll Take my Stand: The South and the Agrarian Tradition* (1930), a provocative collection of twelve essays. Some of the contributions even went so far as to express a preference for the old south before the Civil War. While the Agrarian ideology was quietly dropped in the mid-1930s, the elitism and racial bias continued to inform their literary tastes.

New Criticism was formatively influenced by T.S. Eliot's early literary essays: crucially, his notions of poetic impersonality, the timelessness of great works and the consequent privileging of form over context. In this respect, New Criticism can be usefully considered as a branch of modernist writing. As Louis Menard and Lawrence Rainey explain in *The Cambridge History of Literary Criticism: Modernism and New Criticism* (2000), 'Eliot's criticism was ostensibly formalist, insisting on the recognition of literature on its own terms; it was anti-impressionist and almost scientific-sounding'.[2] It 'seemed a deliberate departure from the sort of appreciatory criticism the turn-of-the-century men and women of letters produced and thus an ideal model for academic criticism', which at that time needed to justify why literary studies should be seen as a rigorous discipline to institutions built on the research models of the natural sciences.[3]

New Criticism overcame the widely held notion that literary studies could only be concerned with subjective impressions (a tenet of aesthetic criticism) by treating literature as a special field in which language functions autonomously, allowing its linguistic structures to be analysed objectively. In this respect, New Criticism had affinities with Russian Formalism, an early twentieth-century movement that sought to make literary study scientific by focusing on the formal devices that distinguish literary language. The most famous trope was 'defamiliarization', the strategy of rendering the familiar unfamiliar and, in the words of Viktor Shklovsky (1893–1984), removing them from 'the automatism of perception'.[4]

The New Critics' methodology derived stimulus from the Cambridge school of 'practical criticism' influentially developed by I.A. Richards (1893–1979). He advocated that close attention should be paid to the text itself on its own terms. In *Principles of Literary Criticism* (1924), Richards approached poems as autonomous, unified structures and explored how their minute particulars interrelate:

■ A single word by itself, let us say 'night', will raise almost as many different thoughts and feelings as there are persons who hear it. [...] But put it into a sentence and the variation is narrowed; put it into the context of a whole passage, and it is still further fixed; and let it occur in such an intricate whole as a poem and the responses of competent readers may have a similarity which only its occurrence in such a whole can secure.[5] □

He encouraged his students to offer readings of anonymised, undated poems and documented and analysed the results of this experiment in *Practical Criticism: A Study of Literary Judgment* (1929), where he explained that 'We pay attention to externals when we do not know what else to do with a poem'.[6]

New Critics rejected what Tate and Ransom's most eminent student Cleanth Brooks (1906–94) famously called 'the heresy of paraphrase' (the idea that the content of a work can be adequately summarised and is somehow separable from form). Instead, they treated literary form as a principle of unity, a 'Well Wrought Urn', which holds all the diverse parts of a work together in harmony, resolving any potentially contradictory elements by appealing to ambiguity, irony and paradox.[7] They advocated close textual analysis at the expense of statements of authorial intent or biographical or historical context. W.K. Wimsatt (1907–75) and Monroe Beardsley (1915–85) coined the phrase 'The Intentional Fallacy' in their celebrated essay of the same name (1946) to describe the false logic of basing critical judgments about the meaning of a literary work on 'external evidence'.[8] They insisted that 'the design or intention of the author is neither available nor desirable as a standard for judging the success of a work of literary art' because such a work is 'detached from the author at birth and goes about the world beyond his power to intend about it or control it'.[9]

New Criticism came to dominate the teaching of literature, particularly in American universities. The approach was promoted in literary quarterlies such as the *Southern Review* (edited by Warren and Brooks, 1935–42), the *Kenyon Review* (edited by Ransom, 1939–69) and the

Sewanee Review (edited by Tate, 1944–46), and undergraduate primers such as Brooks and Warren's *Understanding Poetry* (1938), an anthology with instructive commentary. Brooks was appointed to Yale University in 1947 and Warren joined him there in 1950. As key figures rose to more prominent positions in the academy, New Criticism increased in institutional power and prestige, shaping the analytical practices and literary tastes of a generation.

New Criticism established the primacy of the formally complex branch of modernism from which its critical values were descended, holding difficult, technically innovative literary works that resist amateur readings to be the ones most worthy of exegesis. *Modern Poetry and the Tradition* (1939) by Brooks provides a case in point. It gives special attention to poets who were 'regarded as excessively difficult', principally T.S. Eliot and W.B. Yeats.[10] Not only is Eliot first among the modern critics whose influence Brooks credits: the tradition that Brooks delineates places modern poets as successors to the classical tradition of seventeenth-century wit that Eliot espoused, and the greatest space is given to an elucidation of *The Waste Land*. In addition to difficult writers, the background in Southern Agrarianism drew the New Critics to the formally complex novels of William Faulkner, whose work they interpreted in the light of their own political ends.[11] The canon that the New Critics instituted was white, male and, seemingly, heterosexual.

The inherently class-conscious nature of British society produced 'a discipline far more explicitly concerned with social [...] issues than its American counterpart', as Franklin Court notes in *Institutionalizing English Literature* (1992).[12] The Cambridge academic F.R. Leavis (1895–1978) was an influential figure in this respect. His method was grounded in the close-reading techniques associated with practical criticism, but he opposed the idea that context was irrelevant. Instead he considered reading to be an ethical activity, whereby the critic uses his trained sensibility to scrutinise texts and engage with their literary qualities as a means to assess their moral seriousness. These criteria for appreciation provided the rationale for the literary canon that Leavis formulated and promoted through studies such as: *New Bearings in English Poetry* (1932), in praise of the achievements of Gerard Manley Hopkins (1844–89), Yeats and Eliot; *The Great Tradition: George Eliot, Henry James and Joseph Conrad* (1948); and *D.H. Lawrence: Novelist* (1955), as well as his quarterly review *Scrutiny* (1932–53).

Eliot himself came to have serious misgivings about New Criticism and repudiated the school in his 1956 lecture 'The Frontiers of Criticism':

■ The method is to take a well-known poem [....] without reference to the author or to his other work, analyse it stanza by stanza and line by line, and extract, squeeze, tease, press every drop of meaning out of it that one can. It might be called the lemon-squeezer school of criticism. [...] I imagine that some of the poets (they are all dead except myself) would be surprised at learning what their poems mean [...].[13] □

While lemon-squeezing scholarship that pays close attention to linguistic detail can be very satisfying and pedagogically useful, the New Critics' reluctance to admit contextual information could lead to undiscriminating interpretation. Furthermore, the belief that form is harmoniously unifying had the effect of minimising what is chaotic, unruly, reactive or genuinely radical. The New Critics tamed modernism's rebellious energies, narrowed its scope to formalism and fashioned the movement in their own conservative image.

By the 1960s, new theoretical approaches such as structuralism, poststructuralism and deconstruction offered richer models for analysing literature than New Criticism. However, the legacy of New Criticism endures in the emphasis literary studies as a discipline places on close reading and in the canon it helped to institute. The early dominance of New Criticism also goes a long way towards explaining the tendency to exclude drama from modernist historiography. As Elin Diamond points out, the belief that meaning is intrinsic to text simply cannot account for the contingencies of performance and its 'irreducible material historicity'.[14] The consequence, as Toril Moi notes, is that 'Most books on modernism do not mention theatre at all'.[15] As the materials discussed in Part I of the Guide clearly demonstrate, many of the writers who are best known for their literary achievements also took an active interest in theatre and performance. Revolutions on the modernist stage shaped developments in other genres to such an extent that accounts of literary modernism are greatly impoverished if drama is ignored.

Hugh Kenner

Hugh Kenner has been described as 'the most influential interpreter of Anglo-American literary modernism in the decades after WWII'.[16] He was Cleanth Brooks's graduate student at Yale, but his approach was very much at odds with New Criticism. While Kenner paid very close attention to language and style, he also took account of historical context, biographical details and authorial intention. His conviction that the author mattered was reinforced when he visited Ezra Pound, who advised him 'to visit the great men of your time'.[17] At Pound's behest, Kenner made pilgrimages to see William Carlos Williams, Wyndham Lewis and T.S. Eliot in 1956 to learn from them directly.

Kenner was instrumental in bringing Pound to the attention of the academy. In the 1940s, Pound, then disgraced, was largely ignored by New Critics because his work could not readily be described using their critical vocabulary of wit, irony and paradox, and instead required 'old fashioned, source-hunting scholarship'.[18] Kenner's first book, *The Poetry of Ezra Pound* (1951), made the case that 'There is no great contemporary writer who is less read than Ezra Pound'.[19] It supported that claim to greatness by establishing the 'incomparable assurance' of Pound's melodious verse, his significance as an inventor, an interlingual literary historian and the man 'who picked nearly every winner in his generation', and by offering the first comprehensive account of the *Cantos*.[20] The book was very timely. It followed the controversial award of the 1949 Bollingen prize to Pound for *The Pisan Cantos* (written while Pound was detained in Italy) and it was published at the threshold of a period of academic expansion that saw 'people peering under every cabbage-leaf for "topics"', as Kenner put it.[21] 'Pound before long was a stock on the academic exchange', Kenner recalled, acknowledging the institutional processes that underwrite economies of cultural capital.[22] The publication of Pound's *Literary Essays* (1954), at Eliot's instigation, further helped to rehabilitate Pound's reputation and canonise his ideas about poetry and literary tradition.

Kenner's conversations with Pound at St Elizabeth's formed the basis of *The Pound Era* (1971), a magisterial critical biography of Pound, thirteen years in the making. New Criticism may have established Eliot as its literary star, but Kenner made the case that it was Pound who defined the era, as a poet, theorist, influence and impresario who placed himself at the heart of the modernist vortex and directed its 'patterned energies'.[23] Kenner's argument rested on Pound's gift for renewing the past and bringing it within 'touching distance':[24]

■ Nothing we know the mind to have known has ever left us. Quickened by hints, the mind can know it again, and make it new. Romantic Time no longer thickens our sight, time receding, bearing visions away. Our books of cave paintings are the emblems of its abolition, perhaps the Pound Era's chief theme, and the literary consolidation of that theme stands as the era's achievement.[25] □

While the majority of scholarly writing about modernism is itself highly conventional, *The Pound Era* is strikingly poetic. Kenner took the unusual approach of accumulating luminous details by way of homage to Pound's techniques and conception of history. It begins with an evocative account of Pound's encounter with James in 1914:

■ Toward the evening of a gone world, the light of its last summer pouring forth into a Chelsea street found and suffused the red waistcoat of

Henry James, lord of decorum, *en promenade*, exposing his Boston niece to the tone of things.[26] □

'That is how the past exists', Kenner explained, setting out the case for literary criticism as creative reconstruction: 'The imagination augments, metabolizes, feeding on all it has to feed on, such scraps'.[27] The enduring appeal of *The Pound Era* is as much testament to Kenner's poetic style as his immensely learned, philologically and stylistically attentive, historical and biographical analysis.

Kenner's work on James Joyce also broke new ground. While New Critics had little to say about Joyce's self-consciously autobiographical, pedantically historical fiction, Kenner paid meticulous attention to subtle fluctuations in style, intonation and voice, as well as strategies of restatement and omission. In *Dublin's Joyce* (1956), Kenner proposed that Joyce responded to the particular Dublin habit of using received expressions 'a little ironically' by making 'his prose increasingly patterned and artificial' to the extent that irony and parody become central compositional techniques.[28] 'The language of Dublin *is* the subject', Kenner explained; Joyce's 'books are about words'.[29] Alert to irony, *Dublin's Joyce* was the first study to articulate the now commonplace view that Stephen Dedalus is not straightforwardly heroic. Each chapter of *A Portrait of the Artist as a Young Man* 'closes with a synthesis of triumph which the next destroys', Kenner noted, with the effect that readers' likely 'impulse on being confronted with the final edition of Stephen Dedalus is to laugh'.[30] Over the next four decades, Kenner elaborated and refined the ideas in *Dublin's Joyce*, most famously in *Joyce's Voices* (1978), where he articulated the 'Uncle Charles Principle' (named after the slightly pompous character whose actions are described in the third person, using idioms he might himself have used) that *'the narrative idiom need not be the narrator's'* (Kenner's emphases).[31]

Kenner was prolific and influential. Books such as *Wyndham Lewis* (1954), *Dublin's Joyce, The Invisible Poet: T.S. Eliot* (1959), *Samuel Beckett* (1961), *Joyce's Voices, The Pound Era, Ulysses* (1980) and *A Homemade World* (1975, on William Faulkner, Wallace Stevens, William Carlos Williams, Marianne Moore, Ernest Hemingway and F. Scott Fitzgerald), helped to invent modernism in its institutional form. According to Kenner, 'International Modernism was the work of Irishmen and Americans'.[32] But Kenner's canon was 'not everyone's modernism', as Marjorie Perloff has noted.[33] 'Highly selective in his enthusiasms, Kenner slighted women poets (especially Gertrude Stein) and minority writers'.[34] He also dismissed English modernism as parochial, characterising the Bloomsbury group as insular and class-conscious in *A Sinking Isle* (1987). Although his version of modernism is exclusionary and his approach is often esoteric, readers unfailingly find Kenner's criticism stimulating.

Structuralism, Poststructuralism and Deconstruction

Of course, Hugh Kenner was not the only critic to shape the canon in the decades from 1950–80. In so far as Joyce is concerned, it was Richard Ellmann's masterly critical biography *James Joyce* (1959) that secured Joyce's eminence in the American academy. It reinvented Joyce as an author whose artistic life and works amounted to a unified whole, acclaiming him a great genius and humanist. Ellmann's book marked the beginning of the 'Joyce Industry'. The 1960s saw the coming of a host of North American scholars who would take up the challenge of decoding Joyce's works and solving the 'many enigmas and puzzles' that Joyce had devised to 'keep the professors busy' and ensure his 'immortality'.[35] The decade also saw the inception of two dedicated Joyce studies journals and the initiation of the James Joyce Foundation (1967), as well as the first of a series of international symposia. Joyce had metamorphosed from a subversive revolutionary to a pillar of the establishment.

Joyce is chosen as a case study in this section because his works provided fertile soil for the new paradigm-shifting critical methodologies that took root in France between the late 1960s and the early 1980s and reinvented modernism. They originated in structuralism, which drew on the work of the Swiss linguist Ferdinand de Saussure (1857–1913), whose lectures, reconstructed from students' notes, were published after his death as *Course in General Linguistics* (1916). Saussure proposed that words are arbitrary signs that have no necessary relation to the things they signify. He suggested that their 'precise characteristic is to be what the others are not' and so proposed language to be a system of differences with no positive terms.[36] Far from being a transparent medium that represents the world, Saussure perceived that language organises how we understand the world by determining how meaning is produced. Structuralists applied Saussure's linguistic theories to identify the underlying structures that operate in society, literature and the psyche.

Poststructuralism was a reactive but continuous development. Structuralist theorists quickly realised that any attempt to codify linguistic structures invariably got caught up in the very phenomena it set out to describe, making it impossible to obtain objective knowledge or to produce totalising explanations. Language structures reality, yet no single discourse can claim to be dominant. Subjects too have no core identity that exists outside of language and so their sense of self is produced and modified by language and social relations. Jacques Lacan (1901–81), a psychoanalyst (and erstwhile Surrealist), perceived that the subject is in fact an effect produced by language, and so he recast psychoanalysis as a branch of structuralist and then poststructuralist thought.

Poststructuralism's influence on literary criticism was profound. Poststructuralists approach a literary text in the knowledge that because 'the text reads the theory at the same time as it is read by it [...,] the text constantly overreaches [...] the best critical constructions'.[37] In *Post-Structuralist Joyce* (1984), Derek Attridge and Daniel Ferrer explain that this effect is exaggerated in Joyce's writing:

■ It is impossible to exert any mastery over it, its *shifts* are such that you can never pin it down in any definite place – it always turns up again, laughing, behind your back. In fact, the aim is not to produce a *reading* of this intractable text, to make it more familiar and exorcise its strangeness, but on the contrary to confront its unreadability; not to produce an indefinite accumulation of its meanings (or search for one authentic meaning), but to look at the mechanisms of its infinite productivity [...]; not to reconstruct the world presented by the text, but to follow up within it the strategies that attempt a deconstruction of representation.[38] □

Take Samuel Beckett's famous assessment of *Work in Progress* as a text not written and not to be read, or indeed Kenner's observation 'Joyce's books are about words', and you see how well poststructuralism accords with ideas that are already latent in Joyce's works. It is for this reason that Joyce became 'a stimulus, a focus and a proving-ground' for poststructuralist thinkers such as Hélène Cixous, Julia Kristeva and Jacques Derrida.[39]

Derrida saluted Joyce as 'a great landmark in the history of deconstruction', the branch of poststructuralist theory he initiated in *Of Grammatology* (1967).[40] Deconstruction unpicks oppositions or givens that appear to be natural by revealing that they are in fact constructions produced by the very discourses on which those avowals depend. It mounts a critique of hierarchical binaries, dismantling pairings like signifier/signified, presence/absence, nature/culture, knowledge/belief, male/female, questioning the sovereignty of concepts on the left by showing how they are constructed by their partners on the right. As a consequence, deconstructionists are not interested in topics that deal with concrete specifics such as literary realism or character criticism (which are premised on stable external and internal realities), but instead seek to tease out competing textual significations and reveal ambiguities, paradoxes and contradictions.

Derrida offers a masterclass in this critical approach in '*Ulysses* Gramophone: Hear Say Yes in Joyce' (1984), an intricate, playful performance that responds to *Ulysses* as 'an overpotentialized text that will remind you, at a given moment, that you are captive in a network of language, writing, knowledge, and *even narration*'.[41] The central theme is the role of chance and contingency in networks of communication. As Derek

Attridge explains in his accessible introduction to this difficult essay, Derrida characterises Joyce's oeuvre as 'a derisive mockery of the efforts of those who analyse and systematize, who try to say something *new*' and yet suggests 'it is precisely the overdetermined complexity of this textual program that makes *possible* the new' and sustains the Joyce Industry.[42]

New waves in continental theory took some time to reach British and American shores. Even in the late 1970s, French theory had yet to be accepted as part of the critical mainstream. In *James Joyce and the Revolution of the Word* (1979), Colin MacCabe upbraided Anglo-American commentators for their 'persistent refusal [...] to engage with the radical novelty of Joyce's works', and their transformation of his texts 'into complicated crossword puzzles whose solution is the banal liberal humanism of the critic'.[43] His argument that Joyce was concerned 'not with representing experience through language but with experiencing language through a destruction of representation', met with tremendous resistance in a liberal humanist and residually Leavisite Cambridge, where he was then based.[44] When poststructuralism finally became a widely accepted strategy in Anglo-American circles it restored to modernist literatures the avant-gardism, instability and disunity that New Criticism had diminished.

Pound/Stevens: Whose Era?

The question of whose achievement defined the age was far from settled. Indeed the jury was still out as to whether modernism was a distinctive new phase in cultural life or in fact a continuation of romanticism. In his classic study *Romantic Image* (1957), Frank Kermode (1919–2010) persuasively argued that Imagist poetics were directly descended from the romantic tradition via French Symbolism:

■ The main psychological assumption of Symbolism [...] is essentially that of early Romantic aesthetic: that the human mind is so constituted as to be able to recognize images of which it can have no perceived knowledge – the magic assumption, or the assumption that makes so much of dreams. That the whole work of art should be regarded as such an image would not have surprised Coleridge, nor, for that matter, Blake, though he might have put it very differently. [...] Hulme hands over to the English tradition a modernised, but essentially traditional, aesthetic of Symbolism. [...] In short, the Hulmian image – precise, orderly, anti-discursive, the product of intuition – is the Symbol of the French poets given a new philosophical suit.[45] □

Harold Bloom made the most extreme case for romantic modernism. The foundations were laid in his great revisionist study *Yeats* (1970), where he claimed that the best twentieth-century poets – among them W.B. Yeats, Thomas Hardy (1840–1928) and Wallace Stevens – belonged to the visionary company of the English romantic poets William Blake and Percy Bysshe Shelley. For polemical effect, Bloom made the outlandish suggestion that 'Eliot and Pound may prove to be the Cowley and Cleveland of this age' and 'vanish' out of sight.[46] Bloom restated his position more strongly still in *A Map of Misreading* (1975), kicking against the canon instituted by the New Critics and Hugh Kenner:

■ Modernism in literature has not passed; rather, it has been exposed as never having been there. Gossip grows old and becomes myth; myth grows older and becomes dogma. Wyndham Lewis, Eliot and Pound gossiped with one another; the New Criticism aged them into a myth of Modernism; now the antiquarian Hugh Kenner has dogmatized this myth into the Pound Era, a canon of accepted titans.[47] □

During the 1970s and 1980s, Bloom, Paul de Man, Geoffrey Hartman and J. Hillis Miller (all colleagues at Yale) attempted to adjust the modernist canon and instate Stevens as the supreme poet of the age. Characterising Stevens as the true inheritor of the great American romantic poet Ralph Waldo Emerson (1803–82) in *Wallace Stevens: The Poems of our Climate* (1977), Bloom ventured to suggest that we might begin to refer to 'the Age of Stevens (or shall we say the Stevens Era?)'.[48]

Marjorie Perloff prepared an instructive overview of the quarrel between the Poundians and the Yale Critics in 'Pound/Stevens: Whose Era?' (1984), proposing that 'the very real gap between Pound and Stevens' is 'a gap that perhaps no inclusive definition of Modernism can quite close'.[49] The binary is of course reductive, but the essay highlights the fickle nature of critical fashions. Perloff pointed out that 'no one today [...] seems eager to call the first half of the twentieth century the Eliot Era'.[50] The dawning awareness that modernism is irreducible to any one talent anticipated its multiplication into modernist literatures.

Feminist Theory and Women's Writing

Modernism came into being alongside the 'first wave' of feminism in the guise of figures such as New Women and suffragettes. Its literatures hold especial fascination for feminist critics not only for their historical interest or representations of women's experience, but also for considering the status of women's literary activities in a professionalised literary marketplace.

The modern movement attracted brilliant female commentators and feminist activists from its very beginnings, as the materials in Part I of this Guide attest. However, women's literary achievements have often been side-lined, denigrated or even suppressed by male commentators. 'Not wildly anti-feminist, we are yet to be convinced that any woman ever invented anything in the arts', declared Pound in the pages of the *New Age* with all the bullish confidence invested in his sex.[51]

By the 1970s, between misogynist commentators, the New Critics, the Yale critics and singular scholars like Kenner, modernism in its institutional form had largely been configured by male critics to the glory of male authors. As Bonnie Kime Scott recalls in *The Gender of Modernism* (1990):

■ Modernism as we were taught it at mid-century was perhaps halfway to truth. It was unconsciously gendered masculine. The inscriptions of mothers and women, and more broadly of sexuality and gender, were not adequately decoded, if detected at all.[52] □

She cites Richard Ellmann and Charles Feidelson's influential anthology *The Modern Tradition: Backgrounds of Modern Literature* (1965) as typical in its promotion of a modernism that is staunchly male. It collects manifestos and aesthetic pronouncements from 'the age of Yeats, Joyce, Eliot and Lawrence', and other European male authors besides, but only samples the work of one female writer, Virginia Woolf.[53]

In the 1970s, Anglo-American feminist scholars sought to redress the institutionalised masculine bias by turning from what Elaine Showalter would call 'feminist critique' (analysing and answering the representation of women in literature by male authors) to 'gynocritics' (the study, recovery and revaluation of writing by women, the 'psychodynamics of female creativity', 'the trajectory of the individual or collective female literary career' and 'literary history').[54] In 'Towards a Feminist Poetics' (1979), Showalter argues:

■ If we study stereotypes of women, the sexism of male critics, and the limited roles women play in literary history, we are not learning what women have felt and experienced, but only what men have thought women should be.[55] □

Biographies and critical studies of previously overlooked modernists like Djuna Barnes, Mina Loy and H.D. started to appear in the mid-1970s, bringing their lives and works to attention. Revisionary histories of women's collective contribution to modernism began to appear from the mid-1980s onwards, examining feminine experiences of modernity.

Shari Benstock's classic study *Women of the Left Bank: Paris, 1900–1940* (1987) replies to *The Pound Era* and its narrowing of modernism to a single defining talent by investigating the artistic communities created by the women who gathered in Paris. She analyses the activities of the American, English and French 'writers, publishers, book sellers and *salonières*' who energised the literary life of the city, but were largely 'forgotten by the standard literary histories of this time or rendered inconsequential by memoirs and literary biographies', notably Margaret Anderson, Djuna Barnes, Natalie Barney (1876–1972), Sylvia Beach, Kay Boyle (1902–92), Bryher (pseud. [Annie] Winifred Ellerman (1894–1983)), [Sidonie-Gabrielle] Colette (1873–1954), Caresse Crosby (1891–1970), Nancy Cunard, H.D., Janet Flanner (1892–1978), Jane Heap, Maria Jolas, Mina Loy, Adrienne Monnier (1892–55), Anaïs Nin (1903–77), Jean Rhys (1890–1979), Gertrude Stein, Alice B. Toklas (1877–1967), Renée Vivien (1877–1909) and Edith Wharton (1862–1937).[56] Benstock highlights 'important variations in individual circumstances and lifestyles', noting that many of the expatriates were drawn to Paris for its 'international reputation as the capital of same sex love among women', others for the cultural and personal freedoms it afforded.[57] In this respect, her thesis is similar to that of Gillian Hanscombe and Virginia Smyers, who discerned 'a clear connection between literary endeavour and the shunning of conventionally heterosexual lives' in their account of the artistic and social networks that nourished the creative activities of writers such as Barnes, Beach, H.D., Amy Lowell, Dorothy Richardson and Stein in *Writing for their Lives: The Modernist Woman 1910–1940* (1987).[58]

Benstock's focus is largely biographical, although some space is given to critical discussions of: Stein's activities as a 'linguistic cross-dresser' who 'clothed her homosexuality in heterosexual forms'; H.D.'s divided sexuality and its relation to her experimental poetry; and Barnes's feminist exploration of women's place in society and its effects on perceptions of female body.[59] Benstock also notes the vital roles that Margaret Anderson, Jane Heap, Sylvia Beach and others played in the publication and promotion of *Ulysses*. Exploring the many modernisms these women brought into being through their efforts in creating hubs for social and artistic exchange, publishing daring works and producing writing that challenged the dominant misogynist, heterosexual perspectives of their male contemporaries, Benstock seeks to offer a 'female subtext' that 'exposes all that Modernism has repressed, put aside, or attempted to deny'.[60]

For some feminists, the very existence of patriarchy is sufficient justification to treat women's writing as a distinct phenomenon. The most famous exponents of this view are Sandra Gilbert and Susan Gubar, who made their names with *The Madwoman in the Attic: The Woman Writer and the Nineteenth-Century Imagination* (1979), where they proposed that women write their exclusion from power structures, and their imprisonment in identities, literary forms and traditions created by men, through illness and madness. Gilbert and Gubar restated and elaborated the idea of a female counter-tradition in their weighty three-volume study *No Man's Land: The Place of Women Writers in the Twentieth Century* (1988–94), which sets out to 'theorize about the ways in which modernism, because of the distinctive social and cultural changes to which it responds, is differently inflected for male and female writers'.[61] Their ground-breaking work has been an important reference point for later critics working on gender and sexuality.

Gynocritics tend to find most to praise in texts that affirm their own brand of feminist politics. In the classic gynocritical study *A Literature of their Own* (1977) – which unfolds a tradition of British women's writing in the nineteenth and twentieth centuries – Showalter criticises the techniques that modernist women writers pioneered to represent female consciousness because she feels that they preclude feminist social or political critique. She accuses Virginia Woolf, Katherine Mansfield and Dorothy Richardson of creating 'a deliberate female aesthetic, which transformed the feminine code of self-sacrifice into an annihilation of the narrative self, and applied the cultural analysis of the feminists to words, sentences, and structures of language', complaining that 'the more female this literature became in the formal and theoretical sense, the farther it moved from exploring the physical experience of women'.[62]

Poststructuralists tend to dismiss gynocriticism as theoretically naïve for assuming that language is a transparent form of representation and women's experience is directly recoverable from texts written by women. As Toril Moi points out in *Sexual/Textual Politics* (1985), gynocriticism treats the text as the expression of a unique individual with the consequence that 'all art becomes autobiography, a mere window on to the self and the world, with no reality of its own'.[63] Far from side-stepping patriarchal ideology, and the language and literary forms that underwrite it, Moi argues that gynocriticism in fact affirms the status quo by reducing the text to 'a passive, "feminine" reflection of an unproblematically "given", "masculine" world or self'.[64] By contrast, as Moi explains, French theoreticians regard the avant-garde linguistic forms that modernist writers pioneered to be capable of truly revolutionary critique, irrespective of the author's gender, because they have the power to disrupt, subvert or evade the symbolic order constituted through language and the patriarchal ideology it encodes.[65] According to Lacanian psychoanalysis:

■ [W]oman cannot enter the world of the symbolic, of language, because at the very moment of the acquisition of language, she learns that she lacks the phallus, the symbol that sets language going through a recognition of difference; her relation to language is a negative one, a lack. In patriarchal structures, therefore, woman is located as other (enigma, mystery), and is thereby viewed as outside of (male) language.[66] □

For Julia Kristeva, and other French theorists with an interest in psychoanalytic accounts of gender and patriarchy, 'feminine' comes to designate all radical, disruptive forces that threaten to subvert the structures underwritten by prevailing patriarchal values and discourse:

■ [...] in a culture where the speaking subjects are conceived of as masters of their speech, they have what is called a 'phallic' position. The fragmentation of language in a text calls into question the very posture of this mastery [...].[67] □

Male modernists praised by Kristeva for being open to the 'feminine' and positioning their writing as marginal to the symbolic order include Stephane Mallarmé, Comte de Lautréamont, James Joyce and Antonin Artaud.[68]

Hélène Cixous termed the writing that inscribes the feminine body and female difference *écriture féminine*. The feminine aesthetic is associated with: disruptions to syntax, punctuation, linearity and realism; a refusal of singular, stable points of view and the unified, coherent self; and the embrace of the anti-hierarchical, of indeterminacy, polysemy, fragmentation and the pre-Oedipal (before the child's entrance into the psychosexual order and the symbolic realm of language, where words are figured as sound). Many of these qualities tally with Virginia Woolf's analysis of Dorothy Richardson's 'psychological sentence of the feminine gender'.[69]

Alice Jardine coined the term 'gynesis' to designate the theoretical approach that views the 'feminine' as a discursive effect disrupting the master narratives that secure the symbolic order.[70] Some Anglo-American feminist theorists view gynesis with suspicion for its ideological association of the feminine with the marginal and for its failure to challenge the institutional bias that oppresses women. In *Beyond Feminist Aesthetics* (1989), for instance, Rita Felski counters the 'assertion that experimental writing constitutes the only truly "subversive" and "feminine" textual practice, and that more conventional forms such as realism are complicit with patriarchal systems of presentation'.[71] She argues that the dominant status of realism in women's writing makes it counterproductive for feminists to reject realism as a conservative, masculine form. 'French feminism', Felski argues, 'reveals an overestimation of the radical effects of linguistic indeterminacy which has not come to terms with [...] the political limitations of modernism'.[72]

Since the late 1980s, gynocriticism and gynesis have found an uneasy accommodation. For instance, Scott's landmark critical anthology *The*

Gender of Modernism – written as a corrective to Ellmann and Feidelson's sampler – is firmly rooted in the gynocritical project of recovering women's voices, but remains open to insights from continental theory. In particular, it foregrounds the striking ways in which the 'feminist critical thinking' of H.D., Katherine Mansfield, Mina Loy, Marianne Moore, Gertrude Stein and Virginia Woolf anticipates 'French feminist psychoanalytic and linguistic approaches'.[73] *The Gender of Modernism* 'deliberately features women writers, without strictly limiting itself to them'.[74] 'A major goal of this anthology', as Scott explains, 'is that neglected viewpoints of modernists on their own aesthetic projects should now be known and taken up.'[75] To this end, it offers expert introductions to twenty-six writers whose work is suggestive for a consideration of gender, together with selections from overlooked, out-of-print and previously unpublished materials, particularly from 'marginal genres' such as 'essays, book reviews, interviews, letters, diaries, sketches, even notebooks', to make them newly available to a wide audience.[76] Because relatively little space is given to male writers, the theme of masculinity is almost entirely overlooked and so there is a failure to explore the theme of gender and modernism in its fullest sense.

The *Gender of Modernism* does succeed in imparting a rich sense of the interconnectedness of modernist writers and their aesthetic projects. Scott represents these connections graphically in 'A Tangled Mesh of Modernists', a much-cited diagram constructed by arranging the names of the twenty-six featured authors in a circle alphabetically, together with the names of other figures whose names occur in the book in lower case, and drawing lines to indicate each time an important connection arises.[77] The 'Tangled Mesh' offers an image for the network of diverse talents energising literary culture and decentres modernism by reminding readers that 'Not all strands lead to Eliot, Pound and Joyce'.[78]

Anthologies such as *The Gender of Modernism* have been instrumental in bringing women modernists' works to the fore of the discipline. Even so, it was still not uncommon for distinguished critics working in the 1980s and 1990s to construct modernist lineages that were almost exclusively male. Acclaimed studies in this vein include: Michael Levenson's *A Genealogy of Modernism* (1984), which traces an evolution from literary impressionism to Imagism, Vorticism and classicism, examining Conrad, Ford, Hulme, Pound, Lewis and Eliot's efforts to formulate a new aesthetic; Stan Smith's *The Origins of Modernism: Eliot, Pound, Yeats and the Rhetorics of Renewal* (1994); and Valentine Cunningham's *British Writers of the Thirties* (1987), in which he notes the lack of commentary on women writers but hopes the gap that denotes their absence can be defined so that they 'can be granted the mentions and some of the respect they deserve, and their place marked on the '30s map for future reference'.[79]

As feminist critics refigured modernism to make room for women's writing, they recontoured its temporal boundaries to accommodate earlier and later peaks in production. For instance, in *Refiguring Modernism* (two volumes, 1995) Bonnie Kime Scott enacts a rewriting of modernist literary history from a gynocritical and then a gynetic perspective by looking more deeply into the attachments connecting three female authors – Virginia Woolf, Rebecca West and Djuna Barnes – presenting them 'as central representatives of modernist writing, where typically a cluster of male figures have stood'.[80] Volume One, *The Women of 1928*, takes a psycho-biographical approach to formative relations in the principal writers' lives. It investigates the dysfunctional family setups they endured, their gradual movement out of the influence of confining, directive and sexually exploratory Edwardian literary uncles Arnold Bennett, H.G. Wells (1866–1946), John Galsworthy (1867–1933) and George Bernard Shaw, their positive affiliations to the suffrage movement and to women's social and literary networks, and their interactions with the frequently misogynistic 'Men of 1914'. It builds towards an account of 1928, a highly productive year for Woolf, West and Barnes, who had all by then 'found strategies to succeed as professional writers and a degree of formal license'.[81] Events that year included the publication of West's extended essay *The Strange Necessity*, Barnes's *Ladies Almanack* (a rococo satirical novel centred on the activities of Barney's lesbian salon in Paris), and the 'cultural crisis over lesbian censorship occasioned by the trial of [...] *The Well of Loneliness*', which involved 'Woolf, West and Barnes both in argument and creative writing'.[82] Volume Two, *Postmodern Feminist Readings of Woolf, West and Barnes*, pays close attention to waywardly feminine writing styles, focusing on Woolf's 'rapture with words'; Barnes's preoccupation with 'beasts turning human' and the dissolution of binary categories to develop 'a vast intermediate ground of gender, diversified by racial, homosexual, lesbian and bisexual identifications, and [...] by species and mythic composite animals'; and West's efforts to give 'authority to female experience' by combining the domestic and the political.[83] By centring 'a second rise in modernism' on a moment of lesbian cultural crisis, Scott counters the dominant masculinist criticism that has unfairly privileged the activities of the 'men of 1914' and established 1922 as the high point of modernist production by instituting a new *annus mirabilis* that is female and feminist.[84] From the 1990s onwards, the essential cultural work performed by female modernists could no longer be ignored.

CHAPTER FIVE

Gender and Sexuality in Modernist Literature

Modernism and the Battle of the Sexes

The feminist project of rediscovery, re-evaluation and revision is coextensive with the task of investigating the representation of sexuality and gender. In *No Man's Land*, Gilbert and Gubar ascribe the origins of modernism to the emancipation of women. They cite 'the late nineteenth-century rise of feminism and the fall of Victorian concepts of "femininity"', the emergence of the New Woman, the formation of visible homosexual communities and 'the unprecedented confrontation (by both sexes) with the artifice of gender' in the *fin de siècle*, as well as changes to women's social and economic status, particularly during the First World War when they had access to male professions.[1] Modernity is thus figured as no man's land: both the territory between opposing armies and also a realm that is not male. Gilbert and Gubar argue that, from the late nineteenth century onwards, 'both women and men engendered words and works which continually sought to come to terms with, and find terms for, the ongoing battle of the sexes'.[2] They conclude that '"modernism" is itself [...] for men as much as for women a product of the sexual battle [...], as are the linguistic experiments usually attributed to the revolutionary poetics of the so-called avant-garde'.[3]

The 'masculine' modernism that Gilbert and Gubar identify is paranoid, misogynist and articulated in an aggressively sexualised, phallic language. Evidence that men feared they were losing the battle includes: Filippo Marinetti's 'Contempt for women!'; the prevalence of femicidal fantasies in T.S. Eliot's poetry; D.H. Lawrence's horror at confident, careerist 'cocksure women'; the 'disturbing depictions of female sexuality and aggression' in William Faulkner's *Light in August* (1932); and the proliferation of images of male impotence 'From the betrayed and passive narrator of Ford's *Good Soldier* to cuckolded Leopold Bloom in Joyce's *Ulysses* and the wounded Fisher King in Eliot's *The Waste Land* to the eunuch Jake Barnes in Hemingway's *The Sun Also Rises*, the paralyzed Clifford in Lawrence's *Lady Chatterley's Lover* (1928), and the gelded Benjy in Faulkner's *The Sound and The Fury*'.[4]

Gilbert and Gubar contend that male modernists instituted 'an implicitly masculine aesthetic of hard, abstract, learned verse that is opposed to the aesthetic of soft, effusive, personal verse supposedly written by women and Romantics' in horrified reaction to the social, political and literary gains made by women.[5] In Gilbert and Gubar's reading, 'a reaction-formation against the rise of literary women became not just a theme in modernist writing but a motive for [male] modernism'.[6] The following sections investigate Gilbert and Gubar's thesis that modernism is 'differently inflected for male and female writers' by exploring the politics of modernist form, the proto-modernist dimensions of New Woman fiction, the impact of the First World War on the construction of femininity and masculinity, and the relationship between modernist creativity and sexuality.[7]

Gender and Form

The sheer formalism of modernism has often been interpreted as a means to retreat from pressing realities. Marianne DeKoven elaborates a powerful argument to the contrary in *Rich and Strange: Gender, History and Modernism* (1991). Whereas 'Modernist formal practice has seemed to define itself as a repudiation of, and an alternative to, the cultural implications of late nineteenth- and early twentieth-century feminism and socialism', DeKoven suggests that 'modernist form evolved precisely as an adequate means of representing their terrifying appeal'.[8] She contends that early modernist writers registered antagonistic social pressures from the world beyond the text and held them in unresolved tension. In this respect, 'modernist writing *constitutes itself as* self-contradictory'.[9] DeKoven adapts Derrida's notion of *'sous-rature'* (literally that which is 'under erasure', for instance a crossed-out word that nonetheless remains legible) to describe this unresolved contradictoriness.[10]

The title *Rich and Strange* alludes to Ariel's famous song from *The Tempest*, foretelling the transfiguration into coral and pearls suffered by the body of a father presumed drowned. For DeKoven, the 'unresolved contradiction' 'rich and strange' becomes emblematic of 'modernist writers' irresolvable ambivalence towards the possibility of radical social change'.[11] Furthermore, DeKoven reads the 'sea-change' metaphor as an image for the 'maternal feminine' as 'the repressed other of Western culture'.[12] Drawing on Luce Irigaray's observations concerning the way that the 'maternal feminine' is characteristically represented as something watery, fluid and formless (e.g. amniotic), DeKoven interprets 'sea-change' as an image of the male fear of being subsumed into 'seemingly all-encompassing materiality of the maternal feminine'.[13] This informing cultural myth, which acquires new relevance in the age of feminism and socialism, motivates DeKoven's decision to use 'water imagery as the focus for textual analysis'.[14]

DeKoven's approach is informed by deconstruction, psychoanalysis, biography, sociology and ethnology, focusing on authors' use of language, form and enduring myths and symbols. Examining pairs of texts in turn, one canonical and male, one non-canonical and female, DeKoven traces the emergence of the *sous-rature* in turn-of-the-century and pre-war fiction by Henry James, Charlotte Perkins Gilman (1860–1935), Gertrude Stein, Joseph Conrad, Kate Chopin (1850–1904) and Virginia Woolf. In doing so, De Koven reinscribes the unresolved contradictions modernist texts put under erasure. She argues that these unresolved contradictions are inflected differently for male and female writers:

■ Male modernists generally feared the loss of hegemony the change they desired might entail, while female modernists feared punishment for desiring that utter change.[15] □

DeKoven makes this case most forcibly in her analysis of Gilman's 'The Yellow Wallpaper' (1892) and James's *The Turn of the Screw* (1898), which both feature apparitions who 'are figures of the protagonist's repressed anger at her capitulation to male authority and of her frustrated desire for an eroticized power'.[16] In '"The Yellow Wallpaper"', a female-signed text fearing what it desires, female capitulation is damnation; in *The Turn of the Screw*, a male-signed text desiring what it fears, female (and subaltern) victory is damnation'.[17]

The notion of the 'passage' is crucial to DeKoven's paired readings of Conrad's *The Nigger of the 'Narcissus'* (1897) and Stein's 'Melanctha', as well as Conrad's *Heart of Darkness* (1899) and Woolf's first novel *The Voyage Out* (1915).[18] She draws on Luce Irigaray's notion of the vaginal passage as a conduit between symbolic orders of the mother and the father, figuring 'the possibility of link and movement back and forth between masculine and feminine'.[19] DeKoven explores the passage as the originary birth canal through which modernist literary texts are born to explore how they use the trope of 'racial otherness' to 'connect to the dark and darkly suppressed maternal origin'.[20] DeKoven interprets the tale of black Melanctha's neglected, short-lived baby as a figure for the new kind of narrative that Stein is writing, one which is not yet fully viable, where the maternal 'is the locus of [...] powerful, dark forces that are just as compelling, and potentially liberating, as they are damned'.[21] The birth is contrasted with the extraordinary sequence where the black seaman James Wait is effectively born through a hole in the bulkhead of the *Narcissus*:

■ During the remarkable Cape of Hope gale, the *Narcissus* becomes a woman in labor [...]. Under the extreme duress and life-death liminality of the gale, which images, I would argue, precisely the massive upheaval in culture that is the modernist historical moment, the ship whose name quite literally evokes the endless self-reflexivity of the masculine subject makes visible within itself the buried origin, the 'secret of life' lodged within the threat of death: the maternal womb. The revelation of that womb at the center of the ship and the text occurs as the *Narcissus* reaches the climax of its "downward" (southern) journey *around Africa*: again downwardness [...], darkness [...] and the empowered maternal are conflated [...]. This textual dynamic corresponds of course to historical fact: colonialized nonwhites, the militant working class, and feminist women were the others disrupting white male bourgeois hegemony.[22] □

DeKoven suggests that Rachel Vinrace's journey to South America in *A Voyage Out* and Marlow's trek up the river Congo to the Inner Station of a Belgian ivory-trading company in *Heart of Darkness* also enact 'a return to the terrifying heart of desire, the maternal origin of life that generates [...] disillusionment and death'.[23] For Rachel, the womb-like jungle provides a setting where alternatives to patriarchal, imperial models for relationships can be imagined. Returning to society and its power structures, 'the dualistic trap out of which she is trying to voyage by opening the passage between the masculine-paternal "great world outside" and the feminine-maternal "snug domestic house"' leaves her with one alternative: death.[24] By contrast, Marlow travels up-river through the vaginal passage with the hope of reaching the imperialist ideal embodied in Kurtz, but encounters at the climax the figure of the monstrous maternal in Kurtz's savage, wild-eyed African lover. DeKoven comments that 'through his association with Kurtz, Marlow comes to repudiate what Kurtz represents, forging instead an alternative, new story of gender and race relations, narrated in the impossible dialectic of modernist form'.[25]

DeKoven's study reveals the ways in which early modernists responded to the sea-change that is modernity by cancelling out the historical circumstances that are their ostensible subject. The richness and strangeness of their writings inheres in their irreducibly ambiguous formal appeal to the impossible dialectic represented by the two-way passage and the displacement of anxieties about gender and sexuality onto the colonies and race and vice versa. DeKoven's reading supports Gilbert and Gubar's thesis by presenting a modernism born of the battle of the sexes and inflected differently for men and women, but suggests that it thrives on the conflicts between fear and desire.

New Woman Fiction and Suffrage

The insight that the burgeoning women's movement is a crucial context for modernism has led critics to examine the relations between modernist experimentation and the New Woman fiction of the *fin de siècle*, which explored women's (often frustrated) ambitions beyond the home, marriage and motherhood. Ann Ardis was the first to rethink the familiar periodisation of modern literary history by inscribing the New Woman novel into genealogies of modernism. In *New Women, New Novels: Feminism and Early Modernism* (1990), she explores how 'issues of female identity fuelled tremendous experimentation with narrative form' in the works of writers such as Emma Frances Brooke (1844–1926), Mona Caird (1854–1932), Mary Cholmondeley (1859–1925), Gertrude Dix (1837–98), Ella Hepworth Dixon (1857–1932), Florence Dixie (1855–1905) and Olive Schreiner (1855–1920):[26]

■ New Woman novelists anticipate the reappraisal of realism we usually credit to early-twentieth-century writers. Most obviously, the 'natural' inevitability of the marriage plot is challenged as New Woman novelists 'replace' 'the pure woman', the Victorian angel in the house, with a heroine who is either sexually active outside of marriage or abstains from sex for political rather than moral reasons. In more subtle ways, the Victorian conceptualization of 'character' or identity as something seamless, unified, and consistent over time is also shattered as these novelists demystify the ideology of 'womanliness', an ideology that gives middle-class women 'no life but in the affections'.[27] □

For these reasons, Ardis argues that turn-of-the-century New Women writers are in fact as responsible for 'originating' modernism as better-known figures such as Joseph Conrad and Henry James. She ascribes the general failure to recognise the modernist potential of New Woman fiction to the dominant voices of the conservative commentators who discredited the cultural work these novels performed, devaluing their aesthetic worth by using femaleness as the justification to push them to the margins of literary culture.

Lyn Pykett also emphasises the debt that modernism owes to New Woman fiction in her accounts of the genre. In *Engendering Fictions: The English Novel in the Early Twentieth Century* (1995), a wide-ranging study of the interplay between literary, scientific, sexological, psychoanalytical and social discourses about women and gender in the age of modernism, Pykett makes the case for George Egerton (pseud. Mary Chavelita Dunne Bright, 1859–1945) as 'a very self-consciously innovatory writer who was committed to the development of a female aesthetic'.[28]

■ Her narratives [...] are impressionistic, compressed, concentrated, allusive, elliptical, episodic, and make much use of dream, reverie, and other forms of interiority. [...] The paradigmatic Egertonian story [...] is 'A Cross Line' [...], constructed as a drama in five scenes, or as a musical piece in five movements. Its plot [...] is rudimentary: a woman [...] meets a male stranger [...]; she fantasizes about the other possible lives she might lead; she contemplates escape [...] from the companionable tediousness of her marriage, but becomes resigned to her domestic lot when she discovers (or belatedly acknowledges) [...] that she is pregnant. But to tell the story thus is to mistell it, for the main concern [...] is with the shifting moods of its central female character [...].[29] ☐

For Pykett, 'Egerton anticipates Dorothy Richardson, Virginia Woolf and D.H. Lawrence in getting rid of what Lawrence described as the old stable ego of character, and presents us with a multiplicity of selves, or a subjectivity in process'.[30]

Pykett proceeds to argue that 'Lawrence's condition-of-England novel, *The Rainbow*, is his "New Woman" novel *par excellence*':[31]

■ The emergent narrative of *The Rainbow*, the story of Ursula, is the familiar New Woman story of 'a woman becoming individual, self-responsible, taking her own initiative'. Ursula's story, [...] like that of numerous other heroines of 1890s' fiction (by men and women), is the story of the questing modern woman [...]. Like many New Woman novels, *The Rainbow* ends with a renovatory vision which portends an alliance (in this case a fragile and tenuous one) between the New Woman and the working class.[32] ☐

However, as Pykett notes, '*The Rainbow* also reworks another typical New Woman plot, the "boomerang plot", by means of which the experiments in life of the unconventional heroine blow up in her face, and/or she is boomeranged back into social and gender-role conformity'.[33]

The Rainbow was written at a time when Lawrence was 'sympathetic to the woman's cause' and 'espoused a non-suffragist form of feminism'.[34] He would later declare: 'All fights for freedom that succeed, go too far, and become in turn the infliction of a tyranny [...] like the freedom of women'.[35] Pykett suggests that *The Rainbow* marks 'the end of Lawrence's early attempts to renovate fiction by means of a turn to the feminine', after which his fiction 'seems to take a distinct turn, some would say lurch, to the "male line", first with the search for comradeship between men which is central to *Women in Love*, and then with an increasingly strident valorisation of masculinity and phallicism, and a hostility to the female and the feminine in *Aaron's Rod, Kangaroo* and *The Plumed Serpent*'.[36]

Sally Ledger offers a different perspective on New Woman writing in *The New Woman: Fiction and Feminism at the Fin de Siècle* (1997).

While she agrees with Ardis and Pykett that the New Woman was an important theme for modernism, she places greater emphasis on the New Woman's 'association with mass culture as well as insisting on the *heterogeneity* of the cultural forms deployed by feminist writers at the *fin de siècle*':[37]

> ■ Many New Woman novels were hugely popular best-sellers [...] and whilst George Egerton used the proto-modernist form of the short story, Eleanor Marx's New-Womanish concerns (for example) were mediated through political essays and literary-critical work. Olive Schreiner deployed a multitude of literary forms – the political tract, the realist novel, allegories, dreams and utopias – in order to give voice to her feminism. The New Woman's experimentations with literary form, and her significance in relation to early modernism, constitute one (but not the only) aspect of her modernity: her engagement with public political life and with mass cultural forms are other, equally significant aspects.[38] □

Ledger reminds readers that the majority of fiction by New Woman writers was not formally innovative and that their primary vehicle for feminist expression was realism. She therefore advocates setting the '"modernist" New Woman [...] alongside her "mass cultural", realist sister'.[39] Ledger's account does not invalidate the arguments that Pykett and Ardis make about proto-modernist New Woman fictions, but it alerts us to what is lost when New Woman writing is incorporated wholesale into 'the "modernist" paradigm which reigned supreme in the early part of the twentieth century'.[40]

Gender, Performance and the Body

'Indisputably, the woman question had prime importance for the originators of modern drama'.[41] As Joan Templeton points out in *Ibsen's Women* (1997), a study of the playwright's female characters and their relationships to important women in his life, feminism's challenges to patriarchy preoccupied dramatists of all political persuasions. She cites: Ibsen's innovative and influential plays (most notably *A Doll's House* and *Ghosts*); Strindberg's famous plays of his naturalistic period (for instance *Miss Julie*); the works of the German playwright Gerhart Hauptmann (1862–1946), who 'examined the issues of women's rights (*Before Sunrise*, 1889), and equality in marriage (*Lonely Lives*, 1891), and exposed the viciousness of the double standard (*Rose Bernd*, 1903)'; the work of 'Ibsen's champion' George Bernard Shaw, 'who put varieties of the "New Woman" on the stage in *The Philanderer* (1893), *Mrs Warren's Profession* (1893) and *Candida* (1894)'; and also Oscar Wilde's comedies – *Lady Windermere's Fan* (1892), *A Woman of No Importance* (1893), *An Ideal Husband* (1895) and *The Importance of Being Ernest* (1895) – which all 'expose the unfairness and downright silliness' of sexual double standards.[42]

Penny Farfan expands on the criticism that notes the centrality of female characters in the work of ground-breaking male playwrights in *Women, Modernism, and Performance* (2004) by addressing women's efforts to develop alternative dramatic practices. She examines drama, fiction and dance, as well as a range of performance events such as suffrage demonstrations. In doing so, she accounts for 'the omission of women from accounts of modern theatre history' and clarifies 'the relationship of theatrical and dramatic modernism to more recognized modernism in other fields'.[43] Her first case study is the actress Elizabeth Robins (1862–1952), who identified her star turn as Hedda Gabler as the defining moment in her career, but ultimately found Ibsen's plays wanting as feminist vehicles. 'If we had been thinking politically, concerning ourselves about the emancipation of women, we would not have given the Ibsen plays the particular kind of whole-hearted, enchanted devotion we did give', Robins reflected in an essay of 1928.[44] Farfan argues that Robins's involvement in the suffrage movement led her to reply to Ibsen's shortcomings as a feminist, most particularly his bias towards 'individualism', in her melodramatic, didactic play *Votes for Women!* (first performed in 1907, published in a revised form in 1909). The heroine is Vida Levering, a militant with a past, who successfully convinces an ex-lover with political influence to lobby for women's rights, foregoing her own individual fulfilment to dedicate herself to the feminist cause. The play was notable for its innovative staging as well as its pro-suffrage politics. It utilised a cast of forty actors to dramatise a suffrage rally in Trafalgar Square, where Vida takes the platform 'to express solidarity with women of all classes and to argue the necessity of organization and co-operation'.[45] The reviewer for the *Clarion* [...] described the rally as 'the sensation of the theatrical season'.[46] *Votes for Women!* reached an international audience with productions in Rome and New York in 1909, and became one of the most frequently performed suffrage dramas in America in the 1910s.

Another focus for Farfan is Woolf's imaginative engagement with performance, particularly as it relates to gender. Citing Woolf's essay on French actresses Rachel ([pseud. Elisa-Rachel Félix] 1821–58) and Sarah Bernhardt (1844–1923), Farfan argues that 'Woolf imagined acting in emancipatory terms, suggesting that in impersonating dramatic characters, actresses are, in theory at least, afforded unique opportunities for emotional exploration, heightened experience and self-discovery'.[47] In practice, however, the impoverished roles available to women inhibited artistic self-realisation, as Woolf noted in her essay on Ellen Terry (1847–1928), Britain's leading Shakespearean actress:

■ Something of Ellen Terry it seems overflowed every part and remained unacted. Shakespeare could not fit her; nor Ibsen; nor Shaw.[48] □

Farfan suggests that in Woolf's comic playlet *Freshwater* (written in 1923, then revised for a private performance in 1935), in which Terry figures as the central character, 'Woolf's concept of androgyny is implied as the creative state of mind that cannot find expression in the corporeal and therefore gendered art of acting'.[49]

Performance functions as the central metaphor in Virginia Woolf's last novel *Between the Acts* (1941). Set just before the outbreak of the Second World War, on the day that a village stages its annual play, Woolf's final novel 'incorporates a complete pageant of English literary history staged by the lesbian playwright-director Miss La Trobe'.[50] Farfan argues that Woolf conflates the life stories of characters with literary plots 'to represent the totalizing force that [...] heterosexual romance exerts on all aspects of social life'.[51] The passivity of the spectators, who fail to see their 'passive compliance with the tacitly destructive patriarchal plot [...] that dominates both the pageant and the narrative sections', even when mirrors force 'them to see themselves reflected in the on-stage action', is contrasted with the activity of La Trobe to assert 'not only the force that the conventional structure of the heterosexual relationship exerts on social performers, but also the possibility of its re-plotting and the part that art can play in this vitally important task'.[52] In Farfan's analysis, performance provides Woolf with 'a figure for the common ground "between" the inextricably linked and mutually influential "acts" of making art and everyday living' and 'a site on which to stage a collaboration against the gender politics that lead to war'.[53]

In *Modernism, Technology and the Body* (1998), Tim Armstrong argues that modernism is 'characterized by the desire to *intervene* in the body; to render it part of modernity by techniques which may be biological, mechanical, or behavioural'.[54] He investigates how modernist texts enact experimental procedures that respond to scientific technologies of bodily intervention, such as dietary regimens, early gender-surgery, hormone therapies, rejuvenation operations, electrification and prostheses. His central thesis is that the turn-of-the-century body harboured a crisis: Darwinian science and psychology suggested an underlying primitivism within the body which was 'out of step with the modern, technologically advanced, world'.[55] The stress that civilisation placed on the body was registered by diagnoses like hysteria and neurasthenia, conditions which 'suggested that compensatory action was necessary':[56]

■ Modernity, then, brings both a fragmentation and augmentation of the body in relation to technology; it offers the body as lack, at the same time as it offers technological compensation. Increasingly, that compensation is offered as a part of capitalism's fantasy of the complete body: in the mechanisms of advertising, cosmetics, cosmetic surgery, and cinema; all prosthetic in the sense that they promise the perfection of the body.[57] □

Armstrong investigates 'the problematics of the commoditized body and the gender-politics of Modernism as a whole' by examining the 'textual technologies which directly negotiate between the body and the production of discourse'.[58] He links the way that desire and bodily energy is repeatedly figured in electrical terms in early twentieth-century fiction to the scientific understanding of the body as circuitry, comparing two novels by the American novelist Theodore Dreiser (1871–1945): *Sister Carrie* (1900), where the heroine is 'plugged in' to 'the energies, desires, and rewards' of the electrified city, and *An American Tragedy* (1925), where impulses are controlled by the state power in the guise of the electric chair.[59] Henry James's use of tropes of ingestion, mastication and rumination to describe the textual regulation of his body of work in the prefaces to the New York edition of his works is linked to the dietary regimen he was then following on the advice of Horace Fletcher (1849–1919), who advocated maximum efficiency and minimal waste. James is contrasted with Gertrude Stein, who broke with her Fletcherising brother and also refused to edit, preferring an aesthetic of 'copiousness'.[60] Armstrong argues that 'Stein's continuous present locates itself in the process of the lived body', linking productivity and excretion, and so associating the female body with the free flow of waste products.[61]

The accumulation of detritus and abject body parts in *The Waste Land* – particularly in Eliot's drafts of the poem – is placed in the personal context of the ill health of Eliot's first wife Vivienne, her 'teeth, abscesses, neuralgia, nerves, and menstrual problems'.[62] Pound's surgical excision of waste as he edited the manuscript of *The Waste Land* is framed as an attempt to discipline and purify the unruly (feminine) textual body with virile masculine economy. The 'Steinach Operation' (vasectomy) that W.B. Yeats underwent in the belief that the shift from internal to external secretion would energise his body, mind and writing, provides further evidence of the links between masculinity, phallicism and seminal production. By contrast, Armstrong suggests that Mina Loy's poetry ridicules 'the male aesthetic which founds itself on the objectified feminine body' and satirises the Futurist fascination with the body as a machine.[63] Poems such as 'Parturition' (which describes the experience of childbirth) and 'The Dead' are preoccupied 'with the opening up of the body's boundaries [...] and the traffic across boundaries'.[64] Loy also created her own technique for bodily reform in a manifesto-*cum*-advertisement *Auto-Facial Construction* (1919), which Armstrong interprets as emblematic of her 'determination to represent herself in her own terms'.[65]

Reflecting on prostheses leads Armstrong to consider writing itself as a bodily technology. He examines Stein's early career at the Harvard Psychological Laboratory, suggesting that her research into automatic writing provided a conceptual framework for her own creative processes, whereby the act of writing takes precedence over narrative. The uses to which writers such as Stein, Yeats and André Breton put automatic writing lead Armstrong to reflect: 'At the limits of the body considered as a perceptual apparatus, distraction produces the modern artwork'.[66]

Gender and the Great War

In many accounts of modernism the First World War is presented as a culminating moment of apocalypse that intensified and consolidated an already emergent set of ideas. For instance, Susan Stanford Friedman argues:

■ The starting point of modernism is the crisis of belief that pervades twentieth-century western culture: loss of faith, experience of fragmentation and disintegration, and shattering of cultural symbols and norms. [...] The rationalism of science and philosophy attacked the validity of traditional religious and artistic symbols while the growing technology of the industrialized world produced the catastrophes of war on the one hand and the atomization of human beings on the other. Art produced after the First World War recorded the emotional aspect of this crisis; despair, hopelessness, paralysis, angst [...].[67] □

Motifs of fragmentation and despair reached a peak in the years after the War, as writers struggled to come to terms with the condition of their fractured civilisation and the attendant feelings of nervous dissociation, despair and spiritual dearth.

Gilbert and Gubar present the Great War as 'a climactic episode in a battle of the sexes that had already been raging for years'.[68] They propose that the War is not just an 'apocalypse of masculinism', where traditionally masculine values of soldiering implode, but also an event that led to an 'apotheosis of femaleness' and 'a triumph of women'.[69] In their reading, 'the unmanning terrors of combat lead not just to a generalized sexual anxiety but also to an anger directed specifically against the female'.[70] This anger was born of men's own wretched situation and the perception that women at home were becoming ever more powerful, filling positions as nurses, munitions workers, bus drivers and farm labourers, gaining the vote, and even sending their menfolk to the front as per War Office propaganda such as the 'Women of Britain say – Go!' campaign.[71] For this reason, they conceive the Great War as 'a war between the front and the home front'.[72]

Many critics interpret the War as a revolutionary event in and of itself that changed the literary imagination for good. In *The Great War and Modern Memory* (1975), Paul Fussell argues that there is 'one dominating form of modern understanding; that it is essentially ironic; and that it originates largely in the application of mind and memory to the events of the Great War'.[73] According to Fussell, this mindset was generated by the 'gross dichotomizing' that was a consequence of prolonged trench warfare, under which, from the soldiers' perspective, '"We are all here on this side; "the enemy" is over there'.[74] He argues that the war not only restructured thought, it also generated its own distinctive linguistic manoeuvres. Military terminology, the vocabulary of propaganda and official pro forma such as the Field Service Post Card, together with the combatants' keen sense that they were experiencing 'an unprecedented and […] all-but-incommunicable reality', produced 'an atmosphere of euphemism as rigorous and impenetrable as language and literature skilfully used could make it'.[75]

In *Memories of an Infantry Officer* (1930), Siegfried Sassoon (1886–1967) suggested that 'The man who really endured the War at its worst was everlastingly differentiated from everyone else except his fellow soldiers'.[76] Fussell follows his lead by distinguishing between the male writers who saw active service and the modernists who stayed at home, such as W.B. Yeats, Ezra Pound, Virginia Woolf, D.H. Lawrence, T.S. Eliot and Jmaes Joyce, arguing that the job of memorialising the conflict was 'left to lesser talents' who had borne witness.[77] Fussell also notes the impact of the War on masculinity, particularly with respect to the homoeroticism registered in literary depictions of 'unique physical tenderness, the readiness to admire openly the bodily beauty of young men, the unapologetic recognition that men may be in love with each other'.[78]

In *Modernism, History and the First World War* (1998), Trudi Tate compares a range of writing that attempts to bear witness to the trauma of war and its consequences, including medical journals, psychoanalytic accounts, military histories, memoirs by soldiers and nurses, and fiction by civilians such as Virginia Woolf, H.D., D.H. Lawrence and William Faulkner. Reading these documents together, Tate suggests that 'modernism after 1914 begins to look like a peculiar but significant form of war writing'.[79] However, she carefully distances herself from Fussell's account and from Gilbert and Gubar's binary reading of the Great War as 'a war between the front and the home front'. Tate's starting point is H.D.'s conviction that her child was stillborn following her shock at the news that the 'passenger ship *Lusitania* had been sunk with 1200 casualties' a few days earlier.[80] H.D.'s tragedy is cited as evidence that 'when civilians actually did imagine some of the horrible sights of the Great War, they became susceptible to war neuroses, as *The Lancet* [a medical journal] found itself reporting only a few weeks later'.[81] Tate proceeds to examine 'how civilians are placed as witnesses to, or victims of, the war's trauma'.[82] She compares: H.D.'s depiction of Helforth, a man who suffers from 'hallucinations, a sense of dissociation, loss of certainty about his sexual identity' in adulthood, despite having been too young to fight, whose trauma arises from exposure to propaganda, his association of soldiering with masculinity and his lack of battle experience in 'Kora and Ka' (1934); H.D.'s portrait of Julia, 'a civilian war neurotic', and her soldier husband Rafe, who are both simultaneously 'victim and victimiser, in their marriage, in the war, and in their relationship with others' in *Bid Me to Live* (1960); and 'Mary Postgate' (1915), a striking story by Rudyard Kipling (1865–1936) about a bereaved mother of a Flying Corps serviceman who herself becomes an active participant in the violence when she experiences obscene pleasure at denying medical attention to a fatally injured aviator who has fallen out of a plane and may or may not have bombed her village.[83] The War, Tate argues, 'shapes the ways in which civilians imagine themselves: as distant witnesses but also, increasingly, as military targets'.[84]

As Trudi Tate and Suzanne Raitt argue in their co-edited essay collection *Women's Fiction and the Great War* (1997), transforming 'the actual violence of the Great War into a trope of sex warfare is to deny the specificity of its trauma for men and for women'.[85] The essays they collect emphasise how very different women's experiences and war writings could be, even for women within the same social class. For instance, Helen Small considers the curious case of the anti-suffrage campaigner and formally unadventurous novelist Mrs Humphrey Ward (1851–1920), whose work as a propagandist 'gave her privileged access to precisely the kinds of power and knowledge which she felt ought to be the preserve of men'.[86] Claire Buck explores Radclyffe Hall's sense that the War's call to service had 'special emancipatory status for the female invert'.[87] The War provided the heroine of 'Miss Ogilvy Finds Herself' (1934) and others like her with the opportunity to escape 'claustrophobic domesticity', identify with men and 'do excellent work for the nation', 'asserting their right to serve, asserting their claim for attention'.[88] However, Hall's story focuses on the disillusionment and despair that sets in after the War, when Miss Ogilvy returns from her role as the head of an ambulance unit to be denied the place in society she had fought for. By contrast, Raitt calls attention to the 'ache of war' felt by women like May Sinclair, whose psychoanalytic training led her to dwell on the 'ecstasy of war' and the 'vicarious sexualized enjoyment of male aggression'.[89] Sinclair was fifty-one when the War broke out, and untrained. She used her private influence and financial resources to buy her way to the front, only to experience shame and humiliation and feelings of uselessness when she got there.

Gender and sexual difference enter into Tate's analyses in *Modernism, History and the First World War* as fraught and potentially contradictory categories. For instance, while the figure of the soldier represents 'a powerful social ideal of manhood', for injured servicemen, the 'act of soldiering [...] damaged the bodily basis of masculinity':[90]

■ The Great War was not simply a 'crisis' of masculinity; rather, it made visible – and intensified – differences *within* masculinity in this period. These differences were at once bodily, historical, and imaginary, and they emerge with particular force in the writing of two men who did not go to the war: D.H. Lawrence and William Faulkner.[91] □

Tate contrasts the use of blindness as a symbol of castration in Faulkner's *Soldiers' Pay* (1926), in which blind, disfigured Donald 'is so traumatised by the war that [...] he can do nothing except die', and Lawrence's 'The Blind Man' (1920), in which the protagonist exhibits no signs of mental trauma linked to his wound and even experiences improved relations with his wife, and 'the idea of male castration is externalised in order to be denied'.[92]

Tate's study concludes with an analysis of *Mrs Dalloway*, which, in her reading, 'takes a hard look at those who managed the social and economic aspects of the war and treated the survivors so badly afterwards'.[93] The novel is set on the day that Clarissa Dalloway hosts a party attended by the prime minister. Clarissa is discomforted by talk of the suicide of shell-shock victim Septimus Smith at the party, an event which she both romanticises and also feels as her punishment. Tate questions how far Clarissa can be seen as a victim, noting that she is ignorant of the Armenian Question. As the wife of a parliamentarian, her lack of knowledge is striking. As Tate notes, the Lausanne Treaty (1923) was signed a few weeks after the novel is set. It ignored the plight of the hundreds of thousands of Armenians who were displaced and killed during the War by denying them a homeland. While Woolf presents Clarissa with some sympathy, Tate suggests that *Mrs Dalloway* is in fact a satire that criticises the English ruling-class and their irresponsible attitudes to post-war issues and raises the question of women's relations to structures of power.

Whereas Tate presents modernism as a form of war writing that registers trauma, Vincent Sherry identifies high modernism as a linguistic formation that specifically emerges as a response to the way that the War is conducted on the home front. In *The Great War and the Language of Modernism* (2003), Sherry proposes that the radical stylistic experimentation of the generation of London-based modernist writers who came to artistic maturity in the 1920s was in fact a reaction to the collapse of liberal values and the Enlightenment 'discourse of right reason'.[94] This breakdown occurred in England when the governing Liberal party 'had to maintain support for a war which, by precedent and convention, [...] they ought to have opposed'.[95] Sherry argues that the 'logic' of Liberal policy, as it emerged in journalistic editorials and newspaper reprints of government documents, 'presented arguments of increasingly specious kind': [96]

■ A deep mainstream of established attitudes – call it public reason, call it civic rationality – was convulsing under the effort to legitimize this war.[97] □

Sherry contends that Ezra Pound, T.S. Eliot and Virginia Woolf responded to the 'discrepancy between the intellectual principles and practical actualities of British Liberalism' by imitating and parodying the disintegration of liberal rationalist language and rhetoric, and that it is in rejecting logical and demonstrable consequences that their writing becomes identifiably modernist.[98] His signal example is Eliot's poem 'Gerontion' [elderly man] written in July 1919, the month after the peace treaty to end the Great War was signed in the Hall of Mirrors at Versailles. He presents the poem as Eliot's judgment on contemporary history, its 'cunning passages and contrived corridors', citing the 'wilderness of mirrors' that the speaker encounters as he surveys his conscience.[99] Analysing the contorted syntax of Gerontion's apologetic confession, which takes the form of a 'combat fantasy', invoking 'the maze of trenches' that he would not have encountered, being too old for military service, Sherry probes the disintegration of linear thinking:[100]

■ The 'Neither... Nor... Nor' construction projects a balanced antithesis as the promise of a standard rationalistic grammar. The two participial clauses at the end of the sentence interrupt the movement, however, and frustrate the expectation of a well-measured gesture. The sequences of linguistic reason have again failed to hold the line.[101] □

Sherry's closely attentive readings historicise syntactical twists and grammatical turns in ways that enrich our appreciation of the politics latent in modernist form, even if they risk narrowing modernism to a single cause.

Although they approach their subjects in different ways, the studies surveyed in this section leave us in no doubt that the First World War brought about new literary formations that traversed the writings of combatants and civilians, Georgians and modernists, and that it intervened in the construction of gender, sexual difference, sexuality and gender relations in more complex ways than Gilbert and Gubar's figure of a 'sex war' allows.

Sexualities

The emergence of sexology in the late nineteenth century made a range of sexual practices, behaviours and identities sensationally visible. Characteristically, Gilbert and Gubar take the view in *Sexchanges* (1989) that modernist attitudes to sexuality differ for male and female writers:

■ Confronting drastically changing sex roles as well as dramatically changing definitions of sexuality, and fearing the physical and metaphysical anomaly of no-manhood, modernist men of letters sought to excavate an ontological link between biological sexuality and the traditional sexual ideologies whose disintegration they found so disturbing. A number of their female contemporaries, however, no doubt drawing upon what Freud considered the girl's greater 'bisexuality', sought to disengage anatomy from destiny, postulating an identity whose transcendence of biological sexuality either explicitly or implicitly questions the gender roles prescribed by the conventional sexual ideologies they sought to deconstruct.[102] □

According to Gilbert and Gubar, 'Whether, like Virginia Woolf, women produced extravagant fantasies about gender fluidity; whether – more pragmatically – they experimented with male costume in order to usurp male privilege; or whether they actually believed themselves to have a gender identity at odds with their anatomy', women were more inclined to embrace same-sex desire, transsexualism and transvestism precisely because they presented radical challenges to the patriarchal order.[103]

Sexchanges was published a year before two momentous critiques of feminist accounts of gender: *Gender Trouble* (1990) by Judith Butler and *Epistemology of the Closet* (1990) by Eve Kosofsky Sedgwick. As a poststructuralist, Butler interprets gender as a category that is constituted discursively and sets about deconstructing the rigid divisions between masculine/feminine and male/female. 'Gender', she explains, 'is the cultural meaning that the sexed body assumes'.[104] Gender is performed, not given; made not born:

■ There is no gender identity behind the expressions of gender; that identity is performatively constituted by the 'expressions' which are said to be its results.[105] □

Butler's work presents serious difficulties for gynocriticism, which is premised on stable notions of gender or biological sex as sources of common experience. Accordingly, feminists are now reluctant to '"gender" modernism without "sexing" it, "racializing" it, "Semiticizing" it, "classing" it', as Rachel Blau DuPlessis notes.[106] Most critics now take an intersectional approach to gender, exploring the many overlapping factors which may contribute to an individual's position within hierarchies of power and oppression, as seen in the section on gender and war above.

In *Epistemology of the Closet*, Sedgwick argues that the division of sexual identity as heterosexual/homosexual is a product of the 'New, institutionalized taxonomic discourses – medical, legal, literary, psychological' that 'proliferated and crystallized with exceptional rapidity in the decades around the turn of the [twentieth] century' in a cultural moment when 'the power relations between the genders [...] were in highly visible crisis' and the problematics of sexual perversion were obsessively debated.[107] Sedgwick examines the processes by which heterosexuality was normalised at the expense of homosexuality with reference to the Oscar Wilde trials (1895), suggesting that the effeminate, dandified 'figure of Wilde may have been the most formative individual influence on turn-of-the-century Anglo-European homosexual definition and identity'.[108]

Concealment and discretion were wise precautions for homosexual writers, especially in the wake of Wilde's conviction, with the result that many closeted their sexuality. Sedgwick's readings of works by Wilde, Henry James and Marcel Proust pivot around the idea that 'by the end of the nineteenth century [...] knowledge meant sexual knowledge, and secrets sexual secrets'.[109] She proposes that because homosexuality was constituted as secrecy, 'the special centrality of homophobic oppression in the twentieth century [...] has resulted from its inextricability from the question of knowledge and the processes of knowing in modern Western culture at large'.[110] The consequence, Sedgwick argues, is that 'an understanding of virtually any aspect of modern Western culture must be, not merely incomplete, but damaged [...] to the degree that it does not incorporate a critical analysis of modern homo/heterosexual definition'.[111] This insight is the cornerstone of queer theory, the mode of analysis that Butler and Sedgwick helped to inaugurate. Queer theory examines what Sedgwick calls 'the open mesh of possibilities, gaps, overlaps, dissonances and resonances, lapses and excesses of meaning when the constituent elements of anyone's gender, of anyone's sexuality aren't made (or can't be made) to signify monolithically'.[112] Queer theory asks that critics analyse the works of writers who do not fit heterosexual paradigms and also tease out the homoerotic potentialities of writing that is not explicitly about homosexuality. It provides a framework for locating the homoerotic in texts, which, if closeted or unconscious, may only be legible through gaps, lapses, excesses and overlaps, disclosed through techniques such as fragmentation, dislocation, irresolution and substitution (including symbolism and metaphor).

Because dislocution and fragmentation are recognisably modernist strategies, critics have postulated a vitally creative link between sexual transgression and textual disruption. In *Queer Poetics: Five Modernist Women Writers* (1999), Mary Galvin explores the textual strategies of six writers who occupy different places on what Adrienne Rich calls the 'continuum of lesbian existence'.[113] Galvin starts with the reclusive nineteenth-century American poet Emily Dickinson (1830–86), who developed a passionate friendship with her sister-in-law, and then proceeds to analyse techniques developed by five female modernists: Amy Lowell and Gertrude Stein, who fully identified as lesbians; Djuna Barnes, whose lesbianism was more ambivalent; H.D., whose sexuality was shifting; and finally Mina Loy, who was heterosexual but nonetheless 'enacted a strong questioning of the heterosexist paradigm'.[114] In Galvin's readings, queer feeling finds its formal expression in disruptions to generic and linguistic conventions that dissolve boundaries and categorical distinctions and clear 'a space for a multiplicitous nonheterocentric thinking'.[115] Lowell's sensual 'polyphonic prose' explores the power of the erotic and dissolves 'the distinction between poetic and prosaic discourses'.[116] Stein's writing plays with 'the duplicity of language (its potential for ambiguity, equivocation, unstable meanings)', 'foregoing the hierarchizing structures of grammar' by writing in the 'continuous present' and celebrating 'language in its erotic possibilities'.[117] An example is her poem 'Lifting Belly' (composed between 1915–17). Several roles are mentioned – 'baby, pussy, caesar, bunny, husband, mother, man, bird' – but, as Galvin points out, 'the lack of quotation marks makes it impossible to know which of the lovers to attribute lines to', with the effect that the 'taking on of sexual/ gender roles in the poem is arbitrary and temporary'.[118] Like Bonnie Kime Scott before her, Galvin observes that Barnes transforms 'the ambiguity of language from a medium of coding and disguise into a technique for disrupting the certainty of categorical boundaries'.[119] Galvin notes that this method is particularly foregrounded in *Ladies Almanack*, which parodies the very notion of cataloguing, setting out, as the faux-archaic subtitle explains, (queer) women in *'their Signs and their Tides; their Moons and their Changes; the Seasons as it is with them; their Eclipses and Equinoxes; as well as a full Record of diurnal and nocturnal Distempers'.*[120] In Galvin's reading, Barnes 'developed a technique of reappropriating archaic language styles and forms by which she could write lesbianism into literary existence', implying that it was sexuality that provided the impetus for her discovery of an identifiably high modernist method.[121] Indeed, Garvin proposes that the affinity between modernism and sexual otherness is causal:

■ In a culture structured significantly by heterosexism, the mind that can imagine other sexualities and gender identities must also imagine other ways of speaking, new forms to articulate our visions of difference.[122] □

The disruptions to categorisation enacted by writers like Barnes have given critics pause to consider the kinds of classificatory language they use and the paradigms they impose. By far the largest body of research into homosexual feeling and modernism focuses on female writers. Makiko Minow coined the term 'lesbian modernism' in response to Benstock, Hanscombe and Smyer's identification of lesbianism as a source of radical modernist activity and the ethos that bound together the artistic communities that sustained female modernists, whether they experienced same-sex desire or simply resisted heteronormative expectations by resisting bourgeois marriage and motherhood.[123] Benstock herself later made the case that queer women have been excluded from the male, reactionary, homophobic modernist mainstream to the extent that their work constitutes a genre of its own: 'Sapphic modernism'.[124] The labels have subtly different inflections. As Laura Doan notes:

■ Prior to 1928, and for some years after, the terms "lesbian", "homosexual", "sexual invert" or "Sapphist" often overlapped with one another and [...] did not generally connote a specific sexual behaviour, identity or appearance.[125] □

'Sapphist', the term preferred by Virginia Woolf, refers to Sappho, the sixth century BC Greek poetess of Lesbos. Doan chose to name her book *Fashioning Sapphism* (2001) because 'lesbian' only became formed as a cultural concept during the 1928 trial of *The Well of Loneliness*. By contrast, Gay Wachman entitled her book *Lesbian Empire: Radical Crosswriting in the Twenties* (2002) on the basis that 'knowledge of Latin and Greek was a privilege of upper-class men and a basic component of the systems of exclusion that constituted empire'.[126]

In *Lesbian Empire*, Wachman explores the ways in which modernist writers displace sexual difference onto racial difference. She also identifies a practice of 'lesbian crosswriting', which 'transposes the otherwise unrepresentable lives of invisible, silenced, or simply closeted lesbians into narratives about gay men', as a strategy of ambivalence, disguise or escapism.[127] A prime example is *Mr Fortune's Maggot* (1927), a satire on Christian imperialism by the British novelist Sylvia Townsend Warner (1893-1978), concerning the homoerotic experiences of a male missionary. Jane Garrity also explores 'libidinal cross-identification' in her contribution to *Sapphic Modernities: Sexuality, Women and English Culture* (2006).[128] She examines 'the central and ongoing preoccupation' in the life and work of the British writer Mary Butts (1890–1937) 'with the relationship between women – whether straight, bisexual, or lesbian – and gay men', who 'function variously as signs of degeneracy, embodiments of feminine artifice and excess, symptoms of national distress' and also 'sources of poetic inspiration'.[129] Butts herself had many female lovers and was also married twice: first to John Rodker (1894–1955), who published fine editions of books by Ezra Pound, T.S. Eliot and Wyndham Lewis, and then to Gabriel Aitken (1897–1937), a homosexual artist. As Garrity explains, Butts's best-known experimental story, 'Speed the Plough' (*Dial*, 1921), 'focuses on a shell-shocked, homosexually coded veteran of World War I who reads the popular English society and fashion magazine, *The Sketch*'.[130] He is 'exiled to the country in a therapeutic attempt to restore his shell-shocked mind to sanity' and 'assigned the job of cow milking'.[131] In Garrity's reading, Butts 'utilizes masturbatory imagery to convey the young man's fascination with the "hot milk"' which 'suggests semen', but communicates his loathing for 'the heterosexually coded context in which he is forced to observe the white liquid come into contact with the "huge buttocks" of twenty "female animals"'.[132] The veteran longs for the artifice of the metropolis, where he can express 'his attraction to fashionable femininity and his engagement with consumer culture' which are 'constituent components of his homosexuality'.[133] The story ends with the 'provocative, and arguably masochistic, image of the soldier kneeling submissively pinning a petulant woman's dress', gratified in his decision to 'reject heterosexuality and the nostalgic propaganda of rural England' and return to his previous profession as a dress-shop employee.[134] Garrity speculates, 'Perhaps it is precisely the possibility of masochistic pleasure, Butts suggests, that can subvert conventional notions of the relationship between masculinity, sexuality, and desire'.[135]

The figure of cross-identification unsettles categories such as 'lesbian modernism' and 'sapphic modernism'. While these have been effective banners for advancing the literary reputations of queer women, the risk is that they circumscribe and isolate women's achievements, minimize their wider influence and relevance, and ignore points of intersection with other identities and literatures. More recently, critics steeped in queer theory have taken a broader view still, interpreting modernism as a formation structured by male and female sexual desire in all its deviancy and betweenness.

Joseph Boone argues that modernist innovation is intimately concerned with a new understanding of the workings of the libido in *Libidinal Currents: Sexuality and the Shaping of Modernism* (1998). He explores how incipiently modernist narrative techniques were shaped by 'the psychosexual and libidinal energies that, since the advent of turn-of-the-century sexological and psychoanalytic discourses, have come to be seen as constitutive of human subjectivity'.[136] Examples include James Joyce's radical experiments with form in *Ulysses* to represent 'the atemporal, nonchronological, associative processes of mental and libidinal activity', principally Molly's 'uncensored erotic reveries' in 'Penelope' and the 'perversities surfacing in Bloom's subconscious' in 'Circe', and also the short story 'Smoke, Lilies, and Jade' by Richard Bruce Nugent (1906–87).[137] 'Smoke, Lilies, and Jade' was published in the daring single-issue Harlem Renaissance magazine *Fire!! A Quarterly Devoted to Younger Negro Artists* (1926). It presents the drift of Wildean dandy-aesthete and aspiring artist Alex's movements, thoughts and ambiguous erotic desires, as he rises from bed and cruises Harlem's streets. His 'short, disconnected thoughts' are reported using fragmentary free indirect discourse, punctuated by ellipses, which 'represent bridges or lulls in the process of free association' and signal what is 'unsaid or repressed' as he thinks about his mother, his dead father and his attraction to Beauty (a man) and Melva (a woman).[138] Boone notes that for some readers the arrangement of the ellipses on the page 'evoke the ascending spiral of smoke of the title' and/or Alex's 'footsteps as he meanders throughout the city'.[139] The story is thus a striking instance where 'libidinal currents' literally shape new literary forms, producing 'a poetics of the sexually and textually perverse' that is definitively modernist.[140]

Boone suggests that the 'wayward trajectories the libido etches in the subconscious' raise 'issues of same-sex eroticism and same-sex desire' even in texts that are primarily heterosexual in focus.[141] For instance, *The Awakening* (1899) by Kate Chopin evolves beyond the conventions of nineteenth-century realism by simulating the 'libidinal currents' that underlie the protagonist Edna's erotic awakening by 'strategically arranging episodes, sequences, and images according to an associative rather than causal logic, so that externalized action – the objective plot – bears the imprint of interior, subjective states of mind, unsettling attempts to treat the novel's plot in only mimetic terms'.[142] Edna becomes infatuated with Robert, but Boone contends that it is the intensely sensual feelings activated in the company of female friends that leads her 'to explore her latent eroticism'.[143]

As Colleen Lamos argues, 'there is not, on the one hand, a "homosexual" modernism and, on the other hand, a "heterosexual" modernism, but a single literary corpus that is torn in various ways by the scission between these (supposedly) incongruent longings'.[144] Her book *Deviant Modernism: Sexual and Textual Errancy in T.S. Eliot, James Joyce, and Marcel Proust* (1999) re-evaluates central texts of the modernist canon – Eliot's early poetry up to *The Waste Land*, *Ulysses* and *Remembrance of Things Past* (1913) – revealing them to be sites where homoerotic energies, deviant desires and errant impulses are disavowed, or displaced, and struggle unresolved, as their authors engage with the ongoing cultural crises concerning heterosexual masculine definition.

Lamos focuses on the moments when authors 'swerve from their explicit or implicit intentions'.[145] She argues that writers tend to veer away from the ideals formulated in their critical statements when deviant sexual desires are expressed or inadequately repressed. She calls this phenomenon 'errancy' (as in errors that are also errant or wayward). In Eliot's case, these statements are central to the construction of modernism as monolithic, socially conservative and male. Lamos lists four categories of error that were identified by Eliot in his attempts to establish literary norms premised on the authority of a male tradition: 'emotionalism' (as opposed to impersonality); 'inversions of a literary or natural order, including linguistic, poetic, social and sexual hierarchies'; 'the impure mingling of categories'; and 'the dispersion of what should be a unified whole'.[146] She then explores how the 'errancies' Eliot disavows pervade his writing, suggesting that his personal struggle with female power and homosocial impulses manifests in 'violent abjections of femininity and homophobic displacements of male affection'.[147] For instance, Eliot enclosed his sadistic poem 'The Love Song of St Sebastian', where 'the climax of the speaker's devotion to the woman is her strangulation', in a letter which notes the homoerotic tradition in painting that presents Sebastian as a beautiful youth penetrated by arrows.[148]

Whereas Eliot seeks to ward off error, Joyce embraces it. Lamos notes that Stephen Dedalus regards seeming 'mistakes' as 'portals of discovery'.[149] In her reading of *Ulysses*, the secret to be discovered is its queer subtext. Signs of homosexuality proliferate in the novel, 'disclosed through slips, rumors and misrecognitions' that the main characters work hard to ignore or repress.[150] Lamos proposes that the linguistic errors and errors of judgment that arise in the deliberately ungainly 'Eumaeus' episode are intimately related to the question of homosexuality and the panic it induces in those who fear that they might be implicated if they identify it. For instance, she perceives that although Bloom is intrigued by the sailor, D.B. Murphy, he misses the many homosexual clues that surround him. The chapter ends with Bloom and Stephen walking home together, the older man full of plans to install the younger one in his house and, perhaps, in his wife's bed, a circumstance which suggests to Lamos that the subtext that the novel (almost) represses is the potentially erotic dimension to the relationship between the fatherly Bloom and his pseudo-son Stephen.

A broader account of 'Joyce's inclination and aptitude for queering the dichotomy between the "queer" and the "square/straight", for unsettling the normative and hierarchical distinctions between different modes of sexual expression' can be found in *Quare Joyce* (1998), a collection of essays edited by Joseph Valente, which includes a contribution from Lamos.[151] Joyce emerges as an author who binds same-sex and cross-sex energies in 'complex economies of phobia and frisson, ambivalence and abandon, recognition and disavowal, displacement and overdetermination'.[152] Not only does Bloom's 'phantasmagoric transsexualism in the "Circe" episode of *Ulysses*' breach heterosexual norms, but it exposes gender and sexuality as 'contingent and theatrical'.[153]

'[A]matory and sexual alliances' in Joyce's works 'bear an almost exclusively triangular cast', Valente comments, not only 'Bloom – Molly – Stephen', but 'Bloom – Molly – Boylan', 'Richard – Bertha – Robert' (*Exiles*), 'Stephen – E.C. – Cranly' (*Portrait*), and, incestuously, 'Shem – Issy – Shaun' and 'Anna Livia – Humphrey – Issy' (*Finnegans Wake*).[154] In summary, Joyce 'represents all desire as odd and unruly' and 'resists the idea of coherent sexual orientations'.[155]

Just as male writers do not always repress what is queer, female writers do not always embrace transgressive sexuality to reimagine gender relations. In her contribution to *Sapphic Modernities*, Doan notes that the day before *The Well of Loneliness* was published Radclyffe Hall gave an interview to the *Daily Mail*, seizing 'the opportunity to reassure readers that she was by no means radical, and that, on the contrary, she was eager to endorse the social values of the dominant culture'.[156] In this interview, which was published under the headline 'Woman's Place *Is* the Home', Hall emphasised her especial pleasure in housework. She insisted that her career as a writer seldom interferes with homemaking, but advised 'Very few women can do it!'[157] It is clear from the way she treated housework as a leisure activity (supported by domestic staff) that the balance she achieved is only possible because she enjoyed great privilege. Naturally, Hall courted the hostility of feminists such as Vera Brittain (1893–1970), who 'welcomed Hall's radical call for tolerance of sexual abnormality' in *The Well of Loneliness*, but 'criticized her conservative investment in conventional gender roles', complaining that the novel's female heterosexual characters were 'clinging and "feminine" to exasperation'.[158] Doan concludes: 'Under the influence of women such as Radclyffe Hall [...] sapphic modernity evolved in England as a deeply conservative affair, suspicious of feminism and reluctant to challenge the cultural imperatives represented by the very men keen to silence the dangerous modern woman'.[159]

While sexuality was undoubtedly a font of modernist creativity, it was also a source of anxiety, especially where queer identity was concerned. While writers on the margins of the sexual order were well-placed to question convention, those who hankered after respectability sometimes retreated from the radical implications of same-sex desire. And for all the need for secrecy or discretion stimulated innovation, it also enabled modernism's deep and formative relation to the queer workings of the libido to be pushed to its fringes from the outset. The dawning recognition that modernism may be an art produced at the margins of mainstream culture has invigorated modernist studies over the last three decades. Bringing what was once considered peripheral back into the fold has enabled scholars to overturn old orthodoxies not only as regards to sex and gender, but other identities too. The next chapter continues with the theme of modernism at the margins by investigating the complex yet crucial relations between cultural formations in the modernised cities of Europe and America and those of outlying territories.

CHAPTER SIX

Modernist Geographies and Time Frames

The Imperial Metropolis and the Emergence of Modernism

The beginnings of modernism coincided with the aligned projects of capitalist modernisation and Western imperialism. By the 1970s, modernism had been firmly established as an 'art of cities'.[1] Malcolm Bradbury explains that it emerged in the 'cafés and cabarets, magazines, publishers and galleries' of the great European and North American intellectual, cultural and commercial centres – 'through Berlin, Vienna, Moscow and St Petersburg around the turn of the century and into the early years of the war; through London in the years immediately before the war; through Zürich, New York and Chicago during it; and through Paris at all times'.[2] In the 1980s, scholars began to take account of the ways in which imperialism further concentrated wealth, power and prestige in the great European cities, making them even more attractive to immigrants from outlying regions and colonies. Writing in 1985, Raymond Williams agreed that 'the key cultural factor of the modernist shift is the character of the metropolis', but argued that the 'most important general element of the innovations in form is the fact of immigration to the metropolis'.[3] He emphasised 'how many of the major innovators were [...] immigrants', noting 'the elements of strangeness and distance, indeed of alienation, which so regularly form part of the repertory'.[4] Examples of literary migrants who left the stifling provincialism of their homelands to experience the expressive freedoms and artistic cultures of the metropolitan centres of London and Paris include Katherine Mansfield, Claude McKay, Aimé Césaire (1913–2008, born in Martinique), Jean Rhys (born to a British colonial family in Dominica in the West Indies) and Mulk Raj Anand (1905–2004, born in India).

Raymond Williams suggests that the two-way traffic between Europe and her empires created 'cosmopolitan access to a wide variety of subordinate cultures':[5]

■ The preoccupying visual images and styles of particular cultures did not disappear, any more than the native languages, native tales, the native styles of music and dance, but all were now passed through this crucible of the metropolis, which was in the important cases no mere melting pot but an intense and visually and linguistically exciting process in its own right, from which remarkable new forms emerged.[6] □

For its evident man-madeness, its 'complexity and [...] sophistication of social relations', its cosmopolitanism and the influx of immigrants with different cultural values, modes of expression and ways of knowing, the European metropolis was a space where the organisation of society, culture and language no longer seemed natural and given and could be reshaped anew. Recognising that the imperial metropolis – and its art – was invigorated by forces generated beyond its geographical boundaries, Williams made an urgent call for scholars to challenge 'the metropolitan interpretation of its own processes as universals'.[7] He enjoined them to look at cultures from outside the metropolis, 'from the deprived hinterlands, where different forces are moving, and from the poor world which has always been peripheral to the metropolitan systems'.[8]

Mapping the interplay between the urban modernisms of the West and the cultural life of the outlying areas has revolutionised modernist studies. Engaging with postcolonial theory, cultural studies, literary geography and urban sociology, critics in the last two decades have remapped the field, expanding the national range of modernist literatures and attending to their pressing engagement with the politics of race, place and space.

Primitivism

European and North American scholars of modernism paid little attention to the relationship between modernism, empire and race before the late 1980s, with the result that the institutionalised canon of modernism was as white and as 'first world' as it was male. Race only entered the critical understanding of modernism in the form of primitivism: the imitation of artistic forms from other cultures that appeared 'primitive' to Western eyes. Africa and Polynesia in particular were constructed as repositories of primal expression that were appealingly unspoiled and authentic and yet enthrallingly crude and transgressive in their departure from European representational conventions. Indeed, as Simon Gikandi observes, 'there is now enough documentation to show that almost every major modern writer, painter and theorist posited the exotic and the primitive as an alternative to the Western industrial culture many of them were revolting against'.[9] Tristan Tzara, for one, identified concentration and clarity with negritude in 'Note on Negro Art' (1917), and advised 'From blackness, let us extract light. Simple, rich luminous naivety'.[10] Ezra Pound likewise suggested that 'the artist recognises his life in the terms of the Tahiytian [sic] savage'.[11] T.S. Eliot listed 'Byzantine [...], Polynesian, African, Hebridean, Chinese, etc. etc. say savage and Oriental art in general' when he was asked what he thought comprised modern culture in 1919.[12] And D.H. Lawrence sought the seeds of Western regeneration in the far-flung and – to his mind – primitive societies of ancient Australia in *Kangaroo* (1923). All four interpreted their primitive models freely for purposes that would have been alien to the cultures of origin.

Gikandi notes that Eliot and Lawrence 'were attracted to the Bororo or Aztecs because of what appeared to be the primitive's visible difference from modern civilisation, but it is also clear that the radicalness of this difference depended on Euro-American notions about race – the belief that the primitive constituted a different subject, with a different body, and a different system of cognition'.[13] These theories were premised on hierarchical models of race, whereby white Europeans were assumed to be both intellectually and physically superior and on a higher point on the evolutionary scale than darker-skinned races. They found dubious 'scientific' justification in the mid-nineteenth century in Darwin's theories of evolution and natural selection, and particularly Social Darwinism (the social application of natural selection), which opened up the space for a biological interpretation of human history as determined by competition between 'superior' and 'inferior' races. The racial discourses that underwrote white Western modernists' projection of their own defiant sense of difference onto supposedly primitive cultures were the same discourses that were invoked in support of imperialism and – in America – racial segregation.

In terms of the technical progress of art, idealising the primitive amounted to more than a mere cult of the superficially exotic. In *Avant Garde Theatre, 1892–1992* (1993), Christopher Innes identifies primitivism as the principal force motivating modern theatrical experimentation, from Alfred Jarry and August Strindberg, via Expressionism, to Antonin Artaud, and later avant-garde playwrights and practitioners:

■ [Primitivism] has two complementary facets: the exploration of dream states or the instinctive and subconscious levels of the psyche;

and the quasi-religious focus on myth and magic, which in the theatre leads to experiments with ritual and the ritualistic patterning of performance. These are integrated not only by the Jungian concept that all figures of myth are contained in the unconscious as expressions of psychological archetypes, but also by the idea that symbolic or mythopoeic thinking precedes language and discursive reason, revealing fundamental aspects of reality that are unknowable by any other means. Both are variations of the same aim: to return to man's 'roots', whether in the psyche or prehistory. In theatrical terms this is reflected by a reversion to 'original' forms: the Dionysian rituals of ancient Greece, shamanistic performances, the Balinese dance-drama. Along with anti-materialism and revolutionary politics, the hallmark of avant garde drama is an aspiration to transcendence, to the spiritual in its widest sense.[14] □

The combination of regressive primitivism, aesthetic innovation and political radicalism may seem contradictory, but these three characteristics that define avant-garde theatre are in fact complementary, as Innes explains. The return to primal forms signals 'an attempt to replace the dominant modes of drama – and by extension the society of which these are the expression – by rebuilding from first principles'.[15] The desire to rebuild from underlying principles parallels the scientific ethos of the age, which traces phenomena back to their basis. And this scientific ethos manifests itself in the avant-garde's 'transformation of the stage into a laboratory for exploring fundamental questions about the nature of performance and the relationship between actor and audience'.[16] In Innes's definition, the avant-garde returns to 'the "roots" of theatre – whether in its primitive origins or by divesting it of scenic or illusionistic "accretions" – as much as to the psychological or prehistoric "roots" of man'.[17] What unites avant-garde theatre, in Innes's view, is hostility to Western society and a commitment to 'transforming the nature of theatrical performance'.[18]

Postcolonial Theory

Empire, race and the two-way cultural traffic between imperial powers and colonised territories have become important themes for modernist studies in the wake of postcolonial theory. Postcolonial theory seeks to understand the power relations produced by European imperial expansion. Its insights apply from the very moment of colonial incursion onwards. The foundational text is Edward Said's *Orientalism* (1978), which examines how European discourses of knowledge were used to assemble a prejudicial construction of Eastern culture as 'Other'.[19] Said offers the following summary:

■ At the heart of European culture during the many decades of imperial expansion lay what could be called an undeterred and unrelenting Eurocentrism. This accumulated experiences, territories, peoples, histories; it studied them, classified them, verified them; but above all, it subordinated them to the culture and indeed the very idea of white Christian Europe. [...] All of the subjugated peoples had it in common that they were considered to be naturally subservient to a superior, advanced, developed, and morally mature Europe, whose role in the non-European world was to rule, instruct, legislate, develop, and at the proper times, to discipline, war against, and occasionally exterminate non-Europeans.[20] □

Postcolonial theory interrogates the effects of the hegemonic imposition of Western languages, discourses and cultural practices on the formation of colonial subjects, examining strategies of assimilation and resistance.

Postcolonial theory has triggered debates as to how far Anglo-American and European modernism might be a product of colonial expansion. Imperial domination peaked in the years when modernism was at its height. 'By 1914', Said records, 'Europe held [...] roughly 85 per cent of the earth as colonies, protectorates, dependencies, dominions, and commonwealths'.[21] The Nigerian novelist Chinua Achebe questions whether early European modernism in fact constitutes a form of colonial discourse that replicates and reinforces imperialist ideologies of empire and race in his blistering critique 'An Image of Africa: Racism in Conrad's *Heart of Darkness*' (1977). He denounces Joseph Conrad's novella as 'an offensive and deplorable book' for representing 'Africa as a metaphysical battlefield devoid of all recognisable humanity, into which the wandering European enters at his peril'.[22] 'Can nobody', Achebe asks, 'see the preposterous and perverse arrogance in thus reducing Africa to the role of props for the break-up of one petty European mind?'[23] Noting that the encounter with the colonial Other is a means to confront the savagery barely concealed within the civilised European, Achebe comments: 'It is not the differentness that worries Conrad but the lurking hint of kinship'.[24] Achebe also quashes the idea that African culture is primitive, citing Picasso's celebrated first encounter with West African sculpture (1905) in the guise of an African mask, which provided the germ for Cubism:

■ The mask in question was made by other savages living just north of Conrad's River Congo. They have a name too: the Fang people, and are without a doubt among the world's greatest masters of the sculptured form.[25] □

As Achebe explains, Conrad's depiction of grunting savages is 'grossly inadequate even at the height of their subjection to the ravages of [the Belgian] King Leopold's International Association for the Civilization of Central Africa'.[26]

Said mounts a qualified defence of Conrad in *Culture and Imperialism* (1993), noting that 'Conrad's narrators are not average unreflecting witnesses of European imperialism': 'they worry about it, they are actually quite anxious about whether they can make it seem like a routine thing'.[27] Said maintains that the way that 'Conrad sets the [telling of Marlow's] story on the deck of a boat anchored in the Thames' as darkness falls, gesturing to 'an undefined and unclear world' beyond, encourages readers 'to sense the potential of a reality that seemed inaccessible to imperialism, just beyond its control, and that only well after Conrad's death in 1924 acquired a substantial presence'.[28] For Said, then, it is the formal devices that Conrad uses to draw attention to the constructed nature of 'imperial metropolitan discourse' and a hazy reality beyond that opens up the possibility of critique.[29] Conrad's 'tragic limitation', in Said's view, 'is that even though he could see clearly that on one level imperialism was essentially pure dominance and land-grabbing, he could not then conclude that imperialism had to end so that "natives" could lead lives free from European domination'.[30] For Said, modernist works, and those of Conrad in particular, replace the 'optimism, affirmation, and serene confidence' of high imperialism and instead 'radiate an extreme, unsettling anxiety' concerning the ethics of the self-interested imperialist ideology of progress, commercialism and enlightenment.[31] Indeed, Said suggests, 'many of the most prominent characteristics of modernist culture, which we have tended to derive from purely internal dynamics in Western society and culture, include a response to the external pressures on culture from the *imperium*'.[32]

Irish Modernism

Modernist culture did not only include a response to external pressures from the imperium, but was also generated within, as the richness of Irish modernism attests. Ireland's position in the history of empire is complex. Before the establishment of the Irish Free State in 1922, Ireland was part of the United Kingdom (as formalised through the 1801 Act of Union). It was part of a colonising power, but it was also a colonised territory, ruled from Westminster. For some critics, Ireland's geographical proximity to Britain and complicity in the British imperial enterprise overseas interferes with its claim to postcolonial status.[33] While Ireland's situation was certainly different to that of colonies in

Africa and Asia, to deny the relevance of postcolonial approaches is to overlook the strong evidence that Ireland was an underdeveloped periphery oppressed by its unequal relationship to the modernised imperial centre, London.

Nationalism, Colonialism, and Literature (1990), a three-essay volume introduced by Seamus Deane and issued by the Field Day Theatre Company (founded in 1980 with the aim of responding to Ireland's political situation in a socially, ethically and creatively conscientious manner) is the inaugural postcolonial account of Irish modernism. Deane presents the radical dispossession enacted by colonialism as the primary motivating factor for Irish modernists' extraordinary experiments with language:

■ The recovery from the lost Irish language has taken the form of an almost vengeful virtuosity in the English language, an attempt to make Irish English a language in its own right rather than an adjunct to English itself. [...] Yeats, Joyce, and Synge present its characteristic features most fully, but others do so in slightly less complete array – Wilde [...], Shaw, and Beckett.[34] □

The book's central thesis is that 'the dynamic and central energy' of the remarkable literature that Ireland produced in the first three decades of the twentieth century was 'the attempt to overcome and replace the colonial experience by something other, something that would be "native" and yet not provincial'.[35]

In his contribution, Said presents W.B. Yeats as a postcolonial poet, who, despite his 'settled presence in Ireland, in British culture and literature, and in European modernism', belongs nonetheless to the tradition of 'anti-imperialist resistance' for his role in articulating 'the experiences, the aspirations, and the vision of a people suffering under the dominion of an offshore power' and 'restoring a suppressed history, and rejoining the nation to it'.[36] Fredric Jameson, on the other hand, locates modernism's engagement with imperialism in terms of the way it represents space. In *Howards End* (1910), E.M. Forster presents the intertwined fates of three families in England, the wealthy Wilcoxes, who made their riches in the colonies, the cultured Schlegels and the working-class Basts. As Jameson observes, Forster imagines the colonies beyond the ken of Howards End symbolically with reference to the transport networks and trade routes of Empire that stretch out into infinity, 'beyond the bounds and borders of the national state', a circumstance which points to the spatial disjunction created by imperial conquest.[37] From this proto-modernist text, Jameson draws the conclusion that the colonial system cannot be fully comprehended because so much of it is elsewhere and the experiences of the colonisers and the colonised are mutually unimaginable. Modernism, Jameson proposes, was radically transformed when writers set out to address this disjunction by developing 'a new spatial language', which 'becomes the marker and the substitute [...] of the unrepresentable totality' that is the imperium.[38] Jameson's prime example is *Ulysses*. He proposes that James Joyce overcomes the 'representational dilemmas of the new imperial world system' spatially and linguistically.[39] Joyce simultaneously maps Dublin as a First World metropolis and a colonial city, slyly turning 'imperial relations inside out, appropriating the great imperial space of the Mediterranean [the setting of Homer's *Odyssey*] in order to organize the space of the colonial city'.[40] He also plays with the shared colonial language, eschewing any singular style for a series of 'linguistic games and experiments' with 'impersonal sentence combinations and variations' that place the novel 'beyond all point of view'.[41] As Jameson sees it, imperialism is constitutive of modernist form and style.

Postcolonial readings of Irish literature have been hugely productive in recent years. The greatest body of work has focused on Joyce, undoing the high canonical view that he turned his back on the Irish Literary Revival and later the Irish nationalist cause and sought refuge from political realities by immersing himself in purely aesthetic experimentation. Vincent Cheng's book *Joyce, Race and Empire* (1995) was the first full-length study to argue that 'Joyce wrote insistently from the perspective of a colonial subject of an oppressive empire, and that Joyce's representations of "race" in its relationship to imperialism constitute a trenchant and significant political commentary, not only on British imperialism in Ireland, but colonial discourse in general'.[42] For instance, the Latin mass that Buck Mulligan intones at the beginning of *Ulysses* was originally 'sung by the Hebrews in Babylonian exile', evoking the 'Hebraic history of displacement, diaspora, and struggle for one's homeland and for Home Rule'.[43] Mulligan stands in the Martello Tower, which, to the annoyance of Stephen, is occupied by a British presence (Haines), whose father 'made his fortune by colonial exploitation'.[44]

Cheng explores how Joyce turns the mutually derogatory analogies that Victorians habitually constructed between Irishmen and other races that they considered to be of lower order to suggest 'a solidarity of the marginalized and othered' in his essays and fictional works.[45] He argues that Joyce shows 'the Orientalized construction of Other peoples' to be 'a hegemonic discourse created by colonialism'.[46] For instance, the narrator of the *Dubliners* story 'Araby' longs to attend a bazaar in order to buy something to impress a girl that he likes, conceiving the 'Orient/Other/Exotic' as 'the spiritually liberating alternative to a stifling paralysis' that afflicts Dublin.[47] However, far from living up to the boy's romantic imaginings, 'the bazaar is exemplified by a shabby stall presided over by vulgar English accents'.[48] He leaves empty-handed, angry and self-reproachful. 'Araby', Cheng concludes, 'is finally a parable about Ireland as much as about an Orientalized Other'; 'an Ireland whose soul and self have been debased and prostituted to political and economic imperialism'.[49]

Cheng proceeds to explore how Joyce deconstructs the very notions 'of an essentialist (and suspiciously convenient) distinction between insider and outsider, between native and foreigner, between Self and Other [...]', most particularly in *Ulysses* and *Finnegans Wake*.[50] Cheng observes that Irish-born 'Leopold Bloom finds himself repeatedly stereotyped and essentialized by his fellow male Dubliners as a foreigner and a "dirty Jew", enduring racial slurs and anti-Semitic comments', but notes Bloom's 'self-conscious and unceasing scepticism and questioning of such constructed images' and his ability 'to *imagine* the Other's perspective'.[51] Bloom insists on solidarity and refuses to reproduce the binary hierarchies inherited from the colonial oppressors. For instance, Bloom challenges the Citizen, a Fenian nationalist who asserts the unambiguous purity of the Irish race. Bloom even fantasises about the creation of a New Jerusalem that will unify all the races of the world.[52] As an exile who lived in the cosmopolitan cities of Trieste, Paris and Zürich, Joyce's ambitions for Ireland and Irish literature were international. His subversive, inclusive example would prove crucial for many of the writers emerging from the colonies.

Space, Place and Pace

Jameson's account of modernism and empire inaugurated a 'spatial turn', prompting critics to investigate the social and political significance of the geographies, imaginative and actual, represented in modernist texts, from domestic spaces to urban monuments to the cartographies of empire. Their readings take account of the new philosophies, scientific advances and technologies that transformed how space was conceptualised.

An early study positing a causal link between 'new modes of thinking about and experiencing time and space' and modernist representational strategies is Stephen Kern's *The Culture of Time and Space: 1880–1918* (1983).[53] He sets the spatial disorientations of Cubism and analogous experiments with multi-perspectival, temporally subjective, discontinuous experimental literary forms in many different contexts. They include: Albert Einstein's theories of relativity and the proposition that time dilates according to the relative motion of observed objects, and the notion of the space-time continuum; Henri Bergson's formulation of the real duration of time as it is subjectively experienced; the theory of 'perspectivism' outlined by Spanish philosopher José Ortega y Gasset (1883–1955), which proposes that 'there as many realities as points of view'; 'instantaneous electronic communication, which made simultaneity a reality' and 'extended the present spatially'; the airplanes that enabled travellers to vault 'the traditional geographical barriers between peoples' and brought the faraway near; and X-ray machines that revealed the interior of solid objects.[54] Not only is the new spatial configuration registered in art and literature, but also in theatrical conventions. Of August Strindberg's *A Dream Play,* Kern notes 'Props and sets are transmuted along with the dimensions of time and space. Backdrops rise or separate to reveal new interior spaces, characters age in a few seconds and exit straight through walls'.[55]

Andrew Thacker offers a clear account of the complex theories of spatiality that have helped critics to think about the ways in which modernist texts create 'metaphorical spaces that try to make sense of the material spaces of modernity' in *Moving Through Modernity: Space and Geography in Modernism* (2003).[56] He explains Henri Lefebvre's conception of 'social space' as a 'product literally filled with ideologies', formed through 'spatial practices' ('what people do in spaces'), *'representations of space'* ('space as *perceived* by planners, architects, and governments [...] drawn on plans, maps and diagrams') and *'representational spaces'* ('space as *imagined* by inhabitants' that 'result in symbolic and artistic productions').[57] He touches on Michael Foucault's idea that 'social relations of power infuse all spatial sites and concepts' and his concept of the 'heterotopia' (a real place, which is reimagined so that power relations can be represented, contested and inverted).[58] And he explores Michel de Certeau's distinctions between *space* (constituted by acting or moving subjects) and *place* (a static defined location), and the difference between the *tour* (described by 'the actions of human subjects through spaces') and the *map* ('a totalizing stage on which elements of various origin are brought together to form the tableau of a "state" of geographical knowledge').[59]

Thacker investigates how modernist writers register and interrogate diverse social spaces, oscillating between space and place, tour and map, and the psychic spaces of inner thoughts and external reality. He suggests that the rapid movement between social spaces produces that distinctively modernist 'keenly felt sense of disorientation – at once both thrilling and anxious'.[60] A prime example is *Voyage in the Dark* (1934) by Jean Rhys. In a reversal of the imperialist trope of the voyage out, the white Creole heroine Anna Morgan, the daughter of a planter, voyages *into* the imperial capital to learn how to become an English lady. Instead, she encounters poverty, monotony and xenophobia in London's *demi-monde*. Disorientated by the contrast between 'her dulled existence in England' and recollections of 'her vivid life in Dominica',

Anna's consciousness swings between the two locations, increasingly unable to distinguish which is real and which is a dream.[61] 'The blurring of boundaries', Thacker comments, 'illustrates the disorientating power of modernity' and 'contests the dominant imperial "representation of space"'.[62] As Anna Snaith notes, in London, Rhys's heroine 'feels herself colonized, enslaved', an experience 'that changes the basis of her identification with black West Indians from freedom and vitality to victimization and rebellion'.[63] And so, paradoxically, 'It is in the metropolis – characterized by the economics of empire – that she [Anna Morgan] comes closer to an understanding of slavery'.[64]

Thacker's study focuses on the *flâneurs* and – innovatively – the *voyageurs* who move through the social spaces of modernity, attending to the new technologies of transportation that shaped their experiences of the fast-paced, newly globalised world. He examines the surprising number of Imagist poems by male authors set on urban transport, especially the underground (which Filippo Marinetti praised for providing 'a totally new idea of motion, of speed').[65] What Imagist travel poetry celebrates, Thacker contends, is not necessarily speed, but the underground railway as a spatially disorientating phenomenon that 'profoundly altered the visual experience of space and time in the city' (for instance by cutting travel times and reconfiguring its populous and commercial hubs) and provided a stage for 'a poetic encounter which could stress fixity amid the vertiginous bustle of modernity'.[66] He suggests that the anxiety of the individual amid the crowd manifests in poems like Richard Aldington's 'In the Tube', where confinement and proximity produce a 'gaze of mutual antipathy'.[67] The other passengers are 'punitively anatomised by the poet's gaze' as it is displaced from the row of advertisements to the row of windows, to the row of faces to the row of eyes, 'rendered static and "immobile" [...] within the "swaying train" travelling at speed through the "dingy tunnel"'.[68] The 'people become like adverts, images proclaiming their availability for visual consumption'.[69] Thacker suggests that 'In a Station of the Metro' likewise 'registers the desire to escape the suffocations of the crowd by producing a distance sufficient to view with detachment the faces of other passengers' and that 'Pound's "faces in the crowd" are merely fixed images to be consumed'.[70] Thacker notes that when the poem first appeared in *Poetry*, it was divided 'into six discrete images, six linguistic units parcelled off from one another by blank spaces', each unit 'striving to render only one thing – the faces, the crowd, the petals, the bough', creating 'an innovative representational space in Lefebvre's terms, that was to be developed in Pound's later writings'.[71] It is a key example of the ways in which 'Social space forces itself [...] into the very crevices of the text', revealing how 'the culture of transport affects the spatial form of Imagist poetry'.[72]

The work that has received the most spatial scrutiny is *Ulysses*. It is, in Michael Seidel's words, 'a novel of carefully recorded movements over carefully mapped spaces'.[73] 'To see Joyce at work on the "Wandering Rocks"', Frank Budgen reminisced in 1934, 'was to see [...] a surveyor with theodolite and measuring chain'.[74] The 'Wandering Rocks' consists of eighteen short snapshots of city life, in chronological sequence, interrupted by some thirty-three interpolations, detailing simultaneous events elsewhere, and a coda which presents characters' reactions as the viceregal cavalcade passes them by. And so, as Thacker proposes, 'the spatial form of the novel, as Frank termed it, is [...] intimately connected to the kinds of movements through the social spaces of the city itself'.[75] Thacker argues that the geography mapped in *Ulysses* is actually informed by 'a tour discourse, which emphasises the *movements* and histories by which a particular space or place came into being'.[76] Readers of the novel encounter many tours and spatial stories as the characters move through the city. For instance, the viceregal cavalcade, 'the triumphal display of imperial power through the streets of the subjugated capital', crosses '*Royal* Canal bridge', 'Kingsbridge' and 'Parliament Street', all 'sites redolent of past Irish parliamentary power, as well as toponyms with a suitably regal flavour'.[77] The fact that the real-life procession happened several days before 16 June 1904 and did not involve a viceregal cavalcade, and 'so could not have been seen in either the time or the space of the novel', suggests to Thacker that the coda to 'Wandering Rocks' functions heterotopically to emphasise the spatial form of colonial power.[78]

Thacker is also attentive to the way that Joyce's depiction of Dublin locates 'gender and sexuality within the social spaces of the modernist city'.[79] Griselda Pollock proposes that 'the *flâneur* symbolizes the [male] privilege or freedom to move about the public arenas of the city observing but never interacting, consuming the sights through a controlling but rarely-acknowledged gaze [...] which is both covetous and erotic'.[80] Elizabeth Wilson disagrees, arguing that far from representing 'the triumph of masculine power', the failure of the *flâneur's* gaze to 'annihilate the castrate, woman' and the threat that she poses to the Oedipal order in fact 'represents masculinity as unstable, caught up in the violent dislocations that characterized urbanization'.[81] Thacker draws on Wilson's work to suggest that Bloom's voyeuristic misadventures provide evidence that 'the masculine gaze is foiled by [...] modern metropolitan life'.[82] He cites the time that Bloom stands in line at the butchers and regrets that he cannot catch up with a passing young woman, whose legs he objectifies as pieces of meat, and his later frustration when a woman's expensively stockinged legs are obscured by a passing tram.

Janet Wolff and Griselda Pollock suggest that there could be no female *flâneuse* in the nineteenth century because 'the ideology of women's place in the domestic realm permeated the whole of society' and so women 'were never positioned as the normal occupants of the public realm' and 'did not have the right to look, to stare, scrutinize or watch'.[83] However, as Scott McCracken argues, the rise of socially respectable feminine leisure spaces, such as department stores and tea shops, made the city newly accessible to lower-middle- and middle-class women towards the end of the nineteenth century.[84]

In 'Walking, Women and Writing: Virginia Woolf as Flâneuse' (1992), Rachel Bowlby explores the ways in which Woolf revises the Baudelairean tradition where 'The place of the walker as writer is marked out as a masculine identity which places woman already as part of the representation' (as in Baudelaire's poem '*A une passante*', 'To a Passing Woman' (1861)).[85] She notes that the first thing that Clarissa says in *Mrs Dalloway* is that she loves walking in London. In that same novel, Peter Walsh's pursuit of a *passante* is humorously sent up as the figure of his fantasy rebuffs his gaze. Furthermore, *A Room of One's Own* is structured as an 'imaginary ramble' through 'Oxbridge', London and the British Museum; and Woolf's short story 'Street Haunting: A London Adventure' (1930) presents the five leisurely hours the narrator spends sauntering through London with the only ostensible aim of buying a pencil, explicitly connecting female creativity with 'strolling and story-making'.[86]

African-American Modernism

In spite of New Negro writers' efforts to establish their work as 'the advance-guard of the African peoples', it was not until the publication of Houston Baker's *Modernism and the Harlem Renaissance* (1987) that black American modernism gained wide institutional recognition.[87] Baker challenges those who faulted the Harlem Renaissance 'for its "failure" to produce *vital, original, effective,* or "modern" art in the manner [...] of British, Anglo-American, and Irish creative endeavours'.[88] He asserts that the real subject of Western (white) modernism is not the perilous state of modern civilisation, but more specifically the breakdown of the 'assumed supremacy of boorishly racist, indisputably sexist, and unbelievably wealthy Anglo-Saxon males', a topic that was inimical to black writers.[89] In order to recognise how the African-American artists and writers gathered in Harlem succeeded in 'defining themselves in "modern" terms', Baker argues, that readers must attend to the strategies they used to create a '*modern Afro-American sound,* as a function of a *specifically* Afro-American discursive practice'.[90]

In Baker's formulation, African-American modernism emerges when writers discover 'the mastery of form' and 'the deformation of mastery'.[91] The form that is mastered is the mask of blackface minstrelsy (the nineteenth-century popular entertainment where white actors masqueraded as African-Americans and performed aspects of black folk-culture from dialects to songs and dances). In Baker's reading, this development was 'a primary move in Afro-American discursive modernism', because it enabled writers to conform to the stereotypes that the dominant white culture found reassuring while criticising them from within.[92] Houston dates this move a full fifteen years before Woolf's famous watershed. He echoes her formulation to identify 'a change in Afro-American nature that occurred on or about September 18, 1895', on the day that the political advisor and educator Booker T. Washington (1856–1915) gave the opening address at the Negro exhibit of the Atlanta Cotton States and International Exposition, and adopted the discourse of minstrelsy in order to subvert it.[93] The second move, 'the deformation of mastery', is more radical still. It consists in the deliberate deformation of accepted critical standards by recuperating indigenous sounds and art forms, such as African spirituals and folk songs, that seem inarticulate or deformed to outsiders, as the basis for a proud, modern, black identity, as seen in the writings of W.E.B. Du Bois and Paul Lawrence Dunbar (1872–1906). Baker concludes with a discussion of Alain Locke's *The New Negro*, which followed the precedent set by Du Bois's *The Souls of Black Folk* by including spirituals and folk songs among its anthologised pieces.

Baker's strategy for revising the canon of successful art in *Modernism and the Harlem Renaissance* is to tender a new paradigm that makes no reference to high modernism. For all the mastery of Baker's analysis, he pays no heed to the concerns, friendships, professional encounters and artistic communities that connected African-American writers to their more widely celebrated counterparts. He also treats T.S. Eliot, Joseph Conrad and James Joyce as if they are representatives of the same culture. Baker would later revise this approach, putting the idea of a separate genre defined by a specifically black sound aside to recast it anew in political terms as 'the achievement of a life-enhancing and empowering public sphere mobility and the economic solvency of the black majority'.[94]

In *The Dialect of Modernism: Race, Language and Twentieth-Century Literature* (1994), Michael North reveals 'linguistic mimicry and racial masquerade' to be an unrecognised link connecting high modernism and the Harlem Renaissance.[95] North's starting point is George Bernard Shaw's play *Pygmalion* (1912), in which a professor of phonetics (Henry Higgins) teaches a cockney flower girl (Eliza Doolittle) standard English pronunciation so that she might pass for a duchess. Shaw claimed that the purpose of the play was to dramatise the need for a 'standard English'.[96] North makes the case that the mask of black dialect provided authors with a means to rebel against the strictures of the standard language movement that began in the 1880s as 'Urbanization and mass emigration brought together all sorts of languages, dialects, and idiolects previously separated by space and social difference'.[97]

The imperial promotion of pure English as culturally superior impacted on non-native writers like Conrad, a polyglot whose English was not standard. As North explains, 'to live and write in constant remembrance of linguistic difference, is, as Conrad's friends and associates always reminded him, to be a racial outcast'.[98] North reads Conrad's contradictory presentation of linguistic and racial difference in *The Nigger of the 'Narcissus'* in this light. He argues that Conrad figures his own linguistic 'marginality in the person of a black alter ego', James Wait:[99]

■ Thus he [Conrad] is simultaneously an outside observer, rendering his account in the third person, and an anonymous member of the crew; he is both 'the nigger' and the crew that can barely understand him. And the ship is simultaneously the site of entry for any and all foreigners who may come, Polish or West Indian, a polyglot linguistic community in which communication is carried out in a language that belongs to no one, and a metaphorical version of dear England itself, safe only when it has finally dropped its racial outsiders overboard.[100] □

North presents life aboard the Narcissus as a prototype for the modernism that is shaped by 'the contradictions of European colonialization' and is constituted and yet profoundly disturbed by racial and linguistic difference.[101] This difference, North explains, is both constitutive and radically disruptive of the work announced in the preface to *The Nigger of the 'Narcissus'*: the task of making the reader *see* the *truth* of 'the subtle but invincible conviction of solidarity [...] which binds together all humanity'.[102] It is for this reason, North suggests, that the 'preface remains a valid introduction to the rest of modernism'.[103]

North turns his attention to Pablo Picasso and Gertrude Stein's simultaneous discovery of African art and racial masquerade. He notes that in 1906 'Picasso ended a long struggle with his portrait of Stein by repainting a likeness he had labored over for as many as ninety-two sittings', superimposing 'a flat, expressionless mask with two eye slits cut as against the angle of the rest of the face and body', inspired by ancient Iberian reliefs.[104] It was one of the first incarnations of what would later be called Cubism. Stein likewise 'struggled unsuccessfully to account for an unhappy love affair' and then adopted a black mask and 'rewrote the story [...] as "Melanctha"'.[105] 'In each case', North notes, 'the step away from conventional verisimilitude into abstraction is accomplished by a figurative change of race'.[106]

North proceeds to explore the highly artificial 'dialect mouthed by Stein, Eliot and Pound, and other white writers' that sounded 'a good deal more like Uncle Remus than any actual African-American speaker of the 1920s'.[107] Uncle Remus (a former slave) was the fictional narrator of the popular late nineteenth-century African-American folktales and fables adapted by Joel Chandler Harris (1845–1908), including the Brer Rabbit stories. His patois provided the inspiration for the private language and roles adopted by Ezra Pound (Brer Rabbit) and T.S. Eliot (Possum). North presents Eliot's experiments as a 'blackface comedian' in his obscene unpublished screed about 'King Bolo's big black queen', the references to minstrel songs that were finally removed from *The Waste Land*, and the unfinished dramatic piece *Sweeney Agonistes* (1926–27), which was 'titled in a late typescript "Fragment of a Comic Minstrelsy"', as evidence of the anxious appeal of racial mimicry.[108] The anxiety is registered in Eliot's poem 'The Hollow Men' (1925), which quotes as its first epigraph one of Conrad's most notorious pieces of dialect from *Heart of Darkness*: "Mistah Kurtz – he dead".[109] Here, North suggests, 'Eliot's speaker suffers the utter loss of identity that comes from crossing the line that delimits the races'.[110] This insight leads North to suggest that *The Waste Land* 'was informed from the beginning by the drastically different possibilities opened up by such a transgression: modernist freedom afforded by the drastic mix of styles; the paralyzed horror, the loss of an identity once underwritten by secure racial boundaries'.[111]

North also considers the impact of Anglophilia on American writers who were not expatriates, including key figures in the Harlem Renaissance. He draws attention to how hard it was for Harlem Renaissance writers 'to be both linguistically and stylistically challenging' as they fought their way 'out of the prison of white-created black dialect'.[112] Claude McKay, for instance, was bewildered when his wealthy English patron urged him to drop his standard English 'in favor of the Jamaican dialect'.[113] McKay then produced *Songs of Jamaica* and *Constab Ballads* (both 1912), which 'gained him widespread praise as the first educated black West Indian to bring the dialect into English verse'.[114] He was later advised: 'If you mean to be a modern Negro writer, you should go and meet Gertrude Stein'.[115] As North observes, the need to negotiate 'past two sets of white expectations about the character of black language and art', left 'little free space [...] between traditionalism and modernism'.[116] Recognising this difficulty 'makes it easier to appreciate the true distinction of African-American writing'.[117]

According to North, the only Harlem writer who moved beyond the terms of the linguistic struggle created between the avant-garde's attempts to 'make modernism into a dialect so as to challenge the cultural supremacy of the English' and black writers' attempts to 'make dialect into a modern literature so as to avoid the primitivizing pressures' was Zora Neale Hurston, whose writings celebrate folk expression as mimicry and performance.[118] 'It is this struggle', North contends, 'that allows us to discuss Anglo-American modernism and African-American writing in the same context, and thus to understand how thoroughly each kind of writing was marked, for good or bad, by the other'.[119] 'Modernism', in North's account, 'mimicked the strategies of dialect and aspired to become a dialect itself'.[120] And thus 'linguistic mimicry and racial masquerade were not just shallow fads but strategies without which modernism could not have arisen'.[121]

Global Modernisms

'Across the Empire, during the first half of the twentieth century, colonized élites, articulate though embattled, began to organize cultural revivals, or raised their voices in protest at imperial power', as Elleke Boehmer notes in *Colonial and Postcolonial Literature* (1995).[122] Like the writers of the Harlem Renaissance, their literary struggle was to discover a progressive but authentic voice.

As nationalist anti-imperial campaigns for independence gathered strength and momentum during the 1920s and 1930s, support for empire dwindled. By 1928, Leonard Woolf, a former servant of the British empire, was convinced that 'Imperialism, as it was known in the nineteenth century, is no longer possible, and the only question is whether it will be buried peacefully or in blood and ruins'.[123] Homi Bhabha associates the crisis in colonial authority with *hybridity*, the condition of being caught between the cultural identities that are brought together when colonial powers impose themselves on indigenous populations. In *The Location of Culture* (1994), Bhabha emphasises the disquieting effects the Other sets in motion within colonial discourse: 'In the very practice of domination the language of the master becomes hybrid – neither one thing nor the other'.[124] For all the efforts to manufacture obedient colonial subjects who conform to the dominant culture, colonial superiority is resisted. With 'sly civility', the Other unstably reproduces the identity of the coloniser as mimicry, becoming 'almost the same but not quite', being 'Almost the same but not white'.[125] The act of mimicry reflexively questions the authority of the discourses that colonial powers seek to impose, instilling deep unease. As Bhabha explains, 'mimicry is at once resemblance and menace'.[126]

Movements of opposition and nationalist (or nativist) affirmation inevitably found their literary expression in the hybridity and mimicry that Bhabha describes. As Boehmer explains, 'literary conventions and discourses inherited from the colonizer were appropriated, translated, decentred, and hybridized in ways which we now name postcolonial but were in fact at the time anti-colonial, often opportunistic, tactical, and *ad hoc,* and which formed an important means of self-expression'.[127] Iconoclastic modernist texts supplied emergent writers from the colonies with 'useful decentring strategies, ways of dismantling the dominant patterns of European thought' and 'symbolic languages for interpreting the rapidly changing reality':[128]

> ■ Starting before the Great War but especially during the decades follow-ing, writers like Rabindranath Tagore (India), Claude McKay (Jamaica), Raja Rao (India) and Solomon Plaatje (South Africa) took up the West-ern genres of the novel, sonnet and short story to articulate their own perceptions of cultural space and experience. [...] From the 1930s, for Bengali poets in English such as Bishnu De, the fragmented structures of Eliot's work, and later those of Auden, suggested ways of giving conceptual shape to local urban experience. [...] A later generation of West Indian poets, too, lent an ear to Eliot in their attempt to recon-cile European poetic forms with creole. The allusive, disjunctive style of modernist poetry would also suggest to African writers at the time of independence ways of representing the stark contrasts of their post-colonial experience. As Wole Soyinka put it, from the 1950s onwards Nigerian poets sought to 'regroup images of Ezra Pound around the oil bean and the nude spear'. [...] Again, for Césaire in the 1930s, surreal-ist techniques based on Freudian and Jungian ideas helped to create an 'insurrectional', 'hell-bound' poetry with which to undercut imprisoning forms of Western conceptual thought. Mulk Raj Anand described himself in Joycean terms as forging with the help of modernist techniques 'the uncreated conscience of [his] race'.[129] □

As Simon Gikandi notes, 'The archive of early postcolonial writing in Africa, the Caribbean, and India is dominated and defined by writers whose political or cultural projects were enabled by modernism even when the ideologies of the latter, as was the case with Eliot, were at odds with the project of decolonization'.[130]

Gikandi reflects on the wide appeal of canonical modernism for writers in Africa, the Americas, the Caribbean and the Harlem Renais-sance, in spite of its frequent recourse to 'race as a way of dealing with the pathologies associated with industrial civilisation', in 'Race and the Modernist Aesthetic' (1997).[131] When modernism projected its 'worst fears and anxieties – and sometimes its erotic desires – onto the bodies of (black) others whom it also used as the conduit through which it could psychoanalyse its discontents and, at the same time, as a medium for developing a new language of the self', it connected 'race and aes-thetics at the most fundamental level' and paradoxically 'sought to make blackness an essential condition in the establishment of aesthetic principles'.[132] For all high modernism's Eurocentricism and '(mis)use of black subjects', as Gikandi recognises, its fundamental dependence on blackness enabled the movement 'to be read, especially by colonized black writers, as a mode of liberation of race itself'.[133]

Over the last twenty years, the geographical reach of modernism has been radically expanded as critics have adjusted their focus to include modernisms from beyond the confines of Europe and America. This work has questioned the validity of definitions and genealogies that narrowly focus on Western culture. To give but one example, David Craven proposes that 'the term "modernism" (or *modernismo*) was in fact invented on the periphery of the world economic order by Rubén Darío [(1867–1916)] of Nicaragua, Latin America's first internationally acclaimed modern author', repudiating the notion that non-Western modernisms are reactive and belated.[134] According to Craven, Darío 'inaugurated Latin America's earliest genuine avant-garde movement under the banner of *modernism*' in 1888–89.[135] His *modernismo* 'in such poems as *Azul* (1888) constituted a hybrid fusion of various artistic modes', featuring heterogeneous citations that were European, non-European, precolonial, colonial and postcolonial in origin.[136] (Nicaragua achieved independence from Spain in 1821). Craven argues that the Latin American term *modernismo* then crossed the Atlantic to Barcelona to refer to analogous strategies and thematic concerns in the architectural projects of Antoni Gaudí (1852–1926), which 'are now associated with the European avant-garde and various tendencies of modernism in the more widely acknowledged sense'.[137]

In the last decade, modernist studies has taken what Douglas Mao and Rebecca Walkowitz describe as a 'transnational turn' to explore local modernisms in the context of global modernity, examining 'complex intellectual and economic transactions, among, for example, Europe, Africa, the United States, and the Caribbean'.[138] A landmark text is *Geomodernisms: Race, Modernism and Modernity* (2005), an essay collection edited by Laura Doyle and Laura Winkiel. It seeks to de-Westernise modernism by identifying new strains from overlooked parts of the world and situating celebrated modernist works in alternative transnational genealogies. Contributions encompass 'aesthetic projects in Cuba, Taiwan, China, South Africa, Lebanon, Haiti, Brazil, India, Wyoming, the Congo, London and New York'.[139] What unites the works discussed in *Geomodernisms* is not the moment of their making but 'the persistent, structuring forces of race, place, and modernization within them'.[140]

The focus on modernity dramatically enlarges the timeframe under consideration. Doyle's essay traces 'the key English-language vocabularies of Atlantic modernity' to the 1640s, the rhetoric of the English Civil War, New World slavery and colonising projects, and then situates *Quicksand* (1928) and *Passing* (1929) by the Harlem Renaissance novelist Nella Larsen within the broader 'Atlantic story' of liberty narratives.[141] Other contributions bring later modernisms into focus. Ariela

Freedman explores the 'modernist humanism' of Indian photographer Raghubir Singh (1942–99).[142] Sung-sheng Yvonne Chang considers late twentieth-century modernism in Taiwan New Cinema.[143] Susan Stanford Friedman compares E.M. Forster's *A Passage to India* (1924) with Arundhati Roy's *The God of Small Things* (1997), approaching 'each as a modernist text in its own right, reflecting the modernity of its time and place, as well as the textual and political unconscious of its distinctive geomodernism'.[144]

Modernist Transitions

In 'Periodizing Modernism: Postcolonial Modernities and the Space/ Time Borders of Modernist Studies' (2006), Susan Stanford Friedman advocates 'a planetary approach to modernism', whereby 'the notion of modernism as an aesthetic period' is abandoned and modernism is redefined 'as the expressive dimension of modernity'.[145] This approach necessitates a form of 'cultural parataxis' (placing various artefacts side by side), a practice that 'spatializes modernity as a historical phenomenon emergent around the globe at different times in history', as per Friedman's contribution to *Geomodernisms*.[146] The method of juxtaposing texts from diverse periods and locales is of course a quintessential modernist technique.

Other contributors to the special issue of *Modernism/Modernity* in which Friedman's essay was published view postcolonial literature as a distinct development that transforms the terms of modernism. For instance, Urmila Seshagiri presents Jean Rhys's *Voyage in the Dark* as 'the point when the exhausted limits of modernist form revealed the lineaments of postcolonial fiction'.[147] The 'indeterminate beginning, fractured delivery, and inconclusive ending look back to the techniques that demarcated high modernism from nineteenth-century realism'.[148] At the same time, the act of turning the 'Empire's colonizing gaze back on itself', inverting the perspective which gives 'form to so much experimental modernism', reimagines 'English fiction along a new – and inevitably transnational – axis'.[149] Jahan Ramazani further proposes that 'the hybridizing literary strategies of postcolonial poetry' articulate 'a cross-culturalism still more plural and polyphonic than Euromodernism'.[150] Mindful that many postcolonial writers and theorists are sceptical about the liberational potential of Eurocentric modernism, Simon Gikandi makes the 'bold claim' in his introduction to the special issue that although 'postcolonial criticism has posited modernism as the site of Eurocentric danger', the great irony is that 'without modernism, postcolonial literature as we know it would perhaps not exist'.[151]

Postcolonial writing is often aligned with postmodernism, the broad artistic movement related to the social, political, cultural and philosophical condition of postmodernity (often dated from the end of the Second World War). The 'postmodern' has been defined by Jean-François Lyotard as 'incredulity toward meta-narratives' (the various narrative systems by which human society orders and gives meaning to its experience, including history).[152] One of the first critics to attempt to adumbrate 'postmodernism' as an aesthetic was Ihab Hassan, who contrasted the 'form', 'mastery', 'determinacy', 'hierarchy', 'purpose' and 'depth' associated with modernism with postmodernism's investment in 'play', 'chance', 'dispersal', 'anarchy', 'desire' and 'surface'.[153] While Hassan's list is overly schematic – as he himself acknowledged – it does communicate the sense in which postmodernism felt like a radical new artistic departure in the early 1980s.

The timing of any transition from modernism to postmodernism is a subject of debate. In *Late Modernism: Politics, Fiction, and the Arts between the World Wars* (1999), Tyrus Miller contends that the worldwide crisis and neurasthenia that followed the First World War, together with the apparatus of 'a runaway modernity' – marked by the 'restless, disturbing collective energies of recorded music, fashion, advertising, radio and film', commodification, metropolitan life, the rise of mass politics and the 'loss of a stable, authentic social ground' – eroded the cultural foundations of Anglo-American modernism, which ended shortly after 1922.[154] He proposes that the experimental literatures of the 1920s and 1930s responded to the dissolution of the earlier modernism and its perceived mastery of form by assembling 'fragments into disfigured likenesses of modernist masterpieces'.[155] He designates this new, bitterly satirical and parodic phase in literary culture as 'late modernism'. Miller's exemplary texts include: Wyndham Lewis's anti-modernist polemics *Time and Western Man* and *The Art of Being Ruled* (1926), as well as *The Apes of God* (1930), his savage satire on the Bloomsbury group and the rival literary clique formed by the aristocratic socialites Edith, Osbert and Sacheverell Sitwell (1887–1964, 1892–1969 and 1897–1988); Djuna Barnes's *Nightwood* (1936); and Samuel Beckett's early fiction from *More Pricks than Kicks* (1934) to *Watt* (1953). Miller deftly identifies the qualities that unite these texts: all foreground characters' perspectives (as opposed to the authorial subject) feature 'self-reflexive laughter', 'a loosening of symbolic unity', 'a predominance of grotesque bodies', 'an obsessive depiction of pure corporeal automatism' and present 'subjectivity "at play" in the face of its own extinction'.[156] Late modernism, in Miller's formulation, links 'forward into postmodernism and backward into modernism'.[157]

Anthony Mellors takes issue with Miller's definition of 'late modernism' as a transitional phase and instead uses the term to signify 'the continuation of modernist writing into the war years and until at least the end of the 1970s' in *Late Modernist Poetics* (2005):[158]

■ This was a period of consolidation, when substantial parts of long poems begun before 1939 were composed and published, and new ones were written: *The Cantos, Four Quartets,* Louis Zukofsky's *A,* David Jones's *The Anathemata,* William Carlos Williams's *Paterson,* Charles Olson's *The Maximus Poems,* Basil Bunting's *Briggflatts,* Charles Reznikoff's *Testimony: The United States.* Many poets whose modernist aesthetic was formed earlier in the century developed it beyond the 1930s; some, like Marianne Moore, found a wide audience in later years; others, such as Lorine Neidecker, Nelly Sachs and Bunting, did not publish major work until long afterwards. More significantly, new conceptual, concrete and performance-based poetries inspired by the avant-garde gained international recognition, and younger poets working within modernist traditions appeared, among them Olson, Jack Spicer, Edmond Jabès, Robert Duncan, Anne-Marie Albiach, Paul Celan, Andrea Zanzotto, Charles Tomlinson, Rosemary Tonks and J.H. Prynne.[159] □

As Mellors sees it, 'Miller is right to see the emergence of a troubled, belated version of Anglo-American modernism, but wrong to confine it to the period before World War Two'.[160]

Marjorie Perloff's manifesto *21st Century Modernism: The 'New' Poetics* (2002) advocates dropping 'the tired dichotomy that has governed our discussion of twentieth-century poetics for much too long: that between modernism and postmodernism'.[161] She concedes that 'Postmoderns' like the Projectivists, the Beats, the San Francisco poets, confessional poets and New York School 'were indeed a breath of fresh air' when they arrived on the scene in the late 1950s and 1960s and positioned themselves against modernist and New Critical orthodoxy, but contends instead that it is the avant-garde modernism of the early twentieth century – and the work of trailblazers such as T.S. Eliot, Gertrude Stein, Marcel Duchamp and the Russian Futurist Velimir Khlebnikov (1885–1922) – which inspires the most adventurous American poets of today, among them Susan Howe, Charles Bernstein, Lyn Hejinian and Steve McCaffery.[162]

Recent accounts of the contemporary novel also look beyond 'modernism's conceptual links to, or tenuous divides from, postmodernism' to focus instead on 'its correspondence both with the histories of decolonisation and with the contemporary geopolitical challenges of globalisation'.[163] David James makes the case that engaging with 'the stylistic, thematic and political afterlives of the formal and intellectual ambitions of literary modernism' is vital for building a nuanced account of the development of the novel after 1945 in his introduction to *The Legacies of Modernism: Historicising Postwar and Contemporary Fiction* (2012), an essay collection that traces dialogues between authors from across the twentieth century, including D.H. Lawrence and A.S. Byatt, Virginia Woolf and J.M. Coetzee, and E.M. Forster and Zadie Smith.[164] In *Cosmopolitan Style: Modernism beyond the Nation* (2006), Rebecca Walkowitz explores how the models of 'critical cosmopolitanism' developed in the early modernism of Joseph Conrad, Virginia Woolf and James Joyce, are revived and revised by post-1980s novelists Kazuo Ishiguro, Salman Rushdie and W.G. Sebald. By 'critical cosmopolitanism', Walkowitz means a kind of global political consciousness that 'reflects a conflict about the content and constituency of international experience and an effort to display relationships between everyday, private activities and public, international ones' and that is expressed stylistically in 'the salient features of modernist narrative, including wandering consciousness, paratactic syntax, recursive plotting, collage, and portmanteau language'.[165] Comparing authors from opposite ends of the century who 'write about adverse social conditions – fascism, world war, colonialism, displacement – but also about useless details, trivial sensations, exquisite moments, transient beauty, playful nicknames, and decorative objects', Walkowitz presents modernism as a cosmopolitan style that transcends periodisation.[166] As recent work by Walkowitz, James, Perloff, Friedman, Doyle, Winkiel and others indicates, modernist studies is increasingly reorientating itself to embrace modernity in its many forms.

CHAPTER SEVEN

Modernist Literatures and Mass Culture

The Frankfurt School

The relationship between mass culture and high art was influentially theorised by thinkers affiliated to the Institute of Social Research, which was founded in 1923 under the auspices of the University of Frankfurt to provide a space where Marxist theory could be developed independently from the activities of the organised working class or the communist party. The Institute relocated to New York in 1933, when Hitler rose to power. The members of the so-called Frankfurt School challenged what they saw as the crude economic basis of orthodox Marxism, and instead applied Marxist analysis to the agency of social and cultural formations to understand the workings of mass media. A cornerstone of Frankfurt School thinking – formulated by Theodor Adorno (1903–69) and Max Horkheimer (1895–1973) – was the notion that, far from arising spontaneously from the masses, mass culture is in fact imposed on them from above by the 'culture industry'.[1]

Walter Benjamin (1892–1940) was also affiliated to the Frankfurt School. His celebrated essay 'The Work of Art in the Age of its Techno-logical Reproducibility' (1936) considered the significance of the new processes that enable mass audiences to encounter art:

■ Around 1900 technical reproduction had reached a standard that permitted it to reproduce all known works of art, profoundly modifying their effect [...]. In even the most perfect reproduction one thing is lacking: the here and the now of the work of art – its unique existence in a particular place. It is the unique existence – and nothing else – that bears the mark of the history to which the work has been subject.[2] □

He coined the term 'aura' to describe all that is lost when artefacts are manufactured mechanically, arguing that substituting 'a mass exist-ence for a unique existence [...] detaches the reproduced object from the sphere of tradition', making its historically determined authenticity no longer relevant.[3] For this reason, 'The technological reproducibility of the artwork changes the relation of the masses to art'.[4] Benjamin proposed that when art is presented to a mass audience as a simultaneous, collective experience, for instance when a film is screened in the cinema, 'the conventional is uncritically enjoyed, while the truly new is criticized with aversion', a circumstance that further divides popular and experimental art.[5]

Adorno was struck by Benjamin's essay (which he read in draft form) and sent a critical response to his arguments in a now famous letter. Adorno judged that his friend had overstated the auratic qualities of formally autonomous art and underestimated the ways in which a feeling of 'aura' could be co-opted by mass cultural forms, for instance documentary realist cinema. The intricacies of Adorno's thinking are considerable, but it will suffice to say that Adorno argued that modernist artworks resist the capitalist logic that items are only valuable in so far as they can be exchanged for something else by asserting the autonomy of the formal strategies that distinguish them as high art (for instance, difficulty in literature, dissonance in music and abstraction in painting). For Adorno, this formal resistance to the priorities of the market is what potentially makes modernist artworks socially significant, giving them the power to disrupt or even transcend bourgeois ideology.

Adorno characterised mass culture and modernism as dialectical opposites produced by the forces of modernity:

■ Both bear the scars of capitalism, both contain elements of change. Both are torn halves of freedom, to which however they do not add up.[6] □

The 'torn halves [...] do not add up' to a whole because they both 'bear the scars of capitalism'; a deficiency which no synthesis of their otherwise contrary impulses could overcome.

The Great Divide

Adorno's notion of the autonomous artwork has been central to attempts to theorise the relationships of modernism and mass culture to the avant-garde. In *The Theory of the Avant-Garde* (1974, English translation 1984), Peter Bürger challenges Adorno's thesis by arguing that in bourgeois society the entire institution of art is autonomous from 'the praxis of life' (social practices) and seeks only to change artistic modes of representation.[7] He distinguishes between autonomous modernist art that dissociates itself from practical contexts and radical avant-garde movements such as Dada and Surrealism that attack the bourgeois institution of art and its ideology of aesthetic autonomy by seeking to reintegrate art into 'the praxis of life' and change the way that art functions in society. The presumption that the institution of art is singular, the narrow focus on Dada and Surrealism, and the sharpness of the distinction that Bürger draws between the revolutionary activities of the avant-garde and autonomous modernist art have opened his thesis to attack.[8] As Ástráður Eysteinsson appreciates, it is 'critically stimulating' to recognise that modernist works can also be 'avant-garde in their non-traditional structure and their radicalized correlations of form and content' and that 'while avant-garde movements are historical phenomena in their own right, they are also the salient motors of modernism'.[9]

Bürger's thought-provoking definition of the avant-garde has nonetheless been widely used and so remains crucial for readers of modernism. It was notably taken up by Andreas Huyssen in *After the Great Divide: Modernism, Mass Culture, Postmodernism* (1986), a landmark collection of essays that 'challenge the belief in the necessary separation of high art from mass culture, politics and the everyday'.[10] By the 'great divide' Huyssen means 'the kind of discourse which insists on the categorical distinction between high art and mass culture', which he considers to be crucial to a theoretical and historical understanding of how modernism has been constituted.[11]

Perhaps the most stimulating chapter of *After the Great Divide* for readers of modernist literature is 'Mass Culture as Women: Modernism's Other'.[12] Huyssen begins by investigating 'One of the founding texts of modernism': Gustave Flaubert's *Madame Bovary* (1856).[13] Flaubert desired to write 'a book about nothing, a book without external attachments which would hold together by itself through the internal force of its style', that is, an autonomous work of art.[14] Huyssen notes that while the male author 'emerges as a writer of genuine, authentic literature', Emma Bovary, the female protagonist, 'is positioned as a reader of inferior literature – subjective, emotional and passive'.[15] He then draws attention to Flaubert's handling of 'Emma Bovary's romances (the books *and* the love affairs)' as 'one of the constitutive features of a modernist aesthetic intent on distancing itself and its products from the trivialities and banalities of everyday life' and suggests that, despite Flaubert's professed autonomy, *Madame Bovary* is ultimately concerned with mass culture:[16]

■ Contrary to the claims of champions of the autonomy of art, contrary also to the ideologists of textuality, the realities of modern life and the ominous expansion of mass culture throughout the social realm are always already inscribed into the articulation of aesthetic modernism. Mass culture has always been the hidden subtext of the modernist project.[17] □

Huyssen proceeds to consider historical reasons why 'mass culture is somehow associated with women while real, authentic culture remains the prerogative of men':[18]

> ■ In an age of nascent socialism *and* the first major women's movement in Europe, the masses knocking at the gate were also women, knocking at the gate of a male-dominated culture. [...] The fear of the masses [...] is always also a fear of women, a fear of nature out of control, a fear of the unconscious, of sexuality, of the loss of identity and stable ego boundaries in the mass.[19] □

Huyssen's reading retunes Gilbert and Gubar's premise: it is not simply women who are modernism's Other, but feminised mass culture. Whether female modernists' relationship to mass culture was as vexed as Huyssen supposes it was for male writers is not addressed.

Huyssen contends that 'Modernism constituted itself through a conscious strategy of exclusion, an anxiety of contamination by its other: an increasingly consuming and engulfing mass culture'.[20] His case is that modernism is a reaction formation that defends its claims as true, authentic autonomous art by disdaining the feminised mass culture and its market values, choosing instead to address a select audience. The inextricability of modernism and mass culture puts him in mind of Adorno, who 'never lost sight of the fact that, ever since their simultaneous emergence in the mid-19th century, modernism and mass culture have been engaged in a compulsive *pas de deux* [a dance for two]'.[21] Huyssen declares: 'I still know of no better aphorism about the imaginary adversaries, modernism and mass culture' than Adorno's 'torn halves'.[22]

Huyssen draws a strict distinction between modernism (which he considers to be hostile to mass culture) and the historical avant-garde (which attacks the 'highness of high art' by validating 'other, formerly neglected or ostracized forms of cultural expression' and embracing the popular).[23] He therefore positions postmodernism as the true heir to the avant-garde because it too attempts 'to merge high art and popular culture'.[24] As Lawrence Rainey comments, 'Modernism, in this account, becomes little more than a reactionary, even paranoid fear of popular culture', appearing 'naïve and irredeemably reactionary' by comparison to postmodernism.[25]

After the Great Divide prompted scholars to re-examine the relationship between modernism and mass culture in greater detail, revealing that modernism was not so disdainful of the masses as Huyssen supposed. The following sections introduce key critical studies that situate literary writers and their works in the public world of which they are part, examining the material conditions of their production and dissemination, their place in consumer culture and the literary marketplace, their engagement with emergent mass-media forms such as daily newspapers, advertising and celebrity, and their relations to popular genres such as jazz, music hall and cinema.

Popular Culture and the Public World

'Modernists such as T.S. Eliot [...] emphasized time and again that it was their mission to salvage the purity of high art from the encroachments of [...] modern mass culture', so Huyssen claimed.[26] This thesis – descended from the New Critics who 'required a "serious" Eliot to help them establish a place for modernism (and for the New Criticism) in the academy' – is disputed by David Chinitz in *T.S. Eliot and the Cultural Divide* (2003). Chinitz offers 'a new narrative of Eliot's career' that 'restores the popular elements that previous narratives have suppressed'.[27] He introduces the Eliot who: favoured the 'jazz-banjorine' (an instrument made fashionable by ragtime, the American popular music phenomenon with African-American roots); 'danced all the modern dances', including the foxtrot; loved melodrama and the music-hall, 'comic strips, drama, boxing (on "the sporting page"), and sensational murder stories'; and 'schooled himself for years to write plays that could be mounted as "big budget productions" on Broadway'.[28] This light entertainment Eliot provides a counterpoint to the *Egoist* Eliot who wanted 'to point out that [...] the forces of deterioration are a large crawling mass, and the forces of development half a dozen men', and the curmudgeonly Eliot who remarked gloomily on the modern 'tendency to mass production and lowering of standards'.[29] Exploring different facets of Eliot's personality, Chinitz reveals him to be 'a multidimensional thinker and artist, whose approach to the modern popular' is 'supple, frequently insightful, and always deeply ambivalent'.[30]

Many avant-gardists and progressive intellectuals embraced jazz 'as a symbol of their onslaught against sterile mores and "traditional" aesthetics'.[31] Chinitz observes that the poems in Eliot's early notebook (published as *Inventions of the March Hare* (1996)) 'illustrate the importance of jazz-inflected popular song to the formation of his verse style'.[32] For instance, 'The smoke that gathers blue and sinks' is 'jazz poetry *avant la lettre*', anticipating 'the musical techniques that would be exploited by Langston Hughes at the height of the Jazz Age', while 'Suite Clownesque' (1910) 'includes a vaudeville-comic staging of Prufrock's urban wanderings rendered as Tin Pan Alley pastiche'.[33] (Tin Pan Alley refers to the New York district where popular music publishers and songwriters gathered). Chinitz notes that jazz rhythms also syncopate

The Waste Land, where many lines 'drape loosely over a skeleton of iambic pentameter': [34]

■ Eliot's patented cadence – his characteristic rhythms, the ways he uses rhyme, the tonal contours of his lines – were discovered in the sounds of popular music circa 1911.[35] □

It is American popular culture that gives 'Eliot's poetry its distinctive resonance'.[36]

Chinitz argues that Eliot did not oppose authentic popular culture but 'the respectable mob, the decent middle-class mob' whose 'bourgeois craving for "culture" as a token of respectability' made them averse to 'adventure and experiment'.[37] Indeed, Chinitz suggests that Eliot's early attitude corresponds in many ways to the avant-garde project as defined by Huyssen and Bürger. For instance, Eliot's famous declaration that Joyce's 'mythical method' is 'a step toward making the modern world possible for art' indicates a will (in Bürger's words) to 'reintegrate art into the praxis of life'.[38] After his religious conversion, Eliot's desire to alter the 'praxis of life' was absorbed 'into advocacy of Christianity and the Church', a circumstance which then separated his project from that of the avant-garde. In summary:

■ Although Eliot is often identified as a champion of institutional high art, in reality he offered an increasingly forceful critique of aestheticism and its ideal of artistic autonomy, of modernist hermeticism, and of the prevailing constructs that created an unbridgeable chasm between 'high' culture and 'low'. Eliot regarded the sacralization of high art, which maintained this deleterious cultural divide, as a bourgeois perversion of the nature and function of art.[39] □

As Eliot argued in an essay on 'Marianne Moore' (1923), 'Fine art is the *refinement,* not the antithesis, of popular art'.[40]

Eliot's interest in popular culture is documented in his 1922 essay on Marie Lloyd (1870–1922). Lloyd was a celebrated English music-hall comedienne. Her performances were full of *innuendo* and delighted 'what is called the lower class' (Eliot's words).[41] What Eliot admired – and envied – was Lloyd's 'capacity for expressing the soul of the people'; 'no other comedian succeeded so well in giving expression to the life of that audience, in raising it to a kind of art'.[42] Her success was evinced in the sing-alongs she rallied, which, to Eliot's mind, achieved 'that collaboration of the audience with the artists which is necessary in all art'.[43] For Eliot, her death spelled the demise of a popular culture that 'the encroachment of the cheap and rapid-breeding cinema' was rendering obsolete.[44]

Chinitz proposes that Eliot was never truly comfortable with the select audience modernist poetry attracted and its lack of 'direct social utility'.[45] He suspects that Eliot turned to verse drama in order to 'fill the role on stage left vacant after Marie Lloyd's death' and so 'transcend the [...] stratifications of public taste', which he considered to be 'a sign of social disintegration':[46]

■ A poetic drama rooted in the music hall, in other words, might bridge, or perhaps bypass, the cultural divide and restore to Eliot the popular adulation that was Marie Lloyd's and ought to have been the poet's as well.[47] □

Chinitz suggests that Eliot's unfinished play *Sweeney Agonistes*, with 'its unique blend of forms, incorporating vaudeville, music hall, melo‑ drama, burlesque, jazz, and minstrelsy' was his 'first step *away* from coterie art'.[48] It cleared the ground for popular and commercial successes like *The Cocktail Party*, which reached 'a workable compromise with the expectations of common theater audiences', not just 'the remnants of Marie Lloyd's semi-mythical working class but, for the most part, the very middle class that Eliot and his fellow modernists had despised for so long'.[49] Chinitz concludes, 'the Eliot of the mass-culture critique cannot be taken to represent the whole or the essential Eliot'.[50] Eliot was not averse to the popular *per se*, but to the great divide; the very divide on which Huyssen based his definition of modernism.

Similarly dissatisfied with the 'great divide' that insulates high modernist experiments from newspapers, magazines, popular novels, encyclopaedias, travelogues and the like, Michael North set out with the aim of becoming the 'ideal reader of 1922, with an insomnia so ideal it would be adequate not just to *Ulysses* but to anything else published in the same year'.[51] The result was *Reading 1922: A Return to the Scene of the Modern* (1999). Steeping himself in the Anglo-American cultural life of 1922, he revealed the *annus mirabilis* of modernism to be a year no less remarkable for the advances that were made in the fields of archaeology, anthropology, mass media, advertising and the philosophy of language, and for the rise of 'the three forces that would determine global events until 1945': the Soviet Union, the fascists, and supremacy of the United States as the principal world naval power.[52]

North investigates developments in various disciplines in this foun-dational year. He cites the Austrian philosopher Ludwig Wittgenstein (1889–1951), whose dream of discovering a neutral language of clar-ity and logic is the subject of the *Tractatus Logico-Philosophicus* (English translation 1922). The very attempt to tame language into 'universal familiarity' forced Wittgenstein to confront 'the multiplicity of incom-mensurable language games' and so inverted into a recognition of 'the irreducible foreignness of language'.[53] North explains, 'Poor translation, far from being an annoyance or a difficulty, became the core of a philosophical method', inaugurating what we now call the 'linguistic turn' in philosophy.[54] Likewise, the fieldwork method of modern anthropology, based on immersion in foreign language and culture and popularised by Bronislaw Malinowski (1884–1942) in *Argonauts of the Western Pacific* (1922) and A.R. Radcliffe-Brown (1881–1955) in *The Andaman Islanders* (1922), encountered the 'relativity and contingency of human relations' and so made 'misunderstanding and mistranslation' constitutive of anthropological understanding.[55] Notably, all three studies passed through the hands of the Cambridge linguist C.K. Ogden (1889–1957), who was then collaborating on *The Foundations of Aesthetics* (1922) with I.A. Richards.[56] 'It may be in this fundamental disruption of the universal', North speculates, 'that the year 1922 found its most universal theme'.[57]

Ordinary citizens did not have to travel as far afield as Malinowski and Radcliffe-Brown to encounter the relative, contingent and uncanny nature of modernity:

> ■ Global travel, the self-consciousness taught by anthropology and psychology, the distanciating reduplications of the media all brought awareness to bear on the unaware, the unconscious, the automatically accepted.[58] □

New mass media, like daily newspapers, radio, photography and film, imported these into the heart of everyday, ordinary life. For instance, Lord Northcliffe's Amalgamated Press controlled newspapers such as the *Daily Mail*, the *Daily Mirror*, the *Evening News* and the *Times*, dozens of specialised magazines, and an unending procession of serialised books, including Northcliffe's own anthropological survey *Peoples of All Nations* (1922), while network broadcasting began in 1922 with the creation of the British Broadcasting Corporation.[59]

North redefines literary modernism so that it becomes continuous with other developments in human culture around the globe. He suggests that modernism is implicated in phenomena as various as ladies' fashion trends, BBC radio broadcasts, Hollywood censorship, the first demonstration of sky-writing as an advertising technique (spoofed by Woolf in *Mrs Dalloway*) and the Prince of Wales's much-photographed visit to India (depicted in D.H. Lawrence's poem 'Elephant'). He associates modernism with the struggle to come to terms with the inadequacy of language as theorised by linguists and anthropologists, and he suggests that modernism's aesthetic and promotional techniques are shared with professions that seek to reach the public sphere and tap into the collective unconscious.

North substantiates these claims with reference to the popular craze for all things Egyptian that followed extensive global press coverage of the remarkable discovery of King Tutankhamen's tomb (1922). Egyptomania produced many examples of 'world texts', that is, products circulating within a world economy that incorporate a 'crazy mixture' of diverse cultures, making connections across time.[60] *The Waste Land*, North contends, is directly comparable: 'surely the appeal of an Egyptian handbag depends on allusion just as much as *The Waste Land* does'.[61] Both are 'self-conscious', 'knowing', 'ironic', and make the familiar new.[62] Indeed, North suggests that the *Tutankhamen Rag*, popular with the tourists staying in Luxor's hotels, is of the same order as the jazz hit *That Shakespearean Rag* (1912), which inspired a syncopated line of *The Waste Land*:

■ The existence of something like the Tutankhamen Rag, with all that it implies about the convergence of colonialism and metropolitan fashion, modern science and modern marketing, shows how complex and how quickly changing was the modernity into which Joyce and Eliot introduced their works.[63] □

North proceeds to show that marketing was the key to Egyptomania and the success of *The Waste Land*. Edward Bernays (1891–1995), Sigmund Freud's nephew and the inventor of the term 'public relations', not only commissioned a designer to produce a Tut-themed fashion range, but also 'worked very closely with Liveright in 1919 and 1920'.[64] North suggests that 'the strategies Boni and Liveright used to make *The Waste Land* the poetic equivalent of a best-seller were not so very different from those Bernays was using at the same time to exploit ancient Egypt'.[65] 'Aesthetic modernism may very well be [...] a mockery and a mimicry of strategies of *publicité* and réclame perfected by modern salesmanship', North speculates.[66] 'Such a possibility seems perfectly likely in the case of Joyce, who bases *Ulysses* on parallels between a Greek hero and a modern ad man'.[67]

North also investigates the activities of Gilbert Seldes (1883–1970). As managing editor of the *Dial*, Seldes was heavily involved in the extensive negotiations regarding the publication of *The Waste Land* and the award of the magazine's 1922 prize to Eliot. He inserted an article of his own in the issue of the *Dial* that contained *The Waste Land* and helped to secure the poem's 'nearly instantaneous canonization' by hailing it to be a 'complete expression of the spirit which will be "modern" for the next generation'.[68] That year, Seldes also started work on what would become *The Seven Lively Arts* (1924), 'the first sustained examination and defence of American popular culture', encompassing 'movies, vaudeville, popular music, musical comedy, newspaper columns, and [...] comics'.[69] Remarkably, then, 'the same person who made American popular culture a legitimate object of criticism also played a central role in formulating the public definition of literary modernism, [...] at exactly the same time'.[70] For North, Seldes's career is a signal instance of 'the larger social and cultural connections between popular culture and literary modernism at the moment when both emerged as distinct entities in the public consciousness'.[71]

North's final exercise in recreating what observers of 1922 might have thought about the relationship between literature of the time and other cultural phenomena focuses on the films of Charlie Chaplin (1889–1977). Chaplin's on-screen persona was a product of music-hall theatre. His frenetic antics appealed not only to the masses but to many modernists as well. In a 1923 issue of the *Criterion*, Eliot remarked:

■ The egregious merit of Chaplin is that he has escaped in his own way from the realism of the cinema and invented a rhythm. Of course the unexplored opportunities of the cinema for eluding realism must be very great.[72] □

North explains that the 'repetitiousness' of Chaplin's movements makes 'the whole process of copying, without which movies are unimaginable, visible', defeating 'what would seem the primary power of film, the illusion of presence, of immediacy, that it is able to give'.[73]

Taking in fields as diverse as anthropology and advertising, linguistics and cinema, North's richly inclusive study of 1922 reveals literary modernism to be thoroughly enmeshed in 'the public world of which it was part'.[74] Recognising this fact makes 'it possible to contain within the purview of modernist studies a good deal of material conventionally separated from the extreme literary experimentalism of Eliot, Joyce, or Stein' and move modernism 'Across the great divide'.[75]

Cinema and the Cinematic

Appreciating the synergy between modernist literatures and emergent mass-cultural forms like cinema has revolutionised modernist studies, rendering literary criticism a truly interdisciplinary activity. One such study is David Trotter's *Cinema and Modernism* (2007), which investigates affinities between film technology and modernist aesthetics. He faults previous accounts of modernism and the cinematic for their commitment to 'argument by analogy', whereby experimental literature is said to be '*structured like a film*: it has its "close ups", its "tracks" and "pans", its "cuts" from one "shot" to another'.[76] While the analogy between cinematic montage and modernist juxtaposition is suggestive, Trotter argues that it lacks historical specificity and fails on theoretical grounds too because 'Literature is a representational medium, film a recording medium'.[77] Instead Trotter explores the concerns that film raised as a recording technology:

■ When modernist writers thought of cinema, they thought of an image of the world made automatically: an image which, due to the original and durable excess in it of record over representation, contains either more or less of the world than would the image which would occur under comparable circumstances to a human observer. [...] By obstinately seeing as the human eye does not see, film became a meta-technology: a medium whose constant subject matter was the limits of the human.[78] □

For instance, Marianne Moore comments that film 'reveals the agitation which the eye does not see' in 'Fiction or Nature' (1933), while Virginia Woolf remarks that film shows us 'life as it is when we have no part in it', in her 1926 essay 'The Cinema'.[79]

Trotter's thesis is that 'film's neutrality as a medium' – its delivery of images decoupled from subjectivity – evoked tensions between human presence and absence, immediacy and mechanical mediation, sense and intelligibility.[80] He suggests that writers attempted to re-enact that neutrality in their literature, undertaking a parallel enquiry into 'the age's wilful absorption in the kinds of automatic behaviour exemplified by machinery in general, and by the new technologies of perception in particular'.[81] Trotter examines films that modernist writers could actually have seen to reveal the specifics of James Joyce, T.S. Eliot and Virginia Woolf's engagement with cinema and its representation of space and time.

Joyce was sufficiently interested in film to set up the Cinematograph Volta, Dublin's first cinema, in 1909. Noting that the 'Wandering Rocks' episode of *Ulysses* predates the montage practices developed by the pioneering, internationally acclaimed Soviet film director Sergei Eisenstein (1898–1948), Trotter suggests that Joyce's depiction of the city more closely resembles the turn-of-the-century documentaries of Dublin's bustling streets. In Trotter's analysis, 'Wandering Rocks' is shaped by 'a determination to view the world, for however brief an interval, as a machine would view it'.[82] He argues that the narrative assumes a machine-eye perspective on random objects and citizens, presenting a parallel to the 'least anthropomorphic of camera movements', the lateral tracking shot, which moves 'sideways while looking to the front' and 'found favour with film-makers from 1913 onwards'.[83] Eliot too is revealed to be fascinated by cinematic automatism and the dual accommodation of 'near-tangibility' and 'otherwise unimaginable remoteness'.[84] The view proposed by his early poems such as 'The Love

Song of J. Alfred Prufrock' 'is of consciousness as a space, or event, or drama, of projection', where flickering images are 'thrown technologically onto a screen'.[85]

Trotter suggests that Woolf shared film-makers' 'interest in the ways in which movement [...] defines space' and discovered in early newsreels a means to narrate absence, death and mourning in *To the Lighthouse* (1927).[86] This topic receives more extended treatment in Laura Marcus's *The Tenth Muse: Writing about Cinema in the Modernist Period* (2008), a far-reaching account of the fascinating interactions between cinema and literature in the age of modernism. The first sections examine 'the relationships between early film technologies, the first commentaries on the cinema [...] and literary responses to film in this period, including those of Villiers de l'Isle Adam, H.G. Wells [...], Rudyard Kipling, D.H. Lawrence, H.D., John Rodker and James Joyce'.[87] There follows an account of the potential that Woolf saw in photography and cinematography 'for forms of intense visualization and for radical transitions in time and in space, which could be translated into the novel form'.[88] *Jacob's Room* is read as a novel that self-consciously engages with filmic techniques to explore character as it is externally perceived, depicting the presence of Jacob's absence through glimpses of the always moving world he once occupied. *To the Lighthouse* (1927) is interpreted anew as an exploration of the possible directions that Woolf imagined film might take in her contemporary essay 'The Cinema'. Marcus focuses on the novel's cinematic preoccupation with the play of light, perception, eyelines, sightlines, framing and focus, and in its radical handling of time, death and absence, with particular reference to the middle section of *To the Lighthouse*, 'Time Passes'. This brief interlude races through the ten years that pass between 'The Window', in which the Ramsay family and friends are seen holidaying, and 'The Lighthouse', in which a smaller party returns to the house and the planned trip to the lighthouse finally takes place. 'Time Passes' condenses a decade into a single night in the unoccupied house, gesturing parenthetically to death, childbirth, marriage and the First World War.

The latter half of *The Tenth Muse* provides a comprehensive account of the development of film criticism in cinema's first decades, a discipline that Marcus shows to be shaped to a great extent by modernist writers and their aesthetic values. Marcus variously explores early American considerations of the status of film as an art form, such as Vachel Lindsay's *The Art of the Motion Picture* (1915), Hugo Münsterberg's *The Photoplay: A Psychological Study* (1916) and Gilbert Seldes's *The Seven Lively Arts*, and the discursive strategies that they pioneered to describe the powers of motion, emotion and modes of seeing generated by this new technology. She examines the central role played by the Film Society (founded in London in 1925) in bringing international avant-garde films and the ideas of theorists such as Eisenstein to an English audience, and traces the emergence of film criticism in British periodicals in the 1920s, most particularly *Close Up* (1927–33), the internationally influential avant-garde film journal, founded by Bryher and her husband, the Scottish artist Kenneth Macpherson (1902–71), which counted H.D. (Bryher's lover) and Dorothy Richardson as regular columnists.

Marcus's account of *Close Up* addresses 'the ways in which literary modernism was centrally informed by cinematic consciousness'.[89] *Close Up* ran numerous articles on global cinema, including the first English translations of several of Eisenstein's most influential writings. It drew extensively on 'psychoanalytic theories, Eisenstein's montage theories, and models of space-time, "movement" and "motion", "motion" and "emotion", that had become the currency of early film aesthetics', and adopted a 'dynamic discourse' that registered these concerns stylistically.[90] Marcus notes that the 'favoured mode of much *Close Up* writing in the early period was a form of stream-of-consciousness or interior monologue'.[91] For instance, Richardson's contributions ventriloquised 'a form of demotic, unpunctuated speech intended to represent a feminized, mass cultural reception', while H.D. tended to provide 'a performative running commentary on the process of spectating which became a form of "inner speech", acting as a screen onto which the film images could be projected'.[92] Marcus suggests that the mythic, symbolic and ritualistic dimensions of silent film particularly appealed to H.D.'s Imagist sensibilities and discerns echoes of Gordon Craig's writings on marionette theatre in H.D.'s accounts of 'the bodily hieroglyphics of the film actor'.[93] *The Tenth Muse* ends with a brief chapter on the coming of sound and the critical reception of two early sound films, *The Jazz Singer* (1927) and *Blackmail* (1929). Both Trotter and Marcus attest to the literary potential that modernist writers discerned in filmic technologies and the moving image.

The Middlebrow

'While North persuasively counters Huyssen's construction of modernism as antipathetic to popular entertainment, he does not move beyond Huyssen's conception of early-twentieth-century cultural production as entirely composed of modernist art and popular entertainment', observes Faye Hammill in *Women, Celebrity and Literary Culture between the Wars* (2007).[94] Hammill's study is concerned with the middlebrow, the cultural category at the precarious and unstable interchange of the high and low. The term '"middlebrow" generally refers to a set of institutions and initiatives, including book clubs, extension courses, circulating libraries, lists of "great books", radio book programs, and "outline" books (or accessible introductions to subjects such as philosophy or history), which aimed to make high culture available to a broad public'.[95] She suggests that the 'rise of middlebrow culture in this period performed the very task of destabilizing the categories of high and low which North himself seeks to achieve'.[96] For instance, Virginia Woolf designated the genre as 'betwixt and between' in a letter to the *New Statesman and Nation*, posthumously published in an essay entitled 'Middlebrow' (1932).[97] She disparaged the middlebrow for its 'mixture of geniality and sentiment stuck together with a sticky slime of calves-foot jelly', seeking to emphasise her own distance from it.[98]

As Nicola Humble explains in *The Feminine Middlebrow Novel, 1920s to the 1950s: Class, Domesticity, and Bohemianism* (2001), while 'middlebrow fiction dominated the publishing market' between 1920 and 1950, 'it has been in the main ignored by literary critics and historians', a circumstance that she ascribes to the fact that it 'was largely written and consumed by women'.[99] Humble's aim is to 'rehabilitate both the term and the body of literature' by exploring the social, cultural and political significance of the feminine middlebrow.[100] She successfully recasts this hybrid genre – at once, snobbish and bohemian, conventional and daring, domestic and yet sophisticated – as 'a powerful force in establishing and consolidating, but also in resisting, new class and gender identities'.[101]

By contrast with Humble, Hammill seeks to rehabilitate the middlebrow by nuancing its relations with modernism. She focuses on 'seven high profile women whose books caused a sensation in the early Twentieth Century' – Stella Gibbons (1902–89), Dorothy Parker, Anita Loos (1889–1981), Mae West (1892–1980), L.M. Montgomery (1874–1942), Margaret Kennedy (1896–1967) and E.M. Delafield (1890–1943) – to reflect on celebrity culture, gender, publicity and cultural authority.[102] While these women do not embrace 'a radical modernist aesthetic', Hammill nonetheless insists that these authors are 'stylistically innovative':[103]

■ Several [...] responded to modernist innovation in serious ways, and some of their texts have affinities with experimental narrative projects: West's impressionistic evocations of New York, for example, or Loos's emphasis on the materiality of language. A parodic approach is more characteristic of these authors however: parody of stream of consciousness and free verse occurs in Gibbons, Loos, Delafield, and Parker. Drawing on the more expansive definitions of modernism and modernity which are being developed in recent theory and criticism, it is possible to read them as participants, however tentatively, in modernist experiment.[104] □

Hammill suggests that instead of simply responding to high culture, the middlebrow 'changed the ways in which high culture was understood';

its large audience giving 'some indication of the likely impact of such reformulations of cultural hierarchy':[105]

■ Loos's writing, for example, has interesting resonances with the work of both T.S. Eliot and Gertrude Stein, while Delafield implicitly responds to Virginia Woolf's work in her own texts, with a mixture of admiration and opposition. Gibbons's books have many affinities with those of Evelyn Waugh (who is ambiguously located in relation to modernism), and she also establishes complex intertextual connections with D.H. Lawrence.[106] □

Hammill's book establishes the middlebrow as 'a productive, affirmative standpoint for writers who were not wholly aligned with either high modernism or popular culture', revealing that the 'witty, polished surfaces' of middlebrow writing 'frequently conceal unexpected depths and subtleties'.[107]

Modernism in the Marketplace

In *Institutions of Modernism: Literary Elites and Public Culture* (1998), Lawrence Rainey challenged the once commonly held view that modernism was 'a strategy whereby the work of art resists commodification' by painstakingly recovering the economic and cultural contexts that informed the production and dissemination of canonical works, focusing on the roles played by institutions such as publishing houses, magazines and patron-investors.[108] In doing so, he initiated a materialist turn in modernist studies, inspiring critics to examine the complex relationships between modernist literatures and the marketplaces in which they circulated.

Institutions of Modernism begins by considering the effect of Futurism on Ezra Pound as he grappled with the urgent question of how to make art public practice. In March 1912, Pound gave a series of three lectures in the elite bourgeois realm of the private gallery of Lord and Lady Glenconner in London to 'supplement his income'. Tickets were restricted to fifty and cost 10s 6d for a single lecture. On the day of Pound's second lecture, Filippo Marinetti delivered a lecture on Futurism at Bechstein (now Wigmore) Hall (with a capacity of 550, cheapest admittance 1s). Pound's lecture went unnoticed, but Marinetti's performance was fully reported in the press and he achieved instant notoriety. 'After only six weeks in England', Rainey notes, 'the Futurists had elicited 350 articles in newspapers and reviews and had earned more than 11,000 francs in sales of paintings'.[109] 'Marinetti had achieved his success not by addressing only an educated elite but by speaking in a public forum to a wider audience', and at that moment, it seemed that it was 'no longer the polite salon or the genteel review [...] but the concert hall, the mass circulation newspaper, or perhaps the music hall that might serve as the new agora [public open space] of literary and cultural debate'.[110] Rainey argues that Pound responded by launching 'Imagism in a more systematic and serious way', but defined it in opposition to the programmatic artistic and social ambitions of Futurism.[111]

However, the performances that Marinetti gave at the Coliseum (the largest and grandest music hall in London) in June 1914 were not well received. As Rainey explains, Marinetti had mistaken his audience and 'tried to deliver an academic exposition of Futurist principles'.[112] It seemed that the variety theatre held no future as a public forum for the avant-garde. At this moment, Rainey argues, a new institutional space emerged. He suggests that the modernists responded to 'the growing prominence of the early mass media, the rising pressure of advertising, the unprecedented fusion of information and entertainment, and the challenges presented by a dense, highly differentiated array of institutional arenas in which to speak to an increasingly fragmented public' with a 'tactical retreat into a [...] world of patronage, collecting, speculation, and investment'.[113] Generous subsidies from patron-investors granted writers respite from the immediate pressures of the market economy and simultaneously transformed art 'into a special kind of commodity, a rarity capable of sustaining investment value'.[114] By restricting the supply of these commodities, modernists could then 'exploit the limited demand for modernist literature, turning each book into an objet d'art that acquired potential investment value for collectors'.[115]

Rainey's first example is Sylvia Beach and Adrienne Monnier's scheme to publish *Ulysses* in a deluxe edition of 1,000 copies, a decision that transformed 'the reader into a collector, an investor, or even a speculator'.[116] Book traders quickly began buying and selling volumes for, or in expectation of, large profits. For Rainey, *Ulysses* marked 'the decisive entry of modernism into the public sphere via an identifiable process of commodification'.[117] Further evidence is found in Pound and Eliot's hard-nosed dealings with the managing editors of little magazines and booksellers as they marketed *The Waste Land* 'as a reference point for the assessment of modernism by a wider public'.[118] Rainey notes that the Condé Naste magazine *Vanity Fair* was considered as a potential publisher (circulation 96,500), as was the *Little Review* (circulation 3,000, heavily subsidised by patrons). Eventually an extraordinary deal was negotiated with the *Dial* (circulation 9,500, also heavily subsidised). Eliot would receive 'the second annual Dial Award with its $2,000 prize as payment for the poem'.[119] At that stage, Rainey points out, the editors had not even laid eyes on the manuscript. The prize generated huge publicity, boosting sales of Liveright's extensively advertised commercial edition of the poem. Seven months on, 'Vanity Fair devoted an entire page to reprinting earlier poems by Eliot', with an editorial presenting him as 'the most hotly contested issue in American poetry'.[120] For Rainey, this trajectory is indicative of the ways in which patronage 'facilitated modernism's transition from a literature of an exiguous elite to a position of prestigious dominance'.[121] The transition was supported by the three-step publishing programme which had become normative for the avant-garde by the early 1920s, whereby works were typically published 'first, in a little review or journal; second, in a limited edition of recently collected poems (or as an individual volume if the work was large enough); and third, in a more frankly commercial or public edition issued by a mainstream publisher and addressed to a wider audience'.[122]

The publication histories of *The Waste Land* and *Ulysses* suggest that their instant canonisation may have had as much to do with astute marketing and perceived value as literary excellence. On this basis, Rainey provocatively proposes that 'The best reading of a work may, on some occasions, be one that does not read it at all'.[123] His argument is that examining institutions rather than formal devices is the most direct way to understand modernism as a 'social reality' and probe 'the troublesome place of literary elites in public culture'.[124]

Two further case studies investigate 'the risks that attended the modernist creation of a counter-realm to the public sphere'.[125] First Rainey explores Pound's indebtedness to Averdo Marchetti, a fascist who gave him support as he was writing the so-called 'Malatesta Cantos' in Rimini, Italy (1923). These Cantos (VIII–XI) reflect on 'the life and time of Sigismondo Malatesta, the quattrocentro ruler of Rimini', who 'sponsored the reconstruction of the church of San Francesco' and generously gave the architect and painters free artistic rein.[126] Rainey suggests that Pound's openness to fascism was in part justified by the hope that Mussolini might emulate Malatesta and pursue 'a program of cultural patronage that would turn Italy into an international cultural center'.[127] Succumbing to the illusion of the 'grand myth that the Renaissance was the achievement of a small group of elite spirits', a myth he projected onto Mussolini and Italian fascism, Pound was cut off from 'genuine dialogue with his contemporaries'.[128]

Turning to H.D., Rainey controversially dismisses the critical work that restored her to prominence, ascribing her recent popularity merely to 'the new awareness of ethnicity, race, gender, and sexual preferences'.[129] He suggests that Bryher's lavish patronage 'cast H.D. in the role of a coterie poet, one whose writings circulated, like bonbons at a dinner party, among a cénacle of friends and hangers-on in wealthy bohemia', bereaving her of 'a genuine public' and the 'critical give-and-take' that comes with wide exposure.[130] Rainey contends that Bryher's support led H.D. to 'complacency [...] and solipsistic reverie', obviating the need to make a significant contribution to the invigorating body of critical and theoretical writing that articulated modernist experimentation.[131] While there is no doubt that H.D. was not as prolific as Eliot or Pound, her involvement in the cinematic journal *Close Up* indicates that she was more concerned with public debate than Rainey allows.

In *The Public Face of Modernism: Little Magazines, Audiences and Reception 1905–1920* (2001), Mark Morrison contributes to the re-envisioning of modernism's relationship to mass culture by exploring little magazines' use of commercial publishing and promotional strategies. (The adjective 'little' only applies to the material conditions of publication and not the magazines' ambitions for the public function of art.) Morrison notes that the 'relatively low cost of producing a small-scale magazine [...] and the fantastic successes new advertising techniques and print ventures were having with vast audiences presented the seductive possibility of intervening in public discourse'.[132]

Morrison's study focuses on five little magazines that published work by modernist authors before and during the First World War: 'in London, the *English Review*, *Poetry and Drama*, the *Egoist* and *Blast*; in Chicago, the *Little Review*; and in New York, the *Masses*'.[133] He notes that the form and content of the works published by these magazines indicate a 'complex and fascinating interdependence with the mass market press':[134]

■ Participating in the popular verse-recitation movement of the day, poems in *Poetry and Drama* were written to emphasize aural and recitative qualities; poems like Allen Upward's in the *Egoist* even took the form of advertisement, and Wyndham Lewis's *Enemy of the Stars* and the manifestoes in *BLAST* adopted the language, typographical forms, and visual images of promotional culture; the 'Nausicaa' chapter from *Ulysses* that got the *Little Review* into trouble with New York postal censors used the language, slogans, and images of commercialized youth culture; the poems and cartoons in the *Masses* by Amy Lowell, William Carlos Williams [...] and others drew upon and modified the dialect and racial representations of the commercial magazines; and the modernist covers of the late issues of the *Masses* drew upon and enlivened the popular 'cover girl' strategy that caught readers' eyes.[135] □

Not only did modernists capitalise on the verbal and visual discourses of advertising and promotional culture in their works, they also explored how they might be applied to raise their profile. Writers and editors such as Ford Madox Ford, Ezra Pound, Dora Marsden (1882–1960), Margaret Anderson and Max Eastman (1883–1969) did express concern at 'culture controlled by corporations; public debate constricted by advertisers' prejudices; profit and "the bottom line" sacrificing the original, the creative, to the tried and true, to the "lowest common denominator"; copy that requires little thought and panders to readers' taste for the sensational, uncritical, and merely entertaining'.[136] However, Morrison suggests that many writers and editors 'found the energies of promotional culture too attractive to ignore, especially when it came to advertising and publication techniques' and saw in these the potential to restore a public function to art.[137]

A case in point is the *Freewoman* (1911–12), resurrected as the *New Freewoman* (1913), which attempted to form a 'generally anti-bourgeois oppositional public sphere that would involve not just public discussion of suffrage but would include topics that the bourgeois suffrage magazines would consider "improper", like homosexuality, radical monetary reforms, experimental or radical art and literature, and anti-statist politics'.[138] Morrison explains that suffrage journals such as *Votes for Women* promoted themselves using street sellers with sandwich boards. They reaped enormous revenues from adverts for branded consumer items and department stores by directly recommending that their large middle-class female readership patronise these companies as a way of supporting the cause. The *Freewoman* likewise carried adverts for commercial products and institutions of the countersphere. It 'made more money from advertising revenue than it did from subscriptions', but struggled to build a subscription base because it was not affiliated to any one particular organisation.[139] Marsden tried to attract subscribers by engaging an advertising agent and adopting the 'commercial mass publicity techniques' used by major publishing houses and adapted by suffragist groups.[140] She hired sandwichmen and printed thousands of circulars, as well as posters and fliers, she repackaged the magazine as the *Egoist* (1914) and 'used Imagism like a brand name'.[141] The *Egoist* advertised in other journals with the aim of cultivating a select, 'intelligent', and 'virile' reader, in distinction to the 'feminized mass culture that Huyssen identifies in the period', but failed to attract and maintain a large audience, losing a significant proportion of the female subscribers needed to secure the lucrative advertising revenues from department stores.[142] The magazine folded in 1919. For all the optimism with which early modernists regarded 'the possibility of appropriating some of the institutions of the newly emerging mass publishing world', in fact, as Morrison argues, the 'wide-ranging heterogeneous literary, artistic, political, social and philosophical' concerns voiced in magazines like the *Egoist*, *Little Review* and the *Masses* made it hard to consolidate a singular identity and so 'made the logic of the capitalist press difficult to adopt'.[143]

In *Modernism and the Culture of Celebrity* (2005), Aaron Jaffe reveals how T.S. Eliot, Ezra Pound, James Joyce and Wyndham Lewis fashioned their literary reputations and publicised the project of modernism by exploiting commercial forces to create a market for their work. He argues that these writers established themselves in the transnational economy of celebrity culture by manipulating their 'imprimaturs' (i.e., the personality of the author that is stamped on the literary object). For instance, *A Portrait of the Artist as a Young Man* leads readers to suspect that Joyce is a much better fit than Stephen Dedalus for the stated ambition of becoming Ireland's national writer. Other stories of literary life reveal an awareness 'that too often authors and texts are, like other commodities, put to indiscriminate ends'.[144] A prime example is Henry James's *John Delavoy* (1898), a tale about a novelist who dies unknown and the ensuing stand-off between the mass-circulation magazine editor who wishes to serialise his last work, the deceased's sister, who respects her brother's imprimatur by refusing to supply a personal tribute, and a critic who has prepared an article on the piece of fiction in question.

Jaffe explores how modernists sought to manipulate this literary economy by fetishising authorship. He notes that Pound and Eliot's models for a literary tradition defined through its 'masters' and 'monuments' are 'predicated on certain assumptions about the scarcity of elite literary reputation'.[145] The letterhead that Pound devised when he was the London correspondent for the *Dial* illustrates this principle. It listed the names of prominent modernist contributors as an exercise in branding. What the 'cult of the singular artist' minimises, Jaffe observes, is the importance of collaboration to modernism.[146] To examine this topic, Jaffe follows Rainey in 'not reading', but '*reading other things*' that modernist discourse marks as 'subordinate, minor, un-literary, or worst of all commercial', but which attest to the circumstances of modernist production, circulation and consumption.[147] The memoirs of martyred publishers and publicists, such as Sylvia Beach's *Shakespeare and Company* (1956) and Margaret Anderson's *My Thirty Years War* (1930), reveal the devalued, feminised, 'low literary labour' that underwrote the 'high literary labour of the solitary genius'.[148] By contrast, the assistance that Eliot and Pound offered their contemporaries worked to consolidate their own imprimaturs. Eliot wrote introductions to books by Pound, Djuna Barnes, Marianne Moore, Joyce and Lewis, among others, asserting his authority while implicitly subordinating their texts to his own experience of reading them. Pound promoted his activities through 'a narrative of opposition rather than shared labour', pitting 'form against formlessness, male fixity against female oblivion, the phallic author against the great passive vulva of the London literary scene, Pound, Moore, and Eliot against Amygism [...] and diluted floppiness'.[149] 'The key ingredient in elite modernist reputation', Jaffe argues, 'is not only demonstration of high literary labor through imprimaturs and extant masterpieces, but also the capacity to frame work against contrasting lesser labors of contemporaries'.[150]

Jaffe turns to focus on the glut of new poetry anthologies which exemplify modernist promotion and networking: for instance, *Georgian*

Poetry (5 vols, 1911–22), edited by Edward Marsh (1872–1953), Ezra Pound's *Des Imagistes,* Amy Lowell's *Some Imagist Poets* and Michael Roberts's *New Signatures.* Jaffe argues that the anthologies turned 'hierarchies of reputation' into 'material artefacts' by placing the singular representative modernist *'among* groups of putative subordinates, literary fellow travellers, and also-rans', by embedding 'individual authors in propaganda about new literary brand names'.[151] The prospect of expanded circulation meant that 'an anthology-sized poem – in theory at least – could return exponential gains' in 'financial and promotional terms', as D.H. Lawrence discovered to his delight when his poem 'Snapdragon' appeared in the first volume of *Georgian Poetry.*[152]

Jaffe suggests that while *The Gender of Modernism* aims to promote the work of modernist women, it in fact participates in the same logic as the modernist anthologies that helped to shape the canon. Scott's 'Tangled Mesh' makes working relationships visible, but orders 'literary networks vis-à-vis implicit literary hierarchies of work', so that the most connected authors are the interchanges 'through which the reputations of less "connected" writers are made to circulate'.[153] Likewise, Shari Benstock's laudable attempt to reapportion renown to the women of the left bank nonetheless perpetuates the devaluation of the collaborative work of advertising and marketing on which modernism depended by making female workers accessories to more successful male counterparts. Jaffe concludes his study of celebrity with an account of Wyndham Lewis's 'postwar bid to transform the London museum establishment into a modernist portrait gallery' by co-opting institutional structures to advertise authorial imprimaturs so as to make 'ostensibly unpopular writing both materially possible and culturally defining'.[154] Presenting modernism as a commercial phenomenon driven by authorial imprimatur and celebrity, and sustained by diminishing the collaborative work performed by women, Jaffe hollows out the myths that have conditioned even revisionary attempts to bring modernism to account.

The success of modernism as a global movement can be attributed to its willingness to set aside its anti-bourgeois agenda and assimilate itself into the new capitalist marketplace. Its literatures and promotional practices drew inspiration from and reacted to continuous developments in the public world of which they were part, seeking to intervene in the reception of artistic practices and society and culture at large.

Publishing Modernist Literatures

'We are now at the threshold of a new age for the study of all modernist literature', as Ronald Schuchard has declared.[155] As General

Editor of the seven-volume edition of *The Complete Prose of T.S. Eliot* (to be published by Faber and Faber and Johns Hopkins University Press), Schuchard speaks from a position of knowledge when he says that 'many of the riches are to be found in the untapped archives and unexamined histories of modernist texts'.[156] For instance, it was only when *The Waste Land: A Facsimile and Transcript of the Original Drafts Including the Annotations of Ezra Pound* was published in 1971 that the scale of Pound's editorial midwifery could be evaluated. Only a small percentage of Eliot's prose writings are currently in print and so the *Complete Prose* promises to transform our appreciation of his works. Ongoing major editorial projects include: *The Letters of T.S. Eliot* (also part of the T.S. Eliot Editorial Project, four volumes in print at the time of writing); *The Cornell Yeats*, begun in 1982 with the aim of publishing all extant manuscripts of W.B. Yeats's poetry, most of his plays and selected prose, presenting photographic facsimiles, typescripts and proofs alongside transcriptions, documenting Yeats's creative processes by revealing complicated composition histories; and *The Cambridge Edition of the Works of D.H. Lawrence* (begun in 1981), which collates extant materials, from draft manuscripts to first book publication, identifying errors in transmission, as well as censorship and bowdlerisation by publishers, to present texts that are as close as can presently be determined to those Lawrence would have wished to see in print.

Scholarly editions of modernist texts perform an essential critical function. They mediate the materials that the next generation of literary critics will work on. Textual critics develop editorial principles, which guide them in their attempts to establish the most correct text of works. Editors provide introductions and annotations that offer clarification and illumination, not only of the textual condition of the materials in question, but their cultural context too.

Perhaps the most innovative edition of a literary text yet produced is *Ulysses: A Critical and Synoptic Edition*, edited by Hans Walter Gabler with Wolfhard Steppe and Claus Melchior (1984). The Shakespeare and Company first edition of *Ulysses* was set by French typesetters, who worked with typescripts that bore substantial addenda in Joyce's unclear hand. These typescripts were prepared from Joyce's handwritten drafts, which were themselves heavily revised. Joyce continued to make corrections and additions until three days before the designated date of publication. The first edition was rife with errors, to Joyce's great irritation, and he insisted that 'In a second edition the mistakes must be corrected'.[157] *Ulysses* has since run to many editions, as editors have taken up the challenge of correcting these errors. Gabler sought to get around the problem of discrepancies in textual transmission by instead recreating the genesis of the text from pre-publication documents. This model is very different to the more common Anglo-American practice of textual criticism, whereby an editor takes an authorised document as his/her copy-text – the first edition or ideally the manuscript from which the first edition was composed – which then is edited by reference to later published texts. Instead, Gabler created a genetic edition of the text, by attempting to reconstruct the writing process from the *avant-texte* (pre-publication documents, such as notes, drafts, manuscripts, typescripts, proofs and correspondence). Gabler used the 'Rosenbach Manuscript' (a complete handwritten draft). He then built up the text layer by layer, using information from handwritten notations to typescripts, placards and page proofs. He called this synoptic collation 'a continuous manuscript text for *Ulysses*'.[158] This virtual text – for it has no single direct precedent in any of Joyce's manuscripts – provided the copy-text for Gabler's edition.

In 1986, Gabler brought out an edition of the corrected text of *Ulysses* which simply gave the text of *Ulysses* as Gabler determined it, without annotation. He claimed that his corrected edition presented '*Ulysses* as Joyce wrote it'.[159] Among the myriad corrections Gabler made, his edition famously includes an extra line of dialogue and interior monologue, in which Stephen reflects on love.[160] John Kidd disagreed with Gabler's radical editorial decisions, accused Gabler and his team of errors in execution, and denounced the edition as a scandal.[161] A heated debate ensued. No edition is perfect, but, as Jeri Johnson suggests, Gabler's edition is 'the text most in tune with Joyce's own themes and productions'.[162] The 'Aeolus' episode, set in the offices and print room of the *Evening Telegraph*, epitomises how self-consciously *Ulysses* foregrounds the processes involved in the production and transmission of texts. Gabler's edition had the effect of sensitising scholars of modernism to the interpretive issues raised by textual criticism and encouraging them to study texts as works in process.

New editions of out-of-print works continue to restore commercially unsuccessful modernists to critical attention. For instance, Mina Loy's radical modernism was first rediscovered through Jonathan Williams's 1958 selection *Lunar Baedeker and Time-Tables*. Roger L. Conover's *The Last Lunar Baedeker* (1982) renewed Loy's critical fortunes, but it was not until Conover's *The Last Lunar Baedeker* (1996) that her entire body of published poetry was in print. It is only with the publication of Sarah Crangle's recent edition *Stories and Essays of Mina Loy* (2011), which collects fragmentary writings only previously available in archives, that a rounded assessment of Loy's work can be reached.

Recuperative and revisionary anthologies continue to broaden the range of materials available for university teaching in accordance with the latest methodologies and critical approaches. For instance, Bonnie Kime Scott followed *Gender and Modernism* with the anthology *Gender in Modernism: New Geographies, Complex Intersections* (2007), which takes an intersectional approach to identity by examining gender through its interrelations with other social categories, including 'Sexuality, Race/Ethnicity, Class and Global Situation (inclusive of imperial and capitalist histories)'.[163] Accordingly, the anthology is organised not by author but by theme and/or group identity. Turning to modernity as a complementary field of study, *Gender in Modernism* 'places emphasis on everyday life and takes interest in "low" as well as "high" modernist forms', gathering and introducing material under the categories: 'Modernist/Feminist Activism'; 'Issues of Production and Reception'; 'Diverse Identities and Geographies'; 'War, Technology, and Traumas of Modernity'; and 'Arts and Performances'.[164] The number of authors under consideration is significantly enlarged, including many more women writers, representatives of global modernism, editors, journalists, political organisations, actors, playwrights, visual artists and *cinéastes*, inviting readers to make connections between well-known authors and less familiar figures. The anthology maps the political-cultural work of feminists, suffragists, leftists and colonial subjects, exploring the social and theatrical performance of gendered identities, as they restructure modernism 'to be inclusive of new categories and crossings of disciplines'.[165]

Finally, searchable digital editions of hard-to-access ephemera are making also archival materials newly available to a global audience. The most exciting of these resources to date is surely the Modernist Journals Project (produced in collaboration between Brown University and the University of Tulsa), which makes fully searchable facsimile editions of English-language little magazines such as *Poetry*, *BLAST*, the *Little Review*, and the *Egoist* freely available online.[166] Readers can browse whole issues or search the entire database to summon modernist texts in their original publication context, track critical debates and think about material considerations such as the cost, frequency and visual codes of the magazines, as well as the advertisements that they carried. The three-volume *Oxford Critical and Cultural History of Little Magazines* (2009–13), edited by Peter Brooker and Andrew Thacker, is the ideal companion to this activity, providing insights into the role of independent periodicals in Britain and Ireland, North America and continental Europe.[167]

New editorial initiatives are continuing to change the corpus of modernist literatures as we know it: expanding its texts and adjusting our understanding of the movement that modernised art.

CONCLUSION

Modernism was made in the invigorating plays, prose, poetry and pronouncements of writers who were as critically sophisticated as they were daring and defiant. Modernist drama was nurtured by independent or 'free' theatre companies that resisted the mercantile priorities of crowd-pleasing commercial theatre to present aesthetically and/or socially challenging material. Fiction was released from the strictures of chronological sequence, completed plot and the singularity of stable character as it followed the phases of the mind and renewed the marvellous, the erotic, the ineffable, the contingent and the fleeting at the heart of the everyday. Poets turned away from the lyric 'I' and regular verse, and embraced multiple registers, including common speech. They pioneered innovative forms to articulate the problematically shaky relationship between words and things: from the musical suggestivity of Symbolism, to the allusive dislocation of high modernists such as T.S. Eliot and the non-referential strategies of avant-garde writers.

The modernists were supremely reflexive about their own practice. They kept themselves abreast of new literary movements, they read one another's work with fascination, they were conscious of the need to justify their formal experiments and political agendas to an uninitiated public and to interrogate the social function of art, and they had the technical acumen, passion and flair for publicity to make their voices heard. For these reasons, the modernists were often their own best critics. Indeed, it could be said that the modernists took such an active role in shaping the reception of their works that they invented literary criticism for the modern age. Working as they did in the period that saw the rise of English literature as a scholarly discipline, their pronouncements guided the efforts of the first generation of professional literary scholars, whose methodologies were based on the theories of the writers that they held to be exemplary.

Later critics took their cue from modernist writers and theorists but pushed their ideas further, interpreting literatures anew in the light of emergent cultural theories, many of which were formulated in dialogue with ideas about language, culture and society that were already latent in modernist texts. In the 1970s and 1980s, feminist critics in particular worked to recover the contributions and concerns of then overshadowed modernists from marginalised social groups. In recent decades, the field of study has been expanded and reconfigured in three directions: temporal, spatial and vertical. As Rebecca Walkowitz and Douglas Mao note, the New Modernist Studies encompasses 'artefacts from the middle of the nineteenth century and the years after the middle of the twentieth as well as works from the core period of about 1890 to 1945' and treats modernism as a truly 'transnational' phenomenon that encompasses many alternative traditions.[1] As scholarly enquiry 'increasingly extended to matters of production, dissemination, and reception', the 'great divide' between high art and low popular culture has been disassembled.[2] The success of modernism as a transnational movement is now recognised as testament to its complex engagement with emergent cultures of publicity, advertising and consumer culture as well as its production of truly ground-breaking art. The future of the field inheres in embracing this inclusive, questioning, expansive definition of modernism, examining complex interactions with mass culture, the media and other art forms, learning the languages necessary to undertake truly comparative study of its global manifestations, recovering archival documents, and restoring its rich and manifold historical contexts.

This Guide has offered an indicative history of essential criticism of modernist literatures, showing the ways in which changing critical fashions have made modernism new for successive generations of readers.

Notes

INTRODUCTION

1. Ezra Pound, *Make It New* (London: Faber, 1934).
2. Douglas Mao and Rebecca Walkowitz, 'The New Modernist Studies', *PMLA* 123.3 (May 2008), pp. 737–48.
3. Peter Nicholls, *Modernisms: A Literary Guide*, 2nd rev. edn (Basingstoke: Palgrave Macmillan, 2009).
4. Marjorie Perloff, 'Modernist Studies', in *Redrawing the Boundaries: The Transformation of English and American Literary Studies*, eds Stephen Greenblatt and Giles Gunn (New York: The Modern Language Association of America, 1992), p. 154.
5. Perry Anderson, 'Modernity and Revolution,' *New Left Review* I 144 (March–April 1984), pp. 112–13.
6. Chris Baldick, *The Modern Movement* (Oxford: Oxford University Press, 2004), p. 4.
7. T.E. Hulme, 'Lecture on Modern Poetry', in *The Collected Writings of T.E. Hulme*, ed. Karen Csengeri (Oxford: Clarendon Press, 1994), p. 54.
8. Raymond Williams, 'When Was Modernism?', in *The Politics of Modernism: Against the New Conformists*, ed. Tony Pinkney (London: Verso, 1989), pp. 32, 33, 35, 33.
9. Michael Levenson, *A Genealogy of Modernism: A Study of English Literary Doctrine 1908–1922* (Cambridge: Cambridge University Press, 1994), p. vii.
10. Perloff (1992), p. 158.
11. Joseph Frank, 'Spatial Form in Modern Literature', in *The Widening Gyre* (Bloomington: Indiana University Press, 1963), p. 13.
12. Malcolm Bradbury and James McFarlane, 'The Name and Nature of Modernism', in Malcolm Bradbury and James McFarlane, eds, *Modernism: A Guide to European Literature 1890–1930* (London: Penguin, 1991), p. 23.
13. Bradbury and McFarlane (1991), pp. 29, 25.
14. Williams (1989), p. 31.
15. Christopher Wilk, ed., *Modernism: Designing a New World 1914–1939* (London: V&A Publications, 2006).
16. Nicholls (2009), p. 1.
17. Karl Marx and Friedrich Engels, 'Manifesto of the Communist Party', in *The Marx-Engels Reader*, 2nd edn, ed. Robert Tucker (New York: Norton, 1978), p. 474.
18. Marx and Engels (1978), p. 480.
19. Gustave Le Bon, *The Crowd: A Study of the Popular Mind* (London: Macmillan, 1896), p. 36.
20. Marx and Engels (1978), p. 476.

1   MODERNIST BEGINNINGS

1. Charles Baudelaire, 'The Painter of Modern Life', in *Baudelaire: Selected Writings on Art and Artists*, trans. P.E. Charvet (Cambridge: Cambridge University Press, 1971), p. 403.
2. Baudelaire (1971), pp. 395, 396.
3. Baudelaire (1971), p. 400.
4. Charles Baudelaire, Dedication to *Le Spleen de Paris: Petits poèmes en prose* (1869), quoted in Walter Benjamin, *Selected Writings*, vol. 4, 1839–1940 (Cambridge: Harvard University Press, 2003), p. 320.

5. Georg Simmel, 'The Metropolis and Mental Life', in *Georg Simmel on Individuality and Social Forms*, ed. Donald Levine (Chicago: University of Chicago Press, 1971), p. 325.

6. Victor Hugo to Charles Baudelaire, 6 October 1859, in Claude and Vincentte Pichois, ed., *Lettres à Baudelaire* (Geneva: A la Baconnière, 1973), pp. 188–9.

7. T.S. Eliot, 'Baudelaire' in *Selected Essays* (London: Faber and Faber, 1972), p. 426.

8. Walt Whitman to the Editors of *Harper's Magazine*, 7 January 1860, *The Collected Writings of Walt Whitman: The Correspondence: Volume 1: 1842–1867*, ed. Edwin Haviland Miller (New York: New York University Press, 1961), p. 46.

9. Walt Whitman to William D. O'Connor, 1866, in *Correspondence*, vol. 1 (1961), p. 288.

10. Whit Whitman, 'Preface', *Leaves of Grass*, ed. David Reynolds (Oxford: Oxford University Press, 2005), p. viii.

11. Charles Eliot Norton, review, *Putnam's Monthly* (September 1855) in *Walt Whitman: The Critical Heritage*, ed. Milton Hindus (London: Routledge and Kegan Paul, 1971), p. 24.

12. Rufus Griswold, unsigned review, *New York Criterion* (10 November 1855), in Hindus (1971), p. 32; unsigned review, *Boston Intelligencer* (3 May 1856), in Hindus (1971), p. 61.

13. Whitman (2005), p. v.

14. Langston Hughes, 'The Ceaseless Rings of Walt Whitman' (1946), in *The Collected Works of Langston Hughes: Volume 9: Essays on Art, Race, Politics and World Affairs*, ed. Christopher C. De Santi (Columbia: University of Missouri Press, 2002), p. 484.

15. William Carlos Williams, 'On the American Idiom', in *Interviews with William Carlos Williams: Speaking Straight Ahead*, ed. Linda Welshimer Wagner (New York: New Directions, 1976), p. 59.

16. Théophile Gautier, *Charles Baudelaire: His Life*, trans. Guy Thorne (London: Greening and Co., 1915), pp. 35–6.

17. Arthur Symons, 'The Decadent Movement in Literature', *Harper's Magazine* (November 1893), p. 859.

18. Max Nordau, *Degeneration* (Lincoln: University of Nebraska Press, 1968), p. 5.

19. Nordau (1968), p. vii.

20. Émile Zola, 'Naturalism on the Stage', in *The Experimental Novel and Other Essays*, ed. and trans. Belle M. Sherman (1964), p. 147.

21. André Antoine, 'The Free Theatre' (1890), in *Twentieth-Century Theatre: A Sourcebook*, ed. Richard Drain (Routledge: London and New York, 1995), p. xviii.

22. August Strindberg, Preface to *Miss Julie*, in *Miss Julie and Other Plays*, ed. and trans. Michael Robinson (Oxford: New York: Oxford University Press, 1998), p. 63.

23. Strindberg (1998), p. 63.

24. Sarah Grand, 'The New Aspect of the Woman Question', *North American Review* 158 (1894), p. 271.

25. Strindberg (1998), p. 60.

26. Strindberg (1998), p. 60.

27. Strindberg (1998), p. 61.

28. Henrik Ibsen, 'Notes for the Modern Tragedy', in *A Sourcebook on Naturalist Theatre*, ed. Christopher Innes (London: Routledge, 2000), p. 79.

29. Clement Scott (unsigned), *Daily Telegraph* (8 June 1889), p. 3, in *Ibsen: The Critical Heritage*, ed. Michael Egan (London: Routledge and Kegan Paul, 1972), p. 102.

30. William Archer, 'Ibsen and English Criticism', *Fortnightly Review* xlvi (1 July 1889), pp. 30–7, in Egan (1972) p. 115.

31. Editorial, *Daily Telegraph* (14 March 1891), p. 5, in Egan (1972), p. 190.

32. E.F.S. Piggott, 'Testimony to the 1892 Select Committee on Censorship', quoted in Innes (2000), p. 78.

33. George Bernard Shaw, *The Quintessence of Ibsenism* (London: Tucker, 1891), p. 137.

34. Shaw (1891), p. 16.

35. George Bernard Shaw, Preface, *Mrs Warren's Profession, Bernard Shaw Collected Plays*, vol. 1 (London: Bodley Head, 1970), p. 231.

36. J.T. Grein, quoted in J.L. Styan, *Modern Drama in Theory and Practice* (Cambridge: Cambridge University Press, 1981), p. 60.

37. Bertolt Brecht, 'Three Cheers for Shaw', in *Brecht on Theatre: The Development of an Aesthetic*, ed. and trans. John Willett (London: Methuen, 1964), p. 11.

38. Brecht (1964), p. 10.

39. Walter Pater, *Studies in the History of the Renaissance* (London: Macmillan, 1873), p. viii, p. ix.

40. Pater (1873), p. ix.

41. Pater (1873), pp. 208–9.

42. Pater (1873), pp. 209–10.

43. Pater (1873), p. 213.

44. Henry James, 'The Art of Fiction', in *Partial Portraits* (London: Macmillan, 1894), p. 384.

45. William James, *The Principles of Psychology*, vol. 1 (New York: Holt, 1890), p. 238.

46. James (1894), p. 388.

47. James (1894), p. 390.

48. James (1894), p. 390.

49. Henry James, Preface to *The Spoils of Poynton, The Novels and Tales of Henry James*, vol. 10 (New York: Charles Scribner, 1908), pp. vi, vi, v.

50. Unsigned review, 'Confidence', *New York Herald* (February 1880), p. 8, in *Henry James: The Contemporary Reviews*, ed. Kevin J. Hayes (Cambridge: Cambridge University Press, 1996), p. 87.

51. Unsigned review, '*The Portrait of a Lady* and *Dr. Breen's Practice*', *Atlantic Monthly* (January 1882), p. 128.

52. Julia Wedgwood, *Contemporary Review* (August 1886), pp. 300–1, in Hayes (1996), p. 171.

53. *Lippincott's Magazine* 29 (February 1882), pp. 213–15, in Hayes (1996), p. 144.

54. 'Mr Henry James Exasperates' in Hayes (1996), p. 319.

55. Edmund Gosse, 'America: Mr. Henry James's Impressions', *Daily Mail* (2 February 1907), p. 3, in Hayes (1996), p. xix.

56. Joseph Conrad, Preface, *The Nigger of the 'Narcissus': A Tale of the Sea* (New York: Doubleday, 1914), p. 11.

57. Conrad (1914), p. 14.

58. W.L. Courtney, *Daily Telegraph* (8 December 1897), p. 4, reprinted in *Conrad: The Critical Heritage*, ed. Norman Sherry (London: Routledge & Kegan Paul, 1973), p. 85; Harold Frederic, *Saturday Review* (12 February 1898), p. 211, reprinted in Sherry (1973), pp. 99–100.

59. Conrad (1914), p. 14.

60. Conrad (1914), p. 14.

61. Conrad (1914), pp. 12, 16.

62. Conrad (1914), pp. 13–14.

63. Pater (1873), p. 211.

64. Pater (1873), p. 210.

65. Pater, *The Renaissance: Studies in Art and Poetry*, 2nd rev. edn (London: Macmillan & Co., 1877), p. 233.

66. Yeats (1955), p. 302.

67. Oscar Wilde, *De Profundis*, in *The Complete Works of Oscar Wilde*, vol. 2, ed. Ian Small (Oxford: Oxford University Press, 2000), p. 102.

68. Unsigned review, *Scots Observer* (5 July 1890), p. 181, in *Oscar Wilde: The Critical Heritage*, ed. Karl Beckson (London: Routledge and Kegan Paul, 2001), p. 75; unsigned review, *Daily Chronicle* (30 June 1890), p. 7, in Beckson (2001), p. 71.

69. Oscar Wilde to the Editor of *St James' Gazette* (25 June 1890), in Beckson (2001), p. 67; Oscar Wilde to the Editor of the *Scots Observer* (13 August 1890), in *The Letters of Oscar Wilde*, ed. Rupert Hart-Davis (London: Hart-Davis, 1962), p. 270.

70. Havelock Ellis, *Studies in the Psychology of Sex: Sexual Inversion* (London: The University Press Ltd, 1900), p. 137.

71. Oscar Wilde, 'The Decay of Lying', in *The Complete Works of Oscar Wilde*, vol. 4, ed. Josephine Guy (Oxford: Oxford University Press, 2007), p. 96.
72. Wilde (2007), p. 96.
73. Wilde (2007), p. 79.
74. Wilde (2007), p. 83.
75. Wilde (2007), p. 84.
76. Wilde (2007), p. 103
77. Wilde (2007), p. 90.
78. Strindberg (1998), p. 176.
79. Rudolf Kurz, 'Foreword', *Der Sturm* (March 1910), quoted in Richard Sheppard, 'German Expressionism', in Bradbury and McFarlane (1976), p. 276.
80. Jean Moréas, 'Symbolism', in *Symbolist Art Theories: A Critical Anthology*, ed. Henri Dorra (Berkeley: University of California Press, 1994), p. 151.
81. Baudelaire, quoted in Clive Scott, 'Symbolism, Decadence and Impressionism', in Bradbury and McFarlane (1976), p. 211.
82. Stéphane Mallarmé, 'Crisis in Poetry' in *Mallarmé: Selected Prose Poems, Essays and Letters*, trans. Bradford Cook (Baltimore: Johns Hopkins University Press, 1956), p. 34.
83. Mallarmé (1956), p. 38.
84. Mallarmé (1956), pp. 40–1.
85. Mallarmé (1956), p. 41.
86. Mallarmé (1956), p. 40.
87. Jules Huret, 'Interview with Stéphane Mallarmé', in Dorra (1994), p. 141.
88. Symons (1899), pp. 3–4.
89. Symons (1899), p. 10.
90. Symons (1899), p. 9.
91. Maurice Maeterlinck, quoted in Marvin Carlson, *Theories of Theater* (Ithaca: Cornell, 1984), p. 296.
92. Alfred Jarry, 'Preface', *Ubu Roi*, trans. Beverley Keith and G. Legman (Mineola: Dover Publications, 2003), pp. 2–3.
93. Jarry (2003), p. 2.
94. Arthur Symons, quoted in Karl Beckson, *Arthur Symons: A Life* (Oxford: Clarendon Press, 1997), p. 159.
95. W.B. Yeats, *The Autobiography of W.B. Yeats* (London: Macmillan, 1955), p. 233.
96. W.B. Yeats, Letter to the Editor, *Saturday Review* (5 March 1902), p. 299.
97. Edward Gordon Craig, *On the Art of Theatre* (London: William Heinemann, 1911), p. 140.
98. Edward Gordon Craig, 'The Actor and the *Über-marionette*', *Mask* (April 1908), pp. 3–15.
99. Edward Gordon Craig, *Index to the Story of My Days* (London: Hulton Press, 1957), p. 268.
100. Lady Gregory, *Our Irish Theatre* (New York: G.P. Putnam's Sons, 1913), p. 8.
101. W.B. Yeats to T. Sturge Moore, in *W.B. Yeats and T. Sturge Moore: Their Correspondence, 1901–1937*, ed. Ursula Bridge (New York: Oxford University Press, 1953), p. 156.
102. Gregory (1913), p. 101.
103. J.M. Synge, Preface, *The Playboy of the Western World* (Dublin: Maunsel and Co., 1911), pp. vii, vi.
104. W.B. Yeats, 'The Controversy over the Playboy of the Western World', *Arrow* (23 February 1907), in *Explorations* (London: Macmillan, 1962), p. 225.
105. Constance D'Arcy Mackay, *The Little Theatre in the United States* (New York: Holt, 1917).
106. James (1894), p. 389.
107. T.S. Eliot, review of Peter Quennell, *Baudelaire and the Symbolists*, in *Criterion* (January 1930), p. 357, in *Inventions of the March Hare, Poems 1909–1917*, ed. Christopher Ricks (London: Faber and Faber, 1996), p. 402.
108. T.S. Eliot, *To Criticize the Critic* (London: Faber and Faber, 1965), p. 126.

2 HIGH MODERNISM

1. Virginia Woolf, 'Character in Fiction', in *The Essays of Virginia Woolf: Volume III: 1919–1924*, ed. Andrew McNeillie (London: Hogarth Press, 1988), pp. 420–1.
2. Eliot (1965), p. 58.
3. Woolf, 'Character in Fiction', in *Essays*, vol. 3 (1988), pp. 433–4.
4. William Carlos Williams, 'Recollections', *Art in America* (February 1963), p. 52.
5. Carl Van Vechten, *Music and Bad Manners* (New York: Knopf, 1916), p. 35.
6. T.S. Eliot, 'London Letter', *Dial* (October 1921), pp. 452–5, p. 435.
7. Ford Madox Ford, *Joseph Conrad: A Personal Remembrance* (Boston: Little Brown, 1924), p. 195.
8. Ford Madox Ford, *Memories and Impressions: A Study in Atmospheres* (New York: Harper and Brothers, 1911), p. xviii.
9. Ford, 'On Impressionism', in *Critical Writings of Ford Madox Ford*, ed. Frank MacShane (Lincoln: University of Nebraska Press, 1964), p. 36.
10. Virginia Woolf, 'Modern Fiction', in *Collected Essays*, vol. 2 (London: Hogarth Press, 1966), p. 106.
11. Woolf (1966), p. 110.
12. Elizabeth Bowen, 'The Faber Book of Modern Short Stories' in *The New Short Story Theories*, ed. Charles E. May (Athens: Ohio University Press, 1994), p. 152.
13. Henry James, 'Preface' to 'Lessons of the Master,' in *The Art of the Novel: Critical Prefaces* (New York: Charles Scribner's Sons, 1962), p. 231.
14. Virginia Woolf to Ethel Smyth, 16 October 1930, in *The Letters of Virginia Woolf*, vol. 4, eds Nigel Nicholson and Joanne Trautmann (San Diego: Harcourt Brace Jovanovitch, 1981a), p. 231.
15. Virginia Woolf, *The Diary of Virginia Woolf*, vol. 2, ed. Anne Olivier Bell (Harmondsworth: Penguin, 1981b), pp. 13–14.
16. Winifred Holtby, *Virginia Woolf: A Critical Memoir* (Chicago: Academy Press, 1978), p. 111.
17. T.S. Eliot to Virginia Woolf, 4 December 1922, in *The Letters of T.S. Eliot: Volume I: 1898–1922*, ed. Valerie Eliot (London: Faber and Faber, 1988), p. 607.
18. Unsigned review, 'The Enchantment of a Mirror', *Times Literary Supplement* (26 October 1922), p. 683, in *Virginia Woolf: The Critical Heritage*, ed. Robin Majumdar (London: Routledge and Kegan Paul, 1975), pp. 96–7.
19. Unsigned review, *Pall Mall Gazette* (27 October 1922), p. 6, in Majumdar (1975), p. 99.
20. Rebecca West, review, *New Statesman* (4 November 1922), p. 142, in Majumdar (1975), p. 101.
21. Arnold Bennett, 'Is the Novel Decaying?', *Cassell's Weekly* (28 March 1923), p. 47, in Majumdar (1975), p. 113.
22. Bennett in Majumdar (1975), p. 113.
23. Virginia Woolf, 'Mr Bennett and Mrs Brown', *Nation and Athenaeum* (1 December 1923), 342–3, in Majumdar (1975), p. 118.
24. Katherine Mansfield, *The Letters and Journals of Katherine Mansfield: A Selection*, ed. C.K. Stead (Harmondsworth: Penguin, 1977), pp. 65–6.
25. Mansfield (1977), p. 199.
26. Katherine Mansfield, *Novels and Novelists* (London: Constable, 1930), p. 32.
27. Mansfield (1977), p. 170.
28. Virginia Woolf, 'A Sketch of the Past', in *Moments of Being: Unpublished Autobiographical Writing*, ed. Jeanne Schulkind (New York: Harcourt Brace, 1976), p. 81.
29. James Joyce, *Stephen Hero*, rev. edn, ed. Theodore Spencer (London: Jonathan Cape, 1969), p. 216.
30. James Joyce, 'Drama and Life', *James Joyce: Occasional, Political, and Critical Writing*, ed. Kevin Barry (Oxford: Oxford University Press, 2000), p. 28.
31. James Joyce to Grant Richards, 5 May 1906, in *Letters*, vol. 2 (1966), p. 134.
32. James Joyce to Grant Richards, 5 May 1906, in *Letters*, vol. 2 (1966), p. 134.

33. Ezra Pound, '*Dubliners* and Mr. James Joyce', *Egoist* (15 July 1914), p. 267.

34. Sherwood Anderson to Waldo Frank, 14 November 1916, in *Letters of Sherwood Anderson*, ed. Howard Mumford Jones (Boston: Little, Brown, 1953), p. 5.

35. Sherwood Anderson, *Sherwood Anderson's Memoirs* (New York: Harcourt Brace, 1942), p. 89.

36. Hart Crane, review of *Winesburg, Ohio*, *Pagan 4* (September 1919), pp. 60–1, quoted in Kim Townsend, *Sherwood Anderson* (Boston: Houghton Mifflin, 1987), p. 157; H.L. Mencken, 'Something New under the Sun', *Smart Set* (August 1919), in *The Merrill Studies in Winesburg, Ohio*, ed. Ray Lewis White (Columbus: Merril, 1971), pp. 39–40; Rebecca West, *New Statesman* (22 July 1922), in *Winesburg, Ohio: Text and Criticism*, ed. John Ferres (New York: Viking, 1966), p. 262.

37. Ford Madox Ford, 'Techniques', in *Critical Writings* (1964), p. 68.

38. Ford (1964), p. 68.

39. Ford (1964), p. 69.

40. Valery Larbaud, 'The *Ulysses* of James Joyce', *Criterion* (October 1922), pp. 94–103, in *James Joyce: The Critical Heritage: Volume 1: 1907–27*, ed. Robert Deming (London: Routledge, 2002), p. 253.

41. Quoted in Richard Ellmann, *James Joyce*, rev. edn (New York: Oxford University Press, 1982), p. 519.

42. May Sinclair, 'The Novels of Dorothy Richardson', *Egoist* (April 1918), p. 58.

43. Sinclair (1918), p. 57.

44. Sinclair (1918), p. 57.

45. Sinclair (1918), p. 58.

46. Sinclair (1918), p. 58.

47. Virginia Woolf, *A Writer's Diary: Being Extracts from the Diary of Virginia Woolf*, ed. Leonard Woolf (London: Hogarth Press, 1953), p. 139; Ford (1924), p. 136.

48. Dorothy Richardson, 'Women and the Future: A Trembling of the Veil before the Eternal Mystery of "La Gioconda"', *Vanity Fair* (April 1924), pp. 39–40, in *The Gender of Modernism: A Critical Anthology*, ed. Bonnie Kime Scott (Bloomington and Indianapolis: Indiana University Press, 1990), p. 413.

49. Virginia Woolf, 'Romance and the Heart', *Nation and Athenaeum* (19 May 1923), p. 229, in *Essays*, vol. 3 (1988), p. 367.

50. Richardson (1938), p. 12.

51. Arnold Bennett, 'James Joyce's *Ulysses*', *Outlook* (29 April 1922), pp. 337–9, in Deming (2002), p. 221.

52. Woolf, 'Modern Fiction', *Collected Essays*, vol. 2 (1966), p. 108.

53. Leonard Woolf, *An Autobiography: 1911–1969* (Oxford: Oxford University Press, 1980), p. 120.

54. T.S. Eliot, 'London Letter, August 1922', *Dial* (September 1992), p. 330.

55. D.H. Lawrence to Barbara Low, 16 September 1916, in *The Letters of D.H. Lawrence: Volume II, 1913–16*, eds George Zytaruk and James Boulton (Cambridge: Cambridge University Press, 2002), p. 655.

56. D.H. Lawrence, *'Psychoanalysis and the Unconscious' and 'Fantasia of the Unconscious'*, ed. Bruce Steele (Cambridge: Cambridge University Press, 2004), p. 9.

57. D.H. Lawrence to Bertrand Russell, 8 December 1915, in *Letters*, vol. 2 (2002), p. 470.

58. Lawrence (2004), p. 131.

59. D.H. Lawrence to Arthur McLeod, 23 April 1913, in *Letters*, vol. 2 (2002), p. 543.

60. Robert Lynd, *Daily News* (5 October 1915), p. 6, in *D.H. Lawrence, The Critical Heritage*, ed. R.P. Draper (London: Routledge, 1970), pp. 91–2.

61. James Douglas, *Star* (22 October 1915), p. 4, in Draper (1970), p. 93.

62. Catherine Carswell, *Glasgow Herald* (4 November 1915), p. 4, in Draper (1970), p. 101.

63. D.H. Lawrence, 'The Future of the Novel', in *Study of Thomas Hardy and Other Essays*, ed. Bruce Steele (Cambridge: Cambridge University Press, 1985), p. 152.

64. D.H. Lawrence, 'Morality and the Novel', in Steele (1985), p. 171.

65. Wyndham Lewis, *Time and Western Man* (New York: Harcourt Brace, 1928), p. xiv.

66. Henri Bergson, *Creative Evolution* (New York: Henry Holt, 1911), p. 200.

67. Lewis (1928), pp. 91, 103.

68. Lewis (1928), p. 91.

69. Filippo Tommaso Marinetti, 'The Founding and Manifesto of Futurism', in *Futurist Manifestos*, ed. Umbro Apollonio (London: Thames and Hudson, 1973), p. 21.

70. Marinetti (1973), p. 21.

71. Marinetti (1973), p. 21.

72. Marinetti (1973), p. 21.

73. Filippo Tommaso Marinetti, quoted in Walter Adamson, *Embattled Avant-Gardes: Modernism's Resistance to Commodity Culture in Europe* (Berkeley: University of California Press, 2007), p. 101.

74. Mina Loy, 'Aphorisms on Futurism', *The Lost Lunar Baedeker*, ed. Roger L. Conover (Manchester: Carcanet, 1997), p. 152.

75. Mina Loy, 'Feminist Manifesto', in *The Lost Lunar Baedeker* (1997), pp. 154, 153, 153, 153.

76. Mina Loy (1997), pp. 154, 155.

77. Filippo Tommaso Marinetti, 'Technical Manifesto of Futurist Literature', in *Marinetti Selected Writings*, ed. R.W. Flint (London: Secker & Warburg, 1972), p. 84.

78. Marinetti (1972), pp. 84–5.

79. Marinetti (1972), p. 85, p. 87.

80. Filippo Tommaso Marinetti, 'The Variety Theatre', in Drain (1995), p. 171.

81. Marinetti (1995), p. 173.

82. Filippo Tommaso Marinetti, E. Settimelli and B. Corra, 'The Futurist Synthetic Theatre', in Drain (1995), p. 21.

83. Filippo Tommaso Marinetti, 'The Meaning of the Music Hall, By the Only Intelligible Futurist', *Daily Mail* (21 November 1913), p. 6.

84. Harold Monro, *Poetry and Drama* 1.3 (September 1913), p. 262.

85. D.H. Lawrence to Edward Garnett, in *Letters*, vol. 2 (2002), pp. 182–3.

86. Ezra Pound, 'The New Sculpture', *Egoist* (16 February 1914), p. 68.

87. T.E. Hulme, 'Romanticism and Classicism', in *Collected Writings* (2004), p. 64.

88. Hulme (2001), p. 59.

89. Hulme (2001), p. 61.

90. Ezra Pound, 'A Retrospect' (1954), p. 12.

91. T.S. Eliot, quoted in Ronald Schuchard, *Eliot's Dark Angel: Intersections of Life and Art* (New York: Oxford University Press, 1999), p. 61.

92. 'Poets' Translation Series', *Egoist* (August 1915), p. 131.

93. 'Poets' Translation Series' (1915), p. 131.

94. T.E. Hulme, 'Searchers after Reality, II', *New Age* (19 August 1909), p. 315.

95. F.S. Flint and Ezra Pound, 'Imagisme', *Poetry* (March 1913), p. 199.

96. Ezra Pound to Harriet Monroe, 13 October 1912, in *Letters* (1951), p. 45.

97. Ezra Pound, 'Vorticism', *Fortnightly Review* (1 September 1914), pp. 465–7, in *Gaudier-Brzeska: A Memoir* (Hull: The Marvel Press, 1970), p. 89.

98. Pound (1970), p. 89.

99. Pound (1970), p. 89.

100. Ezra Pound, 'Vortex. Pound', *BLAST* (1914), p. 153.

101. Eliot, 'Hamlet and his Problems', *The Sacred Wood* (London: Methuen, 1920), p. 92.

102. Ezra Pound, 'T.S. Eliot', *Poetry* (August 1917), p. 265–6.

103. [Margaret] Storm Jameson, 'England's Nest of Singing Birds', *Egoist* (November 1915), pp. 175–6, p. 175.

104. Ezra Pound to William Carlos Williams, 19 December 1913, in *Letters* (1951), p. 65.

105. Wyndham Lewis et al., 'Manifesto – I', *BLAST* (1914), p. 13.

106. Ezra Pound, 'Vortex. Pound' (1914), p. 153.

107. Alice Corbin Henderson, 'Imagism: Secular and Exotic', *Poetry* (March 1918), p. 339.

108. Ezra Pound, quoting Eliot, in 'T.S. Eliot', *Poetry* (August 1917), p. 269.

109. Ezra Pound, 'Harold Monro', *Criterion* (July 1932), p. 590.

110. Ezra Pound (and Ernest Fenollosa), *Instigations of Ezra Pound: Together with an Essay on the Chinese Written Character* (New York: Boni and Liveright, 1920), p. 363.

111. Pound (and Fenollosa) (1920), p. 364.

112. Pound (and Fenollosa) (1920), p. 380.

113. Ezra Pound, 'Fenollosa on the Noh', in *The Classic Noh Theatre of Japan*, eds Ezra Pound and Ernest Fenollosa (New York: New Directions, 1959), pp. 69–70.

114. W.B. Yeats, 'Introduction by William Butler Yeats to *Certain Noble Plays of Japan* by Pound and Fenollosa', in Pound and Fenollosa (1959), p. 151.

115. Mabel Dodge Luhan, in *Intimate Memories: Movers and Shakers* (New York: Harcourt Brace and Company, 1936), p. 27.

116. Gertrude Stein, *A Transatlantic Interview* (1946), in Scott (1990), p. 504.

117. Gertrude Stein, *The Autobiography of Alice B. Toklas* (New York: Vintage-Random House, 1933), p. 54.

118. Carl Van Vechten, Introduction, Gertrude Stein, *Three Lives* (Norfolk: New Directions, 1933), p. x; *Literary Digest International Book Review* (May 1923), p. 7.

119. Nella Larsen, Richard Wright and Claude McKay, quoted in John Malcolm Brinnin, *The Third Rose: Gertrude Stein and her World* (London: Weidenfeld & Nicolson, 1960), p. 121.

120. Luhan (1936), p. 28.

121. Mina Loy, 'Gertrude Stein', in Scott (1990), p. 239.

122. Loy in Scott (1990), p. 238.

123. Loy in Scott (1990), p. 241.

124. Gertrude Stein, 'Composition as Explanation', in *A Stein Reader*, ed. Ulla Dydo (Evanston: Northwestern University Press, 1996), pp. 500–1.

125. Gertrude Stein, 'Poetry and Grammar', in *Lectures in America* (New York: Random House, 1935), p. 231.

126. Stein (1935), p. 246.

127. Sherwood Anderson, 'The Works of Gertrude Stein', *Geography and Plays* (New York: Haskell House, 1922), quoted in Brinnin (1960), p. 245.

128. Alfred Kreymborg, 'Gertrude Stein – Hoax and Hoaxtress: A Study of the Woman Whose "Tender Buttons" Has Furnished New York with a New Kind of Amusement', *New York Morning Telegraph* (7 March 1915), p. 6.

129. H.L. Mencken, 'A Cubist Treatise: Baltimore Woman's Book Is as Comprehensible as Paintings', *Baltimore Sun* (6 June 1914), in *The Critical Response to Gertrude Stein*, ed. Kirk Curnutt (Westport: Greenwood Press, 2000), p. 14.

130. Hans Arp, 'Dadaland', in *Arp on Arp: Poems, Essays, Memories* (New York: Viking, 1972), p. 234.

131. Tristan Tzara, 'Dada Manifesto 1918', in *The Dada Painters and Poets: An Anthology*, 2nd edn, ed. Robert Motherwell (New York: Wittenborn, Schultz, 1981), p. 77.

132. Tzara (1981), pp. 81–2.

133. Tzara (1981), p. 77.

134. André Breton, 'After Dada' (1922), in *The Last Steps*, trans. Mark Polizzotti (Lincoln: University of Nebraska Press, 1996), p. 75.

135. Frank Budgen, *James Joyce and the Making of 'Ulysses'* (Bloomington: Indiana University Press, 1960), pp. 67–8.

136. James Joyce to Carlo Linati, 21 September 1920, in *Letters*, vol. 1 (1966), pp. 146–7.

137. James Joyce to Harriet Shaw Weaver, 24 June 1921, in *Letters*, vol. 1 (1966), p. 167.

138. James Joyce to Harriet Shaw Weaver, 6 August 1919, in *Letters*, vol. 1 (1966), p. 129.

139. Stuart Gilbert, *James Joyce's 'Ulysses'* (New York: Viking, 1955), p. 30; James Joyce to Harriet Shaw Weaver, February 1921, in *Letters*, vol. 1 (1966), p. 159.

140. Valery Larbaud, 'The *Ulysses* of James Joyce', *Criterion* (October 1922), pp. 94–103, in Deming (2002), p. 253.

141. Ernest Boyd, *Ireland's Literary Renaissance* (London: Grant Richards, 1923).
142. T.S. Eliot, 'Ulysses, Order, and Myth', *Dial* (November 1923), pp. 480–3, in *Selected Prose of T.S. Eliot*, ed. Frank Kermode (London: Faber and Faber, 1975), p. 175.
143. Eliot (1975), p. 175.
144. Eliot (1975), p. 177.
145. Eliot (1975), pp. 177–8.
146. 'The Scandal of *Ulysses*', *Sporting Times* (1 April 1922), p. 4, in Deming (2002), p. 192.
147. D.H. Lawrence, quoted in Ellmann (1982), p. 615, n.
148. Stuart Gilbert, *James Joyce's 'Ulysses': A Study* (London: Faber, 1930).
149. John Woolsey, 'The Hon. John M. Woolsey's Decision to Lift the Ban on *Ulysses*', eds Nicholas Fargnoli and Michael Patrick Gillespie (Oxford: Oxford University Press, 1995), p. 250.
150. William Archer, 'Great Contribution of "Little Theatres" to our Drama's Future', *New York Evening Post* (24 February 1921), p. 9.
151. Alfred Kreymborg, 'Lima Beans', *The Provincetown Players: A Choice of the Shorter Works*, ed. Barbara Ozieblo (Sheffield: Sheffield Academic Press, 1994), p. 131.
152. Alfred Kremborg, *Troubador: An American Autobiography* (New York: Sagamore Press, 1957), p. 243; William Zorach, *Art Is my Life: The Autobiography of William Zorach* (1967), p. 46.
153. Jean Toomer, 'Negro Psychology in *The Emperor Jones*', in *A Jean Toomer Reader: Selected Unpublished Writings*, ed. Frederick L. Rusch (New York: Oxford University Press, 1993), p. 84.
154. James Weldon Johnson, *Black Manhattan* (New York, Da Capo Press, 1991), p. 185.
155. Jane Heap, 'Dada', *Little Review* (Spring 1922), p. 46.
156. Van Wyck Brooks, *America's Coming-of-Age* (New York: W.B. Huebsch, 1915), pp. 27, 9.
157. Brooks (1915), p. 121.
158. Matthew Josephson, 'The Great American Billposter', *Broom* (November 1922), p. 309.
159. Mina Loy, 'Modern Poetry', in *The Last Lunar Baedecker*, ed. Conover (1997), p. 158.
160. Loy (1997), p. 159.
161. Loy (1997), p. 157.
162. Arthur Kreymborg, *The Troubadour: An Autobiography* (New York: Liveright, 1925), p. 235.
163. Ezra Pound, 'A List of Books', *Little Review* (March 1918), p. 57; Ezra Pound, 'How to Read', in *Literary Essays* (1954), p. 25.
164. Ezra Pound (1918), p. 58.
165. Marianne Moore, 'Poetry', *Others for 1919: An Anthology of the New Verse* (New York: Nicholas Brown, 1920), p. 132.
166. Marianne Moore, 'Comment', *Dial* (May 1927), p. 449.
167. Moore (1920), p. 132.
168. Moore (1920), p. 131.
169. Wallace Stevens, 'About One of Marianne Moore's Poems', *The Necessary Angel* (1951), pp. 91–103, p. 95; William Carlos Williams, 'Marianne Moore', *Selected Essays of William Carlos Williams* (New York: Random House 1954), p. 294.
170. T.S. Eliot, 'Introduction', Marianne Moore, *Selected Poems* (New York: Macmillan, 1935), p. xiv.
171. Wallace Stevens, 'Two or Three Ideas' (1951), in *Opus Posthumous*, ed. Samuel French Morse (New York: Alfred A. Knopf, 1957), p. 215.
172. Stevens (1951), p. 31.
173. Stevens (1951), p. 33.
174. Stevens (1951), p. 32.
175. Matthew Josephson, *Broom* (November 1923), pp. 236–7, in *Wallace Stevens: The Critical Heritage*, ed. Charles Doyle (London: Routledge, 1997), p. 41; Harriet Monroe, 'A Cavalier of Beauty', *Poetry* (March 1924), pp. 322–7, in Doyle (1997), p. 58.
176. Edmund Wilson, 'Wallace Stevens and E.E. Cummings', *Dial* (19 March 1924), pp. 102–3, in Doyle (1997), p. 62.

177. Gorham B. Munson, 'The Dandyism of Wallace Stevens, *Dial* (November 1925), pp. 413–7, in (Doyle 1997), pp. 79, 79, 82.

178. R.P. Blackmur, 'Examples of Wallace Stevens', *Hound and Horn* (Winter 1932), in Doyle (1997), p. 100.

179. T.S. Eliot, 'Tradition and the Individual Talent', in *The Sacred Wood* (1920), p. 46.

180. Eliot (1920), p. 44.

181. Eliot (1920), p. 43.

182. Eliot (1920), p. 48.

183. Eliot (1920), p. 44.

184. Eliot (1920), p. 48.

185. Eliot (1920), p. 48.

186. Eliot (1920), pp. 52–3.

187. Eliot (1920), p. 49.

188. T.S. Eliot, 'Philip Massinger', in *The Sacred Wood* (1920), p. 114.

189. T.S. Eliot in interview, *Yorkshire Post; The Bed Post* (1962), pp. 43–4, in *Inventions of the March Hare*, ed. Ricks (1996), p. xxiv.

190. Ezra Pound to Felix Schelling, 9 July 1922, in Paige (1951), p. 248.

191. J.C. Squire, 'Poetry', *London Mercury* (October 1923), pp. 655–6, in *T.S. Eliot: The Contemporary Reviews*, ed. Jewel Spears Brooker (Cambridge: Cambridge University Press, 2004), p. 115; Louis Untermeyer, 'Disillusion vs. Dogma', *Freeman* (17 January 1923), p. 454, in Brooker (2004), pp. 93, 94, 94.

192. T.S. Eliot, 'The Metaphysical Poets', *Selected Prose* (London: Faber, 1975), p. 65.

193. T.S. Eliot, 'Notes on *The Waste Land*', *The Complete Poems and Plays* (London: Faber and Faber 1969), p. 76.

194. J.G. Frazer, *The Golden Bough: A Study in Magic and Religion*, ed. Robert Fraser (Oxford: Oxford University Press, 1998), p. 12.

195. Frazer (1998), p. 804.

196. Edmund Wilson, 'The Poetry of Drouth', *Dial* (December 1922), pp. 611–16, in Brooker (2004), pp. 84–5.

197. Wilson (2004), p. 84.

198. Wilson (2004), pp. 86–7.

3   MODERNISM AFTER 1922

1. William Carlos Williams, *The Autobiography of William Carlos Williams* (New York: New Directions Publishing, 1967), p. 174.

2. Ezra Pound, 'Provincialism the Enemy 1', *New Age* (12 July 1917), p. 245.

3. Williams (1970), p. 24.

4. William Carlos Williams, 'Spring and All', in *Imaginations* (1970), p. 131.

5. Williams (1970), pp. 131, 136.

6. Williams (1970), p. 101.

7. Williams (1970), pp. 91, 120.

8. William Carlos Williams, *In the American Grain* (New York: New Directions, 1959), p. 109.

9. D.H. Lawrence, 'American Heroes', *Nation* (14 April 1926), pp. 413–14, *William Carlos Williams: The Critical Heritage*, ed. Charles Doyle (London: Routledge & Kegan Paul, 1980), p. 90.

10. Lawrence, 'American Heroes', in Doyle (1980), p. 90.

11. Alfred Kreymborg, *Our Singing Strength: An Outline of American Poetry* (1620–1930) (New York: Coward-McCann, 1929), pp. 500–4, quoted in Doyle (1980), p. 118.

12. Philip Blair Rice, review, *Nation* (28 March 1934), pp. 365–6, in Doyle (1980), p. 128.

13. Rice, in Doyle (1980), p. 129.

14. George Oppen to Mary Ellen Solt, 16 February 1961, *The Selected Letters of George Oppen*, ed. Rachel Blau DuPLessis (Durham: Duke University Press, 1990), p. 47.

15. Louis Zukofsky, *Prepositions: The Collected Critical Essays of Louis Zukofsky*, expanded ed. (Berkeley: University of California Press, 1981), p. 12.

16. Zukofsky (1981), p. 12.
17. William Carlos Williams, *Paterson* (New York: New Directions, 1963), p. 3.
18. Wallace Stevens, 'Preface', William Carlos Williams, *Collected Poems 1921–31* (New York: The Objectivist Press, 1934), in Doyle (1980), p. 125.
19. Philip Cohen and Doreen Fowler, 'Faulkner's Introduction to *The Sound and the Fury*', *American Literature* 62.2 (June 1990), p. 276.
20. Evelyn Scott, 'On William Faulkner's *The Sound and the Fury*' (New York, October 1929), in *William Faulkner: The Critical Heritage*, ed. John Bassett (London: Routledge & Kegan Paul, 1975), p. 77.
21. Scott, in Bassett (1975), p. 78.
22. Henry Nash Smith, review of *The Sound and the Fury*, *Southwest Review* (Autumn 1929), pp. iii–iv, in Bassett (1975), p. 87.
23. John McClure [pseud. Julia K. Wetherill Baker], 'Literature and Less: A Page on Books of the Day', *Times-Picayune* (29 June 1930), p. 23, in *Icon Critical Guides: The Sound and the Fury and As I Lay Dying*, ed. Nicolas Tredell (Duxford, Cambridge: Icon Books, 1999), p. 24.
24. William Faulkner in interview, *Faulkner in the University*, eds Frederick Gywn and Joseph Blotner (Charlottesville: University of Virginia Press 1959), pp. 273–4.
25. Tzara (1981), p. 79.
26. André Breton, 'The Second Manifesto of Surrealism', in *Manifestos of Surrealism*, trans. Richard Seaver and Helen Lane (Ann Arbor: University of Michigan Press, 1972), p. 160.
27. André Breton, 'The Mediums Enter', *Littérature* 6 (November 1, 1922), in *The Lost Steps*, trans. Mark Polizzotti (Lincoln: University of Nebraska Press, 1996), pp. 89–95.
28. André Breton, 'First Manifesto of Surrealism', in Seaver and Lane (1972), p. 26.
29. Breton (1972), p. 14.
30. Comte de Lautréamont, *Maldoror*, trans. Alexis Lykiard (Cambridge, MA: Exact Change, 1994), p. 193.
31. Antonin Artaud, 'Theatre and Cruelty', in *The Theatre and Its Double*, trans. Victor Corti (London: Calder and Boyars, 1993), p. 64.
32. Artaud, 'Theatre and Cruelty' (1993), p. 65.
33. Antonin Artaud, 'The Theatre of Cruelty (First Manifesto)', in Corti (1993), pp. 70–1.
34. Artaud, 'On the Balinese Theatre', in Corti (1993), p. 37.
35. Artaud, 'Theatre and Cruelty' (1993), p. 66.
36. Wyndham Lewis, *Blasting and Bombardiering* (London: Eyre & Spottiswoode, 1937), p. 252, p. 289.
37. Lewis (1937), pp. 252, 258.
38. Ezra Pound, '*Credit Power and Democracy* by Major. C. H. Douglas and A. R. Orage [sic]', *Contact* 4 (1921), p. 1.
39. T.S. Eliot, 'Last Words', *Criterion* (January 1939), p. 271.
40. T.S. Eliot, Preface, *The Sacred Wood* (London: Methuen, 1928), p. viii.
41. T.S. Eliot, *The Use of Poetry and the Use of Criticism* (London: Faber and Faber, 1933), p. 153.
42. William Carlos Williams, 'It's about "Your Life and Mine, Darling"', review of T.S. Eliot, *The Cocktail Party*, *New York Evening Post* (12 March 1950), p. 18, in Michael Grant, *T.S. Eliot: The Critical Heritage* (London: Routledge & Kegan Paul, 1982), p. 601.
43. F. Scott Fitzgerald, 'Echoes of the Jazz Age', in *The Crack-Up, with other Uncollected Pieces, Note-Books and Unpublished Letters*, ed. Edmund Wilson (New York: New Directions, 1956), p. 13.
44. Fitzgerald (1956), p. 14.
45. Fitzgerald (1956), p. 15.
46. H.L. Mencken, *The Smart Set* (August 1920), p. 140, in Jackson R. Bryer, ed., *F. Scott Fitzgerald: The Critical Reception* (New York: Burt Franklin, 1978), p. 28.
47. Isabel Paterson, 'Up to the Minute', *New York Herald Tribune* (19 April 1925), p. 6, in Bryer (1978), p. 200; 'The First Reader – Great Scott', *New York World* (22 April 1925), p. 13, in Bryer (1978), p. 204.
48. F. Scott Fitzgerald to Ludlow Fowler, August 1924, in *Correspondence of F. Scott Fitzgerald*, eds Matthew Bruccoli and Margaret Duggan (New York: Random House, 1980), p. 145.

49. F. Scott Fitzgerald to Maxwell Perkins, mid July 1922, in *Correspondence* (1980), p. 112.
50. T.S. Eliot to F. Scott Fitzgerald, 31 December 1925, in Wilson (1965), p. 310; Gertrude Stein to F. Scott Fitzgerald, 22 May 1925, in Wilson (1956), p. 308.
51. Ernest Hemingway, 'Introduction', *Men at War* (New York: Crown, 1942), p. xv.
52. Ernest Hemingway, *The Sun Also Rises* (New York: Grosset and Dunlap, 1926), p. 174.
53. George Plimpton, 'The Art of Fiction, XXI: Ernest Hemingway', *Paris Review* 5 (Spring, 1958), pp. 60–89, p. 84.
54. Edmund Wilson, 'Mr. Hemingway's Dry-Points', *Dial* (October 1924), pp. 340–1, in *Hemingway: The Critical Heritage*, ed. Jeffrey Meyers (London: Routledge & Kegan Paul, 1982), p. 63.
55. Wilson, in Meyers (1982), p. 63.
56. Paul Rosenfeld, *New Republic* (25 November 1925), pp. 22–3, in Meyers (1982), p. 67.
57. Rosenfeld, in Meyers (1982), pp. 67–9.
58. Allen Tate, 'Hard-boiled', *Nation* (5 December 1926), pp. 642–4.
59. Edmund Wilson, 'Ernest Hemingway: Gauge of Morale', *Atlantic* (July 1939), pp. 36–46, in Meyers (1982), p. 303.
60. Wyndham Lewis, *Men without Art* (New York: Russell and Russell, 1934), pp. 24, 29.
61. Dorothy Parker, *PM* (20 October 1940), p. 42, in Meyers (1982), p. 315.
62. W.E.B. Du Bois, *The Souls of Black Folk: Essays and Sketches* (Chicago: A. C. McClurg & Co. 1903), p. vii.
63. Du Bois (1903), p. 11.
64. Du Bois (1903), p. 8.
65. Langston Hughes, 'The Negro Artist and the Racial Mountain', in De Santi (2002), p. 34.
66. Jean Toomer, *The Wayward and the Seeking: A Collection of Writings by Jean Toomer*, ed. Darwin Turner (Washington: Howard University Press, 1980), p. 123.
67. W.E.B. Du Bois, 'The Younger Literary Movement' (1924), in *The New Negro: Readings on Race, Representation, and African American Culture: 1892–1938*, eds Henry Louis Gates and Gene Andrew Jarrett (Princeton: Princeton University Press, 2007), p. 219.
68. Jean Toomer, letter to the *Liberator*, August 1922, quoted in Michael North, *The Dialect of Modernism: Race, Language & Twentieth-Century Literature* (New York: Oxford University Press, 1994), p. 162.
69. Publicity clipping for *Cane*, quoted in North (1994), p. 164.
70. Alain Locke, 'The New Negro', in *The New Negro: An Interpretation*, ed. Alain Locke (New York: Atheneum, 1969), p. 14.
71. Locke (1969), p. 4.
72. Alain Locke, 'Negro Youth Speaks', in Locke (1969), p. 50.
73. Locke (1969), p. 51.
74. H.L. Mencken, 'The Aframerican: New Style', *American Mercury* (February 1926), pp. 254–5, in *The New Negro: Readings on Race, Representation, and African American Culture*, eds Henry Louis Gates and Gene Andrew Jarrett (Princeton: Princeton University Press, 2007), p. 227.
75. Mencken (1926), in Gates and Jarrett, eds (2007), p. 228.
76. Carl Van Vechten, 'Uncle Tom's Mansion', *New York Herald Tribune* (20? December 1925), in Gates and Jarrett, eds (2007), p. 224.
77. Van Vechten (1925), in Gates and Jarrett, eds (2007), p. 225.
78. W.E.B. Du Bois, 'Books', *Crisis* (December 1926), p. 81.
79. Zora Neale Hurston, 'Characteristics of Negro Expression', in *Negro*, ed. Nancy Cunard (London: Wishart, 1934), pp. 24, 28.
80. Hurston (1934), p. 28.
81. Hurston (1934), p. 28.
82. Hurston (1934), p. 28.
83. Alain Locke, review of *Their Eyes Were Watching God*, *Opportunity* (1 June 1938), in *Zora Neale Hurston: Critical Perspectives Past and Present*, eds Henry Louis Gates, Jr and K.A. Appiah (New York: Amistad, 1993), p. 18.

84. Alice Walker, *In Search of Our Mothers' Gardens: Womanist Prose* (New York: Harcourt, 1983), p. 86.
85. Radclyffe Hall, *Radclyffe Hall's 1934 Letter about the Well of Loneliness*, ed. Polly Thistlewaite (New York: Lesbian Herstory Educational Foundation, 1994), in *Gender in Modernism: New Geographies, Complex Intersections*, ed. Bonnie Kime Scott (Urbana and Chicago: University of Illinois Press, 2007), pp. 325–6.
86. Leonard Woolf, 'The World of Books. *The Well of Loneliness*', *The Nation and Athenaeum* (4 August 1938), p. 593.
87. James Douglas, 'A Book that Must Be Suppressed', *Sunday Express* (19 August 1928), in *Palatable Poison: Critical Perspectives on 'The Well of Loneliness'*, eds Laura Doan and Jay Prosser (New York: Columbia University Press, 2001), p. 37.
88. Rebecca West, *Ending in Earnest: A Literary Log* (Freeport: Books for Libraries, 1967), p. 9.
89. E.M. Forster and Virginia Woolf, 'The New Censorship', *Nation & Athenaeum* (8 September 1927), p. 629.
90. Forster and Woolf (1927), p. 629.
91. Forster and Woolf (1927), p. 629.
92. Forster and Woolf (1927), p. 629.
93. Virigina Woolf, *A Room of One's Own and Three Guineas*, ed. Morag Shiach (Oxford: Oxford University Press, 2000), p. 106.
94. Woolf (2000), pp. 100, 99.
95. Woolf (2000), pp. 113–14.
96. Michael Roberts, ed., *New Signatures* (London: Hogarth Press, 1935), pp. 12, 19, 11, 11.
97. Quoted in Valentine Cunningham, ed., *The Penguin Book of Spanish Civil War Verse* (London: Penguin, 1980), pp. 49–50.
98. C. Day-Lewis, *Revolution in Writing* (London: The Hogarth Press, 1938).
99. George Orwell, 'Inside the Whale', in *Collected Essays* (London: Martin Secker and Warburg, 1961), p. 141.
100. Orwell (1961), p. 152.
101. Virginia Woolf, 'The Leaning Tower', *Collected Essays*, vol. 2 (1966), pp. 172, 176, 176, 176.
102. Orwell (1961), p. 157.
103. Orwell (1961), p. 139.
104. Orwell (1961), p. 157.
105. Orwell (1961), p. 158.
106. Woolf (1966), p. 181.
107. Eugène Jolas, *Man from Babel*, eds Andreas Kramer and Rainer Rumold (New Haven: Yale University Press, 1998), p. 2.
108. Eugène Jolas, 'The Revolution of the Word: Proclamation', *transition* 16/17 (June 1929), p. 13.
109. James Joyce to Harriet Shaw Weaver, 24 November 1926, in *Letters of James Joyce*, vol. 3, ed. Richard Ellmann (New York: Viking, 1966), p. 146.
110. Samuel Beckett, 'Dante...Bruno. Vico.. Joyce', in *Our Exagmination Round His Factification for Incamination of 'Work in Progress'* (London: Faber and Faber, 1972), pp. 14–15.
111. Samuel Beckett in interview with Israel Shenke, *New York Times* (5 May 1956), section II, p. 1, p. 3, reprinted in *Samuel Beckett: The Critical Heritage*, eds L. Graver and R. Federman (London: Routledge, 1997), p. 162.
112. Elliot Paul, 'Mr. Joyce's Treatment of Plot', in *Our Exagmination* (1972), p. 134.
113. Oliver St. John Gogarty, review, *Observer* (7 May 1939), p. 4, in Deming (1997), p. 675; Richard Aldington, review, *Atlantic Monthly* (June 1939, clxiii, n.p.), in Deming (1997), p. 690.
114. Harry Levin, 'On First Looking into *Finnegans Wake*', *New Directions in Prose and Poetry* (1939), pp. 253–87, in Deming (1997), p. 699.

4   THE MAKING OF MODERNIST CANONS

1. John Crowe Ransom, 'Waste Lands', *New York Evening Post Literary Review* 3 (July 14), pp. 825–6; Allen Tate, 'Waste Lands', *New York Evening Post Literary Review* 3 (4 August 1923), p. 886.

2. Louis Menand and Lawrence Rainey, 'Introduction', in *The Cambridge History of Literary Criticism: Modernism and the New Criticism*, eds. A. Walton Litz, Louis Menand and Lawrence Rainey (Cambridge: Cambridge University Press, 2000), p. 10.

3. Menard and Rainey (2000), p. 10.

4. Viktor Shklovsky, 'Art as Technique', in *Russian Formalist Criticism: Four Essays*, eds Lee Lemon and Marion Reis (Lincoln: University of Nebraska Press, 1965), p. 13.

5. I.A. Richards, *Principles of Literary Criticism* (London: Kegan Paul, Trench, Trübner, 1924), p. 4.

6. Richards (1924), p. 16.

7. Cleanth Brooks, *The Well Wrought Urn: Studies in the Structure of Poetry* (New York: Harcourt, Brace and World, 1947).

8. William K. Wimsatt and Monroe C. Beardsley, 'The Intentional Fallacy', *Sewanee Review* 54.3 (1946), p. 477.

9. Wimsatt and Beardsley (1946), p. 468, p. 470.

10. Cleanth Brooks, *Modern Poetry and the Tradition* (Chapel Hill: The University of North Carolina Press, 1939), p. x.

11. Lawrence H. Schwartz, *Creating Faulkner's Reputation: The Politics of Modern Literary Criticism* (Knoxville: The University of Tennessee Press, 1988).

12. Franklin E. Court, *Institutionalizing English Literature: The Culture and Politics of Literary Study, 1750–1900* (Stanford: Stanford University Press, 1992), p. 2.

13. T. S. Eliot, 'The Frontiers of Criticism', *On Poetry and Poets* (London: Faber and Faber, 1957), p. 113.

14. Elin Diamond, 'Modern Drama/Modernity's Drama', in *Modern Drama*, eds Ric Knowles, Joanne Tompkins and W.B. Worthen (Toronto: University of Toronto Press, 2003), p. 5.

15. Toril Moi, 'Ibsen, Theatre, and Ideology of Modernism,' *Theatre Survey* 45.2 (November 2004), p. 247.

16. John Paul Riquelme, 'Introduction to Reading Modernism, After Hugh Kenner', *Modernism/Modernity*, 12.3 (September 2005), p. 459.

17. Hugh Kenner, 'The Making of the Modernist Canon', *Chicago Review*, 34. 2 (1984), p. 59.

18. Kenner (1984), p. 59.

19. Hugh Kenner, *The Poetry of Ezra Pound* (Norfolk: New Directions, 1951), p. 16.

20. Kenner (1951), pp. 16, 32.

21. Kenner (1984), p. 58.

22. Kenner (1984), p. 58.

23. Hugh Kenner, *The Pound Era* (Berkeley: University of California Press, 1971), p. 145.

24. Kenner (1971), p. 554.

25. Kenner (1971), p. 554.

26. Kenner (1971), p. 3.

27. Kenner (1971), p. 5.

28. Hugh Kenner, *Dublin's Joyce* (Bloomington: Indiana University Press, 1956), pp. 34, 13.

29. Kenner (1956), p. 12.

30. Kenner (1956), p. 129, p. 132.

31. Hugh Kenner, *Joyce's Voices* (Berkeley: University of California Press, 1978), pp. 18, 17.

32. Kenner (1984), p. 53.

33. Marjorie Perloff, 'Reading Modernism, After Hugh Kenner (1923–2003): Hugh Kenner and the Invention of Modernism', *Modernism/Modernity*, 12.3 (September 2005), p. 466.

34. Perloff (2005), p. 466.

35. James Joyce, quoted in Ellmann (1982), p. 521.
36. Ferdinand de Saussure, *Course in General Linguistics*, ed. and trans. Wade Basklin (London: Peter Owen, 1959), p. 117.
37. Derek Attridge and Daniel Ferrer, eds, *Post-Structuralist Joyce: Essays from the French* (Cambridge: Cambridge University Press, 1984), p. 10.
38. Attridge and Ferrer (1984), p. 10.
39. Attridge and Ferrer (1984), p. ix.
40. 'The Villanova Roundtable: A Conversation with Jacques Derrida', in *Deconstruction in a Nutshell: A Conversation with Jacques Derrida*, ed. John Caputo (New York: Fordham University Press, 199), p. 26.
41. Jacques Derrida, '*Ulysses* Gramophone: Hear Say Yes in Joyce', in *Acts of Literature*, ed. Derek Attridge (London, Routledge: 1992), p. 281.
42. Derek Attridge, 'Introduction to *Ulysses* Gramophone: Hear Say Yes in Joyce' in *Acts of Literature* (1992), p. 254.
43. Colin MacCabe, *James Joyce and the Revolution of the Word* (Basingstoke: Macmillan, 1979), p. 3.
44. MacCabe (1979), pp. 3, 4.
45. Frank Kermode, *Romantic Image* (London: Routledge and Kegan Paul, 1957), pp. 110–30.
46. Harold Bloom, *Yeats* (New York: University of Oxford Press, 1970), p. v.
47. Harold Bloom, *A Map of Misreading* (New York: Oxford University Press, 1975), p. 28.
48. Harold Bloom, *Wallace Stevens: The Poems of our Climate* (Ithaca: Cornell University Press, 1977), p. 152.
49. Marjorie Perloff, 'Pound/Stevens: Whose Era?', *New Literary History* 13.3 (Spring, 1982), p. 485.
50. Perloff (1982), p. 506.
51. B.H. Dias (pseud. Ezra Pound), 'Art Notes', *New Age* (1 August 1918), p. 223.
52. Scott (1990), p. 2.
53. Richard Ellmann and Charles Feidelson, eds, *The Modern Tradition: Backgrounds of Modern Literature* (London: Oxford University Press, 1965), p. vi.
54. Elaine Showalter, 'Towards a Feminist Poetics', in *The New Feminist Criticism: Essays on Women, Literature and Theory*, ed. Elaine Showalter (London: Virago, 1985), p. 128.
55. Elaine Showalter (1985), p. 130.
56. Shari Benstock, *Women of the Left Bank: Paris, 1900–1940* (London: Virago, 1987), pp. ix, 19.
57. Benstock (1987), pp. 9, 47.
58. Gillian Hanscombe and Virginia Smyers, *Writing for their Lives: The Modernist Woman 1910–1940* (London: The Women's Press, 1987), p. xv.
59. Benstock (1987), pp. 188, 189.
60. Benstock (1987), p. x.
61. Sandra Gilbert and Susan Gubar, *No Man's Land: The Place of the Woman Writer in the Twentieth Century*, 3 vols (New Haven: Yale University Press, 1988–1994): vol. 1, *The War of the Words* (1988), p. xii; vol. 2, *Sexchanges* (1989); vol. 3, *Letters from the Front* (1994).
62. Elaine Showalter, *A Literature of their Own* (London: Virago, 1977), pp. 33, 34.
63. Toril Moi, *Sexual/Textual Politics: Feminist Literary Theory* (London and New York: Routledge, 2001), p. 8.
64. Moi (2001), p. 8.
65. Moi (2001), p. 166.
66. E. Ann Kaplan, 'Is the Gaze Male?', in *Desire: The Politics of Sexuality*, eds Ann Barr Snitow, Christine Stansell and Sharon Thompson (Virago: London, 1984), p. 331.
67. Julia Kristeva, 'Oscillation between Power and Denial', in *New French Feminisms*, eds. Elaine Marks and Isabelle de Courtivron (Amherst: University of Massachusetts Press, 1980), p. 165.
68. Julia Kristeva, *Revolution in Poetic Language*, trans. Margaret Waller (New York: Columbia University Press, 1984).
69. Woolf, 'Romance and the Heart', in *Essays*, vol. 3 (1988), p. 367.

70. Alice Jardine, 'Gynesis', *Diacritics* 12.2 (1982), pp. 54–65.
71. Rita Felski, *Beyond Feminist Aesthetics: Feminist Literatures and Social Change* (Cambridge: Harvard University Press, 1989), p. 7.
72. Felski (1989), pp. 5–6.
73. Scott (1990), pp. 13, 13, 198.
74. Scott (1990), p. 7.
75. Scott (1990), p. 12.
76. Scott (1990), pp. 7, 8.
77. Scott (1990), p. 10.
78. Scott (1990), p. 11.
79. Valentine Cunningham, *British Writers of the Thirties* (Oxford: Oxford University Press, 1989), p. 27.
80. Scott, *Refiguring Modernism: Volume One, The Women of 1928* (Bloomington: Indiana University Press, 1995), p. xvi.
81. Scott (1995), vol. 1, p. xxxvii.
82. Scott (1995), vol. 1, p. xxxvii.
83. Bonnie Kime Scott, *Refiguring Modernism, Volume Two: Postmodern Feminist Readings of Woolf, West and Barnes* (Bloomington: Indiana University Press, 1995), pp. xvi, 73, xvi.
84. Scott (1995), vol. 1, p. xxxvii.

5 GENDER AND SEXUALITY

1. Gilbert and Gubar (1988), p. xii; (1989), p. xii.
2. Gilbert and Gubar (1988), p. xii.
3. Gilbert and Gubar (1988), p. xii.
4. Gilbert and Gubar (1988), pp. 22, 37, 38, 35, 36.
5. Gilbert and Gubar (1988), p. 154.
6. Gilbert and Gubar (1988), p. 156.
7. Gilbert and Gubar (1988), p. xii.
8. Marianne DeKoven, *Rich and Strange: Gender, History and Modernism* (Princeton: Princeton University Press, 1991), p. 4.
9. DeKoven (1991), p. 24.
10. DeKoven (1991), p. 4.
11. DeKoven (1991), p. 4.
12. DeKoven (1991), p. 27.
13. DeKoven (1991), p. 33.
14. DeKoven (1991), p. 33.
15. DeKoven (1991), p. 4.
16. DeKoven (1991), p. 39.
17. DeKoven (1991), p. 63.
18. DeKoven (1991), p. 68.
19. DeKoven (1991), p. 85.
20. DeKoven (1991), p. 68.
21. DeKoven (1991), p. 79.
22. DeKoven (1991), pp. 76–8.
23. DeKoven (1991), p. 85.
24. DeKoven (1991), p. 134.
25. DeKoven (1991), p. 115.
26. Ann Ardis, *New Women: New Novels: Feminism and Early Modernism* (New Brunswick: Rutgers University Press, 1990), p. 169.
27. Ardis (1990), p. 3.
28. Lyn Pykett, *Engendering Fictions: The English Novel in the Early Twentieth Century* (London: Arnold, 1995), p. 61.
29. Pykett (1995), pp. 62–3.

30. Pykett (1995), p. 63.
31. Pykett (1995), p. 123.
32. Pykett (1995), p. 124.
33. Pykett (1995), p. 124.
34. Pykett (1995), p. 123.
35. D.H. Lawrence, 'The Real Thing' (1930), quoted in Pykett (1995), p. 137.
36. Pykett (1995), pp. 125, 126.
37. Sally Ledger, *The New Woman: Fiction and Feminism at the Fin de Siècle* (Manchester: Manchester University Press, 1997), p. 6.
38. Ledger (1997), p. 6.
39. Ledger (1997), p. 194.
40. Ledger (1997), p. 194.
41. Joan Templeton, *Ibsen's Women* (Cambridge: Cambridge University Press, 1997), p. 324.
42. Templeton (1997), p. 324.
43. Penny Farfan, *Women, Modernism and Performance* (Cambridge: Cambridge University Press, 2004), p. 117.
44. Elizabeth Robins, *Ibsen and the Actress* (London: Hogarth Press, 1928; rpt. New York: Haskell House, 1973), p. 31, quoted in Farfan (2004), p. 12.
45. Farfan (2004), p. 25.
46. Unsigned review, *Clarion* (19 April 1907), p. 3, quoted in Farfan (2004), p. 25.
47. Farfan (2004), p. 8.
48. Virginia Woolf, 'Ellen Terry', *Collected Essays*, vol. 4 (London: Hogarth Press, 1967), p. 72, quoted in Farfan (2004), p. 60.
49. Farfan (2004), p. 8.
50. Farfan (2004), p. 9.
51. Farfan (2004), p. 95.
52. Farfan (2004), pp. 96, 96, 95.
53. Farfan (2004), pp. 99, 100.
54. Tim Armstrong, *Modernism, Technology and the Body: A Cultural Study* (Cambridge: Cambridge University Press, 1998), p. 6.
55. Armstrong (1998), p. 3.
56. Armstrong (1998), p. 3.
57. Armstrong (1998), p. 3.
58. Armstrong (1998), pp. 9, 6.
59. Armstrong (1998), p. 29.
60. Armstrong (1998), p. 66.
61. Armstrong (1998), p. 68.
62. Armstrong (1998), p. 70.
63. Armstrong (1998), p. 117.
64. Armstrong (1998), p. 119.
65. Armstrong (1998), p. 121.
66. Armstrong (1998), p. 187.
67. Susan Stanford Friedman, *Psyche Reborn: The Emergence of H.D.* (Bloomington: Indiana University Press, 1981), p. 97.
68. Gilbert and Gubar (1989), p. 260.
69. Gilbert and Gubar (1989), p. 262.
70. Gilbert and Gubar (1989), p. 260.
71. Gilbert and Gubar (1989), p. 282.
72. Gilbert and Gubar (1989), p. 302.
73. Paul Fussell, *The Great War and Modern Memory* (London: Oxford University Press, 1975), p. 35.
74. Fussell (1975), p. 75.
75. Fussell (1975), pp. 174, 175.

76. Siegfried Sassoon, *Memoirs of an Infantry Officer* (New York, 1937), p. 280, quoted in Fussell (1975), p. 90.

77. Fussell (1975), pp. 313–14.

78. Fussell (1975), p. 270.

79. Trudi Tate, *Modernism, History and the First World War* (Manchester: Manchester University Press, 1998), p. 3.

80. Tate (1998), p. 10.

81. Tate (1998), p. 11.

82. Tate (1998), p. 10.

83. Tate (1998), pp. 21, 31, 29, 32–40.

84. Tate (1998), p. 40.

85. Suzanne Raitt and Trudi Tate, 'Introduction', *Women's Fiction and the Great War*, eds Suzanne Raitt and Trudi Tate (Oxford: Clarendon Press 1997), p. 15.

86. Raitt and Tate (1997), p. 13.

87. Claire Buck, '"Still Some Obstinate Emotion Remains": Radclyffe Hall and the Meanings of Service', in Raitt and Tate (1997), p. 13.

88. Radclyffe Hall, 'Miss Ogilvy Finds Herself' (1932), *The Norton Anthology of Literature by Women*, eds Sandra M. Gilbert and Susan Gubar (New York: Norton, 1985), p. 1447, quoted in Buck (1997), p. 180.

89. Suzanne Raitt, '"Contagious Ecstacy": May Sinclair's War Journals', in Raitt and Tate (1997), p. 67.

90. Tate (1998), p. 97.

91. Tate (1998), p. 96.

92. Tate (1998), p. 117.

93. Tate (1998), p. 153.

94. Vincent Sherry, *The Great War and the Language of Modernism* (New York: Oxford University Press, 2003), p. 9.

95. Sherry (2003), p. 9.

96. Sherry (2003), p. 9.

97. Sherry (2003), p. 9.

98. Sherry (2003), p. 21.

99. T.S. Eliot, 'Gerontion', *Collected Poems 1909–1962* (1963; rpt. London: Faber, 1974), p. 40, quoted in Sherry (2003), p. 6.

100. Sherry (2003), p. 6.

101. Sherry (2003), p. 13.

102. Gilbert and Gubar (1989), pp. 326–7.

103. Gilbert and Gubar (1989), p. 327.

104. Judith Butler, *Gender Trouble: Feminism and the Subversion of Identity* (London: Routledge, 1990), p. 6.

105. Butler (1990), p. 25.

106. Rachel Blau DuPlessis, *Genders, Races, and Religious Cultures in Modern American Poetry, 1908–1935* (Cambridge: Cambridge University Press, 2001), p. 6.

107. Eve Kosofksy Sedgwick, *Epistemology of the Closet* (London: Harvester Wheatsheaf, 1991), p. 2.

108. Sedgwick (1991), p. 213.

109. Sedgwick (1991), p. 73.

110. Sedgwick (1991), pp. 33–4

111. Sedgwick (1991), p. 1.

112. Eve Kosofksy Sedgwick, *Tendencies* (London: Routledge, 1994), p. 8.

113. Adrienne Rich, 'Compulsory Heterosexuality and the Continuum of Lesbian Existence', *Signs: Journal of Women in Culture and Society* 5.4 (1980), pp. 631–60.

114. Mary Galvin, *Queer Poetics: Five Modernist Women Writers* (Westport and London: Greenwood Press, 1999), p. 8.

115. Galvin (1999), p. 9.
116. Galvin (1999), p. 7.
117. Galvin (1999), pp. 7, 45, 47.
118. Galvin (1999), p. 49.
119. Galvin (1999), p. 8.
120. Djuna Barnes, *Ladies Almanack* (Elmswood Park: Dalkey Archive Press, 1992), title page.
121. Galvin (1999), p. 8.
122. Galvin (1999), p. xii.
123. Makiko Minow, 'Versions of Female Modernism: Review Article', *News from Nowhere* 7 (1989), p. 67.
124. Shari Benstock, 'Expatriate Sapphic Modernism: Entering Literary History', in *Lesbian Texts and Contexts: Radical Revisions*, eds Karla Jay and Joanne Glasgow (London: Onlywomen Press, 1992), p. 183.
125. Laura Doan, *Fashioning Sapphism: The Origins of a Modern English Lesbian Culture* (New York and Chichester: Columbia University Press, 2001), p. xxi.
126. Gay Wachman, *Lesbian Empire: Radical Crosswriting in the Twenties* (New Brunswick: Rutgers University Press, 2001), p. 5.
127. Wachman (2001), p. 37.
128. Jane Garrity, 'Mary Butts's "Fanatical Pédérastie": Queer Urban Life in 1920s London and Paris', in *Sapphic Modernities: Sexuality, Women and English Culture*, eds Laura Doan and Jane Garrity (New York: Macmillan, 2006), p. 249.
129. Garrity (2006), pp. 233, 235.
130. Garrity (2006), p. 237.
131. Garrity (2006), p. 239.
132. Garrity (2006), p. 239.
133. Garrity (2006), p. 238.
134. Garrity (2006), pp. 240–1.
135. Garrity (2006), p. 241.
136. Joseph Boone, *Libidinal Currents: Sexuality and the Shaping of Modernism* (Chicago: University of Chicago Press, 1998), p. 3.
137. Boone (1998), p. 152.
138. Boone (1998), pp. 224–5.
139. Boone (1998), p. 225.
140. Boone (1998), p. 419.
141. Boone (1998), pp. 7, 14.
142. Boone (1998), p. 78.
143. Boone (1998), p. 81.
144. Colleen Lamos, 'Queer Conjunctions in Modernism', in Scott (2007), pp. 336–7.
145. Colleen Lamos, *Deviant Modernism: Sexual and Textual Errancy in T.S. Eliot, James Joyce, and Marcel Proust* (Oxford: Clarendon Press, 1999), p. 1.
146. Lamos (1999), p. 18.
147. Lamos (1999), pp. 110–11.
148. Lamos (1999), p. 77.
149. James Joyce, *Ulysses: The Corrected Text*, ed. Hans Walter Gabler, with Wolfhard Steppe and Claus Melchior (New York: Garland, 1986), p. 399, quoted in Lamos (1999), p. 121.
150. Lamos (1999), p. 123.
151. Joseph Valente, 'Joyce's (Sexual) Choices: A Historical Overview', ed. Joseph Valente, *Quare Joyce*, (Ann Arbor: University of Michigan Press, 1998), p. 4.
152. Valente (1998), p. 5.
153. Valente (1998), p. 5.
154. Valente (1998), p. 5.
155. Christopher Lane, 'Afterword: "The Vehicle of a Vague Speech"', in Valente (1998), pp. 276, 284.

156. Laura Doan, '"Woman's Place Is the Home": Conservative Sapphic Modernity', in Doan and Garrity (2006), p. 104.
157. 'How Other Women Run their Homes' (Interview with Radclyffe Hall), *Daily Mail,* May 11 (1927), p. 19, quoted in Doan (2006), p. 99.
158. Vera Brittain, *Time and Tide* (August 10, 1928), quoted in Doan (2006), p. 104.
159. Doan (2006), p. 105.

6   MODERNIST GEOGRAPHIES AND TIME FRAMES

1. Malcolm Bradbury, 'The Cities of Modernism', in Bradbury and McFarlane (1991), p. 96.
2. Bradbury (1991), p. 96.
3. Raymond Williams, 'Metropolitan Perceptions and the Emergence of Modernism', in *The Politics of Modernism* (1989), p. 45.
4. Williams (1989), p. 45.
5. Williams (1989), p. 44.
6. Williams (1989), p. 46.
7. Williams (1989), p. 47.
8. Williams (1989), p. 47.
9. Simon Gikandi, 'Race and the Modernist Aesthetic', *Writing and Race*, ed. Tim Youngs (London: Longman, 1997), p. 151.
10. Tristan Tzara, 'Note on Negro Art', *Seven Dada Manifestos and Lampisteries*, trans. Barbara Wright (London: Calder, 1977), p. 57.
11. Ezra Pound, 'The New Sculpture', *Egoist* (16 February 1914), p. 68.
12. T.S. Eliot to Mary Hutchinson, 11? [sic] July 1919, in *Letters*, vol. 1 (1988), p. 317.
13. Gikandi (1997), p. 151.
14. Christopher Innes, *Avant Garde Theatre, 1892–1992* (London: Routledge, 1993), p. 3.
15. Innes (1993), p. 3.
16. Innes (1993), p. 9.
17. Innes (1993), p. 9.
18. Innes (1993), p. 4.
19. Edward Said, *Orientalism* (New York: Pantheon Books, 1978).
20. Edward Said, 'Yeats and Decolonization', in *Nationalism, Colonialism, and Literature*, Seamus Deane, Terry Eagleton, Fredric Jameson and Edward Said (Minneapolis: University of Minnesota Press, 1990), p. 72.
21. Edward Said, *Culture and Imperialism* (London: Vintage, 1994), p. 6.
22. Chinua Achebe, 'An Image of Africa: Racism in Conrad's *Heart of Darkness'*, *Massachusetts Review* (Winter, 1997), p.788.
23. Achebe (1977), p. 788.
24. Achebe (1977), p. 783.
25. Achebe (1977), p. 791.
26. Achebe (1977), p. 791.
27. Said (1994), p. 32.
28. Said (1994), p. 32.
29. Said (1994), p. 32.
30. Said (1994), p. 34.
31. Said (1994), p. 227.
32. Said (1994), p. 227.
33. See, for instance, Bill Ashcroft, Gareth Griffiths and Helen Tiffin, *The Empire Writes Back: Theory and Practice in Post-Colonial Literatures* (London: Routledge, 1989); Liam Kennedy, *Colonialism, Religion and Nationalism in Ireland* (Belfast: The Queen's University of Belfast, 1996).
34. Seamus Deane, 'Introduction', *Nationalism, Colonialism, and Literature* (1990), pp. 3–19, p. 10.
35. Deane (1990), p. 3.

36. Edward Said, 'Yeats and Decolonization', in *Nationalism, Colonialism, and Literature* (1990), pp. 69, 70, 69, 92.
37. Fredric Jameson, 'Modernism and Imperialism', in *Nationalism, Colonialism, and Literature* (1990), p. 57.
38. Jameson (1990), p. 58.
39. Jameson (1990), p. 59.
40. Jameson (1990), p. 64.
41. Jameson (1990), p. 62.
42. Vincent Cheng, *Joyce, Race and Empire* (Cambridge: Cambridge University Press, 1995), n.p.
43. Cheng (1995), p. 151.
44. Cheng (1995), pp. 151–2.
45. Cheng (1995), p. 27.
46. Cheng (1995), p. 170.
47. Cheng (1995), p. 79.
48. Cheng (1995), p. 99.
49. Cheng (1995), p. 98.
50. Cheng (1995), p. 11.
51. Cheng (1995), pp. 185, 179.
52. Cheng (1995), p. 6.
53. Stephen Kern, *The Culture of Time and Space, 1880–1918* (Cambridge, MA: Harvard University Press, 1983), p. 1.
54. Kern (1983), pp. 151, 8, 6, 81, 7.
55. Kern (1983), p. 202.
56. Andrew Thacker, *Moving through Modernity: Space and Geography in Modernism* (Manchester: Manchester University Press, 2009), p. 3.
57. Thacker (2009), p. 17; Henri Lefebvre, 'Reflections on the Politics of Space', *Antipode* 8.2 (May 1976), p. 31, quoted in Thacker (2009), p. 17; Thacker (2009), pp. 19–20.
58. Thacker (2009), pp. 23, 24–7.
59. Thacker (2009), p. 34; Michael de Certeau, *The Practice of Everyday Life*, trans. Steven Randall (Berkeley: University of California Press), p. 121, quoted in Thacker (2009), p. 34.
60. Thacker (2009), p. 7.
61. Thacker (2009), p. 203.
62. Thacker (2009), pp. 204, 203.
63. Anna Snaith, 'A Savage from the Cannibal Islands: Jean Rhys and London', in *Geographies of Modernism: Literatures, Cultures, Spaces*, eds Peter Brooker and Andrew Thacker (London: Routledge, 2005), pp. 84, 85.
64. Snaith (2005), p. 85.
65. Interview with Marinetti, *Evening News* (4 March 1912), p. 3, quoted in Thacker (2009), p. 86.
66. Thacker (2009), pp. 89, 86.
67. Thacker (2009), p. 93.
68. Thacker (2009), p. 94.
69. Thacker (2009), p. 94.
70. Thacker (2009), pp. 99, 101.
71. Thacker (2009), pp. 102, 101, 101.
72. Thacker (2009), p. 104.
73. Michael Seidel, *Epic Geography: James Joyce's 'Ulysses'* (Princeton: Princeton University Press, 1976), p. ix.
74. Budgen (1960), p. 124.
75. Thacker (2009), p. 133.
76. Thacker (2009), p. 131.
77. Thacker (2009), pp. 138–9.

78. Thacker (2009), p. 139.
79. Thacker (2009), p. 141.
80. Griselda Pollock, *Vision and Difference: Femininity, Feminism and the Histories of Art* (London: Routledge, 1988), p. 67.
81. Elizabeth Wilson, 'The Invisible *Flâneur*', *New Left Review* 191 (January–February 1992), p. 109.
82. Thacker (2009), p. 143.
83. Janet Wolff, 'The Invisible *Flâneuse*: Women and the Literature of Modernity', *Theory Culture and Society* 2.3 (1985), p. 37; Pollock (1988), p. 71.
84. Scott McCracken, 'Voyages by Teashop: An Urban Geography of Modernism', in Brooker and Thacker (2005), pp. 86–98.
85. Rachel Bowlby, 'Walking, Women and Writing: Virginia Woolf as Flâneuse', *New Feminist Discourses: Critical Essays on Theories and Texts*, ed. Isobel Armstrong (London: Routledge, 1992), p. 29; Charles Baudelaire, *Les Fleurs du mal* (1861), reprinted in *Oeuvres complètes* (Paris: Seuil, 1968), p. 101.
86. Bowlby (1992), pp. 35, 44.
87. Alain Locke, (1969), p. 14.
88. Houston Baker, *Modernism and the Harlem Renaissance* (Chicago: University of Chicago Press, 1987), p. xiii.
89. Baker (1987), p. 4.
90. Baker (1987), p. xvi.
91. Baker (1987), p. xvi.
92. Baker (1987), p. 17.
93. Baker (1987), p. 8.
94. Baker (1987), p. 33.
95. Michael North, *The Dialect of Modernism: Race, Language and Twentieth-Century Literature* (New York: Oxford University Press, 1994), n.p.
96. George Bernard Shaw, *Collected Plays with their Prefaces*, 7 vols. (New York: Dodd, Mead, 1975), vol. 4, p. 800, quoted in North (1994), p. 12.
97. North (1994), p. 15.
98. North (1994), p. 52.
99. North (1994), p. 53.
100. North (1994), p. 57.
101. North (1994), p. 76.
102. Joseph Conrad, *The Nigger of The 'Narcissus'*, ed. Robert Kimbrough (New York: Norton, 1979), pp. 145–6, quoted in North (1994), p. 38.
103. North (1994), p. 40.
104. North (1994), p. 61.
105. North (1994), p. 61.
106. North (1994), p. 61.
107. North (1994), n.p.
108. North (1994), pp. 9, 10, 87.
109. North (1994), p. 86.
110. North (1994), p. 86.
111. North (1994), p. 86.
112. North (1994), n.p.
113. North (1994), p. 100.
114. North (1994), p. 101.
115. Claude McKay, *A Long Way from Home* (New York: Lee Furman, 1937), p. 248, quoted in North (1994), p. 115.
116. North (1994), p. 123.
117. North (1994), n.p.
118. North (1994), p. 174.

119. North (1994), n.p.
120. North (1994), n.p.
121. North (1994), n.p.
122. Elleke Boehmer, *Colonial and Postcolonial Literature: Migrant Metaphors* (Oxford: Oxford University Press, 1995), p. 99.
123. Leonard Woolf, *Imperialism and Civilization* (London: Hogarth Press, 1928), p. 17.
124. Homi Bhabha, *The Location of Culture* (London: Routledge, 1994), p. 33.
125. Bhabha (1994), pp. 93, 86, 89.
126. Bhabha (1994), p. 86.
127. Boehmer (1995), p. 100.
128. Boehmer (1995), p. 131.
129. Boehmer (1995), pp. 100–31.
130. Simon Gikandi, 'Preface: Modernism in the World', *Modernism/Modernity* 13.3, Special Issue: Modernism in the World (September 2006), p. 420.
131. Gikandi (1997), p. 158.
132. Gikandi (1997), pp. 158, 152.
133. Gikandi (1997), p. 159.
134. David Craven, 'The Latin American Origins of "Alternative Modernism"', in *The Third Text Reader on Art Culture and Theory* (London: Continuum, 1996), p. 24.
135. Craven (1996), p. 25.
136. Craven (1996), p. 25.
137. Craven (1996), p. 25.
138. Mao and Walkowitz (2008), p. 738.
139. Laura Doyle and Laura Winkiel, 'Introduction: The Global Horizons of Modernism', in *Geomodernisms: Race, Modernism, Modernity*, eds Laura Doyle and Laura Winkiel (Bloomington and Indianapolis: Indiana University Press, 2005), p. 1.
140. Doyle and Winkiel (2005), p. 4.
141. Laura Doyle, 'Liberty, Race, and Larsen in Atlantic Modernity: A New World Genealogy', in Doyle and Winkiel (2005), p. 51.
142. Ariela Freedman, 'On the Ganges Side of Modernism: Raghibur Singh, Amitav Ghosh, and the Postcolonial Modern', in Doyle and Winkiel (2005), p. 120.
143. Sung-sheng Yvonne Chang, 'Twentieth-Century Chinese Modernism and Globalizing Modernity: Three Auteur Directors of Taiwan New Cinema', in Doyle and Winkiel (2005), pp. 133–50.
144. Susan Stanford Friedman, 'Paranoia, Pollution and Sexuality: Affiliations between E.M. Forster's *A Passage to India* and Arundhati Roy's *The God of Small Things*', in Doyle and Winkiel (2005), pp. 246–7.
145. Susan Stanford Friedman, 'Periodizing Modernism: Postcolonial Modernities and the Space/Time Borders of Modernist Studies', *Modernism/Modernity* 13.3 (September 2006), p. 432.
146. Susan Stanford Friedman (2005), p. 246.
147. Urmila Seshagiri, 'Modernist Ashes, Postcolonial Phoenix: Jean Rhys and the Evolution of the English Novel in the Twentieth Century', *Modernism/Modernity* 13.3 (September 2006), p. 487.
148. Seshagiri (2006), pp. 488–9.
149. Seshagiri (2006), p. 489.
150. Jahan Ramazani, 'Modernist Bricolage, Postcolonial Hybridity', *Modernism/Modernity* 13.3 (September 2006), p. 449.
151. Simon Gikandi, 'Preface: Modernism in the World', *Modernism/Modernity*, 13.3 (September 2006), p. 421.
152. Jean-François Lyotard, *The Postmodern Condition: A Report on Knowledge*, trans. Geoff Bennington and Brian Massumi (Manchester: Manchester University Press, 1984), p. xxiv.
153. Ihab Hassan, *The Dismemberment of Orpheus: Toward a Postmodern Literature*, 2nd edn (Madison: University of Wisconsin Press, 1982), pp. 267–8.

154. Tyrus Miller, *Modernism: Politics, Fiction, and the Arts between the World Wars* (Berkeley: University of California Press, 1999), pp. 7, 43.
155. Miller (1999), p. 14.
156. Miller (1999), pp. 62–4.
157. Miller (1999), p. 7.
158. Anthony Mellors, *Late Modernist Poetics* (Manchester: Manchester University Press, 2005), p. 19.
159. Mellors (2005), p. 19.
160. Mellors (2005), p. 22.
161. Marjorie Perloff, *21st-Century Modernism: The "New" Poetics* (Oxford: Blackwell, 2002), pp. 1–2.
162. Perloff (2002), p. 2.
163. David James, 'Introduction: Mapping Modernist Continuities', *The Legacies of Modernism: Historicising Postwar and Contemporary Fiction* (Cambridge: Cambridge University Press, 2012), p. 2.
164. James (2012), n.p.
165. Rebecca Walkowitz, *Cosmopolitan Style: Modernism beyond the Nation* (New York: Columbia University Press, 2006), p. 2.
166. Walkowitz (2006), p. 32.

7   MODERNIST LITERATURES AND MASS CULTURE

1. Theodor Adorno and Max Horkheimer, 'The Culture Industry: Enlightenment as Mass Deception', *Dialectic of Enlightenment*, trans. John Cumming (London: Verso, 2010), pp. 120–67.
2. Walter Benjamin, 'The Work of Art in the Age of its Technical Reproducibility', in *Selected Writings: Volume 4, 1938–1940*, ed. Michael Jennings (Cambridge: The Belknap Press of Harvard University Press, 2003), p. 253.
3. Benjamin (2003), p. 254.
4. Benjamin (2003), p. 264.
5. Benjamin (2003), p. 264.
6. Printed in Walter Benjamin, *Gesammelte Schriften*, vol. 1, part 3 (Frankfurt am Main: Suhrkamp, 1974), p. 1003, quoted in Andreas Huyssen, *After the Great Divide* (Bloomington: Indiana University Press, 1986), p. 24.
7. Peter Bürger, *The Theory of the Avant-Garde*, trans. Michael Shaw (Minneapolis: University of Minnesota Press, 1984), p. 49.
8. See Menand and Rainey (2000), pp. 4–6; Richard Murphy, *Theorizing the Avant-Garde* (Cambridge: Cambridge University Press, 1999), pp. 3, 27.
9. Ástráður Eysteinsson, *The Concept of Modernism* (Ithaca: Cornell University Press, 1992), p. 178.
10. Huyssen (1986), p. x.
11. Huyssen (1986), p. viii.
12. Huyssen (1986), pp. 44–62.
13. Huyssen (1986), p. 44.
14. Huyssen (1986), p. 54.
15. Huyssen (1986), p. 46.
16. Huyssen (1986), p. 47.
17. Huyssen (1986), p. 47.
18. Huyssen (1986), p. 47.
19. Huyssen (1986), pp. 47–52.
20. Huyssen (1986), p. vii.
21. Huyssen (1986), p. 57.
22. Huyssen (1986), pp. 57.
23. Huyssen (1986), p. 61.
24. Huyssen (1986), p. 60.

25. Lawrence Rainey, *Institutions of Modernism: Literary Elites and Public Culture* (New Haven: Yale University Press, 1998), p. 2.

26. Huyssen (1986), p. 163.

27. David Chinitz, *T.S. Eliot and the Cultural Divide* (Chicago: University of Chicago Press, 2003), p. 13.

28. Chinitz (2003), pp. 19, 27, 24, 8.

29. T.S. Eliot, 'Observations', *Egoist* 5 (1918), pp. 69–70, quoted in Chinitz (2003), p. 63; 'T.S. Eliot, 70 Today, Concedes He Looks on Life More Genially', *New York Times* (26 September 1958), p. 29, quoted in Chinitz (2003), p. 157.

30. Chinitz (2003), p. 5.

31. Chinitz (2003), p. 30.

32. Chinitz (2003), p. 33.

33. Chinitz (2003), pp. 37, 33.

34. Chinitz (2003), p. 28.

35. Chinitz (2003), p. 38.

36. Chinitz (2003), p. 38.

37. T.S. Eliot, 'London Letter [April 1922]', *Dial* (May 1922), pp. 510–11, quoted in Chinitz (2003), p. 58.

38. Chinitz (2003), p. 82.

39. Chinitz (2003), pp. 13–14.

40. T.S. Eliot, 'Marianne Moore', *Dial* (December 1923), p. 594, quoted in Chinitz (2003), p. 59.

41. T.S. Eliot, 'Marie Lloyd', in *Selected Essays* (New York: Harcourt Brace, 1960), p. 405, quoted in Chinitz (2003), p. 92.

42. Eliot, 'Marie Lloyd' (1960), p. 406, quoted in Chinitz (2003), p. 91.

43. Eliot, 'Marie Lloyd' (1960), p. 407, quoted in Chinitz (2003), p. 92.

44. Eliot, 'Marie Lloyd' (1960), p. 407, quoted in Chinitz (2003), p. 92.

45. Eliot, *The Use of Poetry and the Use of Criticism*, (1933), p. 147, quoted in Chinitz (2003), p. 103.

46. Chinitz (2003), pp. 103–4; Eliot (1933), p. 147, quoted in Chinitz (2003), p. 104.

47. Chinitz (2003), p. 104.

48. Chinitz (2003), p. 121.

49. Chinitz (2003), p. 16.

50. Chinitz (2003), p. 187.

51. Michael North, *Reading 1922: A Return to the Scene of the Modern* (New York: Oxford University Press, 1999), p. v.

52. North (1999), p. 7.

53. North (1999), pp. 39, 45, 39.

54. North (1999), p. 39.

55. North (1999), pp. 64, 46.

56. North (1999), p. 8.

57. North (1999), p. 171.

58. North (1999), p. 203.

59. North (1999), pp. 126, 15.

60. North (1999), p. 26.

61. North (1999), p. 26.

62. North (1999), p. 26.

63. North (1999), p. 27.

64. North (1999), p. 24.

65. North (1999), p. 24.

66. North (1999), p. 26.

67. North (1999), p. 26.

68. North (1999), p. 141; Gilbert Seldes, 'Nineties—Twenties—Thirties', *Dial* 73 (November 1922), p. 577, quoted in North, p. 141.

69. Charles Maland, *Chaplin and American Culture: The Evolution of a Star Image* (Princeton: Princeton University Press, 1989), p. 88, quoted in North (1999), p. 140; North, p. 140.
70. North (1999), p. 141.
71. North (1999), p. 141.
72. T.S. Eliot, 'Dramatis Personae', *Criterion* (April 1923), p. 306, quoted in North (1999), p. 171.
73. North (1999), p. 171.
74. North (1999), p. vii.
75. North (1999), pp. 209, 140.
76. David Trotter, *Cinema and Modernism* (Oxford: Blackwell, 2007), p. 1.
77. Trotter (2007), p. 3.
78. Trotter (2007), p. 4.
79. Marianne Moore, 'Fiction or Nature?', in *Complete Prose*, ed. Patricia C. Willis (London: Faber and Faber, 1987), pp. 303–8, quoted in Trotter (2007), p. 4; Virginia Woolf, 'The Cinema', in *The Crowded Dance of Modern Life*, ed. Rachel Bowlby (Harmondsworth: Penguin Books, 1993), pp. 54–8, quoted in Trotter (2007), p. 12.
80. Trotter (2007), p. 10.
81. Trotter (2007), p. 10.
82. Trotter (2007), pp. 113–14.
83. Trotter (2007), pp. 103, 103, 12.
84. Trotter (2007), p. 12.
85. Trotter (2007), pp. 126, 132.
86. Trotter (2007), p. 160.
87. Laura Marcus, *The Tenth Muse: Writing about Cinema in the Modernist Period* (Oxford: Oxford University Press, 2007), p. 13.
88. Marcus (2007), p. 11.
89. Marcus (2007), p. 16.
90. Marcus (2007), pp. 320, 343.
91. Marcus (2007), p. 343.
92. Marcus (2007), pp. 359, 364.
93. Marcus (2007), p. 42.
94. Faye Hammill, *Women, Celebrity and Literary Culture between the Wars* (Austin: University of Texas Press, 2007), p. 10.
95. Hammill (2007), p. 20.
96. Hammill (2007), p. 10.
97. Virginia Woolf, 'Middlebrow', in *The Death of the Moth, and Other Essays* (London: Hogarth, 1942), p. 115.
98. Woolf (1942), p. 117.
99. Nicola Humble, *The Feminine Middlebrow Novel 1920s to 1950s: Class, Domesticity and Bohemianism* (Oxford: Oxford University Press, 2001), pp. 1–2.
100. Humble (2001), p. 1.
101. Humble (2001), p. 3.
102. Hammill (2007), p. 2.
103. Hammill (2007), p. 5.
104. Hammill (2007), p. 9.
105. Hammill (2007), p. 11.
106. Hammill (2007), p. 9.
107. Hammill (2007), p. 6.
108. Terry Eagleton, 'Capitalism, Modernism, and Postmodernism', in *Modern Criticism and Theory: A Reader*, ed. David Lodge (London: Longman, 1988), p. 392, quoted in Rainey (1998), p. 3.
109. Rainey, *Institutions of Modernism* (1998), p. 28.
110. Rainey (1998), pp. 12, 28.
111. Rainey (1998), p. 30.

112. Rainey (1998), p. 35.
113. Rainey (1998), pp. 4, 5.
114. Rainey (1998), p. 39.
115. Rainey (1998), p. 154.
116. Rainey (1998), p. 53.
117. Rainey (1998), p. 44.
118. Rainey (1998), p. 78.
119. Rainey (1998), p. 88.
120. Rainey (1998), p. 91; 'A Group of Poems by T.S. Eliot', *Vanity Fair* (June 1923), p. 67, quoted in Rainey (1998), p. 92.
121. Rainey (1998), p. 91.
122. Rainey (1998), p. 99.
123. Rainey (1998), p. 106.
124. Rainey (1998), pp. 4, 5.
125. Rainey (1998), p. 170.
126. Rainey (1998), p. 108.
127. Rainey (1998), p. 141.
128. Rainey (1998), pp. 169, 170.
129. Rainey (1998), p. 148.
130. Rainey (1998), p. 148.
131. Rainey (1998), p. 170.
132. Mark Morrison, *The Public Face of Modernism: Little Magazines, Audiences and Reception 1905–1920* (Madison: University of Wisconsin Press, 2001), p. 9.
133. Morrison (2001), p. 10.
134. Morrison (2001), p. 5.
135. Morrison (2001), p. 6.
136. Morrison (2001), p. 5.
137. Morrison (2001), p. 6.
138. Morrison (2001), p. 92.
139. Morrison (2001), p. 91.
140. Morrison (2001), pp. 92, 102.
141. Morrison (2001), p. 103.
142. Morrison (2001), pp. 102, 106.
143. Morrison (2001), pp. 11, 204, 204.
144. Aaron Jaffe, *Modernism and the Culture of Celebrity* (Cambridge: Cambridge University Press, 2005), p.33.
145. Jaffe (2005), p. 4.
146. Jaffe (2005), p. 96.
147. Jaffe (2005), p. 6.
148. Jaffe (2005), p. 100.
149. Jaffe (2005), p. 133.
150. Jaffe (2005), p. 4.
151. Jaffe (2005), p. 138.
152. Jaffe (2005), p. 143.
153. Jaffe (2005), p. 168.
154. Jaffe (2005), pp. 4, 201.
155. Ron Schuchard, 'American Publishers and Transmission of T.S. Eliot's Prose: A Sociology of English and American Editions', in *Modernist Writers and the Marketplace*, eds Ian Willison, Warwick Gould and Warren Cherniak (Basingstoke: Palgrave Macmillan, 1996), p. 195.
156. Schuchard (1996), p. 195.
157. James Joyce to Harriet Shaw Weaver, *Letters*, vol. 1 (1966), p. 183.
158. Hans Walter Gabler with Wolfhard Steppe and Claus Melchior, eds, *Ulysses: A Critical and Synoptic Edition* (New York and London: Garland, 1984), p. 1895.

159. Hans Walter Gabler, quoted 'Afterword', in James Joyce, *Ulysses: The Corrected Text*, (London: Bodley Head, 1986), p. 649.
160. Joyce (1986), p. 161.
161. John Kidd, 'The Scandal of *Ulysses*', *New York Review of Books* (30 June 1988), pp. 32–9.
162. Jeri Johnson, 'Composition and Publication History', James Joyce, *Ulysses: The 1922 Text*, ed. Jeri Johnson (Oxford: Oxford University Press, 1993), p. lvii.
163. Scott (2007), p. 11.
164. Scott (2007), pp. 13, 14.
165. Scott (2007), p. 3.
166. http://dl.lib.brown.edu/mjp/journals.html.
167. Peter Brooker and Andrew Thacker, eds, *The Oxford Critical and Cultural History of Modernist Magazines*, 3 vols (Oxford: Oxford University Press, 2009–2013), vol. 1, *Britain and Ireland 1880–1955* (2009); vol. 2, *North America 1894–1960* (2012); *Europe 1880–1940* (2013).

CONCLUSION

1. Mao and Walkowitz (2008), p. 738.
2. Mao and Walkowitz (2008), p. 738.

Select Bibliography

I t is not practical to list all the primary materials by the many modernist writers and contemporary critics consulted in the writing of a book with such a broad and inclusive remit. For ease of reference, all the major manifestos and critical essays that are discussed in Part I of the Guide are catalogued in the index, where they appear under the principal author's name. Bibliographical details for the quotations that appear in Part I of the Guide can be found in the endnotes.

The Reader's Guide to Essential Criticism Series contains several other volumes that will interest readers who are keen to find out more about the reception histories of works by individual authors, including Joseph Conrad, Virginia Woolf, D.H. Lawrence, T.S. Eliot, William Faulkner, F. Scott Fitzgerald and Walt Whitman. Another valuable resource for tracing the contemporary reception of select writers is the Critical Heritage Series, which amasses reviews from newspapers and literary quarterlies. Readers are also advised to consult scholarly editions of authors' letters, diaries, essays and manifestos, as well as the gatherings of critical documents in anthologies such as:

Apollonio, Umbro, ed., *Futurist Manifestos* (London: Thames and Hudson, 1973).
Drain, Richard, ed., *Twentieth-Century Theatre: A Sourcebook* (Routledge: London and New York, 1995).
Faulkner, Peter, ed., *A Modernist Reader: Modernism in England 1910–1930* (London: Batsford, 1986).
Innes, Christopher, ed., *A Sourcebook on Naturalist Theatre* (London: Routledge, 2000).
Kolocotroni, Vassiliki, Jane Goldman and Olga Taxidou, eds, *Modernism: An Anthology of Sources and Documents* (Edinburgh: Edinburgh University Press, 1998).
Matthews, Steven, *Modernism: A Sourcebook* (Basingstoke: Palgrave Macmillan, 2008).
Motherwell, Richard, *The Dada Painters and Poets: An Anthology*, 2nd edn (New York: Wittenborn, Schultz, 1981).
Rainey, Lawrence, ed., *Modernism: An Anthology* (Oxford: Blackwell, 2005).
Seaver, Richard, and Helen Lane, trans. *Manifestos of Surrealism* (Ann Arbor: University of Michigan Press, 1972).
Scott, Bonnie Kime, ed., *The Gender of Modernism: A Critical Anthology* (Bloomington and Indianapolis: Indiana University Press, 1990).
Scott, Bonnie Kime, ed., *Gender in Modernism: New Geographies, Complex Intersections* (Urbana and Chicago: University of Illinois Press, 2007).
Whitworth, Michael, ed., *Modernism* (Oxford: Blackwell, 2007).

The Modernist Journals Project is a superb resource for following the critical debates that were conducted in little magazines (http://dl.lib. brown.edu/mjp/journals.html).

CHAPTER FOUR: THE MAKING OF MODERNIST CANONS

Benstock, Shari, *Women of the Left Bank: Paris, 1900–1940* (London: Virago, 1987).

Bloom, Harold, *Wallace Stevens: The Poems of Our Climate* (Ithaca: Cornell University Press, 1977).

Ellmann, Richard, and Charles Fiedelson, eds, *The Modern Tradition: Backgrounds of Modern Literature* (London: Oxford University Press, 1965).

Gilbert, Sandra, and Susan Gubar, *No Man's Land: The Place of the Woman Writer in the Twentieth Century*, 3 vols (New Haven: Yale University Press, 1988–1994): vol. 1, *The War of the Words* (1988) ; vol. 2, *Sexchanges* (1989); vol. 3, *Letters from the Front* (1994).

Kenner, Hugh, *The Pound Era* (Berkeley: University of California Press, 1971).

Kermode, Frank, *Romantic Image* (London: Routledge and Kegan Paul, 1957).

Levenson, Michael, *A Genealogy of Modernism: A Study of English Literary Doctrine 1908–1922* (Cambridge: Cambridge University Press, 1994).

Menard, Louis, and Lawrence Rainey, eds, *The Cambridge History of Literary Criticism: Modernism and the New Criticism* (Cambridge: Cambridge University Press, 2000).

Scott, Bonnie Kime, ed., *The Gender of Modernism: A Critical Anthology* (Bloomington and Indianapolis: Indiana University Press, 1990).

Scott, Bonnie Kime, *Refiguring Modernism*, 2 vols (Bloomington: Indiana University Press, 1995): vol. 1, *The Women of 1928*; vol. 2, *Postmodern Feminist Readings of Woolf, West and Barnes*.

Smith, Stan, *The Origins of Modernism: Eliot, Pound, Yeats and the Rhetorics of Renewal* (London: Harvester Wheatsheaf, 1994).

CHAPTER FIVE: GENDER AND SEXUALITY

Ardis, Ann, *New Women: New Novels: Feminism and Early Modernism* (New Brunswick: Rutgers University Press, 1990).

Armstrong, Tim, *Modernism, Technology and the Body: A Cultural Study* (Cambridge: Cambridge University Press, 1998).

Boone, Joseph, *Libidinal Currents: Sexuality and the Shaping of Modernism* (Chicago: University of Chicago Press, 1998).

DeKoven, Marianne, *Rich and Strange: Gender, History and Modernism* (Princeton: Princeton University Press, 1991).

Doan, Laura, *Fashioning Sapphism: The Origins of a Modern English Lesbian Culture* (New York: Columbia University Press, 2001).

Farfan, Penny, *Women, Modernism and Performance* (Cambridge: Cambridge University Press, 2004).

Galvin, Mary, *Queer Poetics: Five Modernist Women Writers* (Westport and London: Greenwood Press, 1999).

Lamos, Colleen, *Deviant Modernism: Sexual and Textual Errancy in T.S. Eliot, James Joyce, and Marcel Proust* (Oxford: Clarendon Press, 1999).

Pykett, Lyn, *Engendering Fictions: The English Novel in the Early Twentieth Century* (London: Arnold, 1995).

Raitt, Suzanne, and Trudi Tate, eds, *Women's Fiction and the Great War* (Oxford: Clarendon Press 1997).

Tate, Trudi, *Modernism, History and the First World War* (Manchester: Manchester University Press, 1998).

CHAPTER SIX: MODERNIST GEOGRAPHIES AND TIME FRAMES

Baker, Houston, *Modernism and the Harlem Renaissance* (Chicago and London: University of Chicago Press, 1987).

Boehmer, Elleke, *Colonial and Postcolonial Literature: Migrant Metaphors* (Oxford: Oxford University Press, 1995).

Cheng, Vincent, *Joyce, Race and Empire* (Cambridge: Cambridge University Press, 1995).

Deane, Seamus, Terry Eagleton, Fredric Jameson and Edward Said, *Nationalism, Colonialism, and Literature* (Minneapolis: University of Minnesota Press, 1990).

Doyle, Laura, and Laura Winkiel, eds, *Geomodernisms: Race, Modernism, Modernity*, (Bloomington and Indianapolis: Indiana University Press, 2005).

Gikandi, Simon, ed., *Modernism/Modernity* 13.3, MSA Special Issue: Modernism and Transnationalisms (September 2006).

Bradbury, Malcolm, and James McFarlane, eds, *Modernism: A Guide to European Literature: 1890–1930* (London: Penguin, 1991).

James, David, *The Legacies of Modernism: Historicising Postwar and Contemporary Fiction* (Cambridge: Cambridge University Press, 2012).

Mellors, Anthony, *Late Modernist Poetics* (Manchester: Manchester University Press, 2005).

Miller, Tyrus, *Modernism: Politics, Fiction, and the Arts between the World Wars* (Berkeley: University of California Press, 1999).

North, Michael, *The Dialect of Modernism: Race, Language and Twentieth-Century Literature* (New York: Oxford University Press, 1994).

Thacker, Andrew, *Moving through Modernity: Space and Geography in Modernism* (Manchester: Manchester University Press, 2009).

Walkowitz, Rebecca, *Cosmopolitan Style: Modernism beyond the Nation* (New York: Columbia University Press, 2006).

Williams, Raymond, *The Politics of Modernism: Against the New Conformists*, ed. Tony Pinkney (London: Verso, 1989).

CHAPTER SEVEN: MODERNIST LITERATURES AND MASS CULTURE

Bürger, Peter, *The Theory of the Avant-Garde*, trans. Michael Shaw (Minneapolis: University of Minnesota Press, 1984).

Chinitz, David, *T.S. Eliot and the Cultural Divide* (Chicago: University of Chicago Press, 2003).

Hammill, Faye, *Women, Celebrity and Literary Culture between the Wars* (Austin: University of Texas Press, 2007).

Huyssen, Andreas, *After the Great Divide: Modernism, Mass Culture, Postmodernism* (Bloomington: Indiana University Press, 1986).

Jaffe, Aaron, *Modernism and the Culture of Celebrity* (Cambridge: Cambridge University Press, 2005).

Marcus, Laura, *The Tenth Muse: Writing about Cinema in the Modernist Period* (Oxford: Oxford University Press, 2007).

Morrison, Mark, *The Public Face of Modernism: Little Magazines, Audiences and Reception 1905–1920* (Madison: University of Wisconsin Press, 2001).

North, Michael, *Reading 1922: A Return to the Scene of the Modern* (New York: Oxford University Press, 1999).

Rainey, Lawrence, *Institutions of Modernism: Literary Elites and Public Culture* (New Haven: Yale University Press, 1998).

Trotter, David, *Cinema and Modernism* (Oxford: Blackwell, 2007).

Index